Cover photo: Revoir Historical Collection, Red Wing

***The front cover shows Josephine Keye and her daughters trying to cool down on a hot, sticky day in 1907. The girls were Harriet, about 4, and Pauline, about 2. They were wading in Wells Creek, on their farm near Frontenac. The book's title comes from the message of Joe Lommel Jr. on July 18, 1973. He was painting the outside of his parents' tavern in Luxemburg, near St. Cloud, and his mother said he could go swimming when he had used up his bucket of paint. To see how he did it, see the back cover.***

# Too Hot, Went to Lake

# Too Hot, Went to Lake

## *Seasonal Photos from Minnesota's Past*

By Peg Meier

Design/Jarrett Smith

Printer/Meyers Printing Company

Published by Neighbors Publishing
P.O. Box 15071
Minneapolis, MN 55415

Second printing



0-933387-03-2 Too Hot, Went to Lake

Neighbors Publishing
P.O. Box 15071
Minneapolis, MN 55415

In memory of Anna Schulz Bierbaum and Ida Schulz Bohnhoff, my maternal grandmother and her sister. They loved old photographs, and they loved me.

# Table of contents

"One of the most interesting results of the ease and cheapness with which photographs are produced is the prompting which it will give many persons to have their likenesses taken frequently during their lives. What would a man value more highly late in life than this accurate record of the gradual change in his features from childhood to old age? What a splendid illustration would such a series of photographs make in every household. First the new-born babe in his mother's arms; then the infant creeping on the floor; next the child tottering by the mother's apron; then the various phases of boyhood, till the sprouting beard tells of the time when the plans and hopes of life began to take form and purpose; another portrait with softer locks and eyes is now coupled with the series, and the stern warfare with the world begins; the features henceforth grow harder and more severe; lines slowly come into the forehead and grey hairs mingle with the locks; the lines grow deeper and the head whiter, till the babe is changed into the wrinkled and grey old man, so different but still the same! Even when life is closed the power of the photographer has not ceased. The fixed features that return no answering glance to the last fond look of surviving love are caught and indelibly preserved to its memory."

**— "Scientific American" of Aug. 9, 1862**

# Introduction

## Old photos and detective work

Old photographs are like mystery tales. Their secrets make us curious, and they require detective work to figure out. With proper sleuthing, some of the mysteries in old photos can be solved.

Sometimes it seems that more pieces of information are missing from photos than are available. By the time they reach historical societies or are passed on to the grandchildren of the subjects, valuable knowledge is missing: Who's that standing next to Aunt Esther? Are those people from grandma's or grandpa's side of the family? Was this picture taken at the lake cabin the family used to rent up north every summer or at the Lake Superior place they stayed in that hot summer when dad was a baby? What the *heck* was this guy doing in that picture?

The tools used to research old photos are some of the same ones detectives use. A magnifying glass, for one. It's amazing to see the details that pop up with magnification.

And it's interesting to check the handwriting on the back of the photos for more than an account of who is in the picture. For instance, if that's really Ruth's writing, why did she identify everyone except her Uncle Charlie? Was that from the time she was mad at him?

A good detective does research. Libraries and historical societies are invaluable resources. You can track down information with old city directories, history books, telephone books and newspapers of the period. Your library is likely to have books that show how automobiles, toys, clothing and hairstyles have changed over the decades; they can help you figure out when a photo was shot.

Objects in photos can give clues about prized possessions. Although some studio photographers had a prop or two that every kid in town was posed with, more casual snapshots taken by friends or family members can reveal beloved treasures. Children tended to choose a favorite doll or bicycle. Adults wore their best clothes and jewelry to prove their prosperity, and they held special items, such as heirlooms from the Old Country. Farmers liked to pose in their best-looking fields. And after the turn of the century, nearly everybody wanted their pictures taken with automobiles, the symbol of American culture.

It helps when studying family pictures to understand the Standing Operating Procedures of early photography. By reading this book, you'll pick up some clues. An example: Wedding photos from the 1800s usually show the bride standing next to her seated husband. Why? One reason was to show off the full beauty of her wedding gown. Another was to allow her to breathe deeply in her whale-bone corset.

Of course, the best technique to interpret old photos may be good old-fashioned interrogating. Ask people. Does your great-aunt remember this scene? Do the staff members or volunteers at your hometown historical society recognize this as their main street? Do your cousins think this scene looks familiar? Can gardeners or farmers identify what was growing in the plot behind grandma?

Sometimes it pays to visit the scene of the crime, hmmm, that is, the place where you suspect the photo was taken. Was the door in this picture part of the family homestead that's still standing? Do the brick buildings in this shot match up with the row of stores that exist to this day in St. Paul?

It pays to use your gut instincts too. Let your imagination fly: Was this woman happy or just pretending? Do these two people seem to be a long-married couple? Study the arrangement of people. In group shots, people tend to stand next to the individuals they especially like. People who don't like each other place themselves in distant parts of the frame. Or, if forced to stand next to each other, they leave a gap between them. Does the body language of the people in your 1935 family reunion reveal who they love? Who they can't stand?

Remember that in even a photograph posed by a professional, the shooter didn't have complete control of the subjects. The photographer may have said, "Stand there, look here, put your chin up, smile," but each person stood differently, lifted the chin a certain way and had a unique smile. Personalities reveal themselves in photos, and a good photo detective makes use of the information.

Oh, one other clue to old photos. Check the ears. Bodies change, faces change, but ear shapes, especially the lobes, stay the same through life. Or so say some photo experts. Ears don't provide as reliable clues as fingerprints or DNA, but what the heck, studying ears in old family photos is bound to provide a few laughs. Trust me on that one.

## Some clues to this book

**How we chose the photographs.** Jarrett Smith, who designed this book, and I like "people photos" — pictures of ordinary folks living their lives. During our five years of research, we looked at many thousand images of Minnesotans, and we picked the ones that stirred our hearts. When we saw these photos for the first time, we said "Wow!" or "Look at this one!" or "Too sad!" or "This one's a hoot!"

We wanted to give you an idea of what life might have been like for you if you'd been born a few generations earlier. We like photos of families, people having fun, people working, people relaxing.

Style is hard to define, but here were some of our less emotional criteria: We wanted photos that tell something about Minnesota people. That give a feeling for the times and places. That bring back memories. That are clear and sharp and composed well. We skipped over photographs of Minnesota's architecture, scenery and dignitaries. You can find them in lots of other books.

**Where we found the photos.** The majority are from the Minnesota Historical Society, which has been collecting photographs since the Civil War. The society has more than 250,000 images. The generous photo librarians and archivists there led us to some gems. Others we uncovered in the society's files.

Also, I drove around the state finding photos. Some county historical societies have lovely old pictures. I was especially impressed with the collections of these counties — Brown, Clay, Fillmore, Goodhue, Lake, Otter Tail, Stearns and Winona — plus the regional collections of the Iron Range Research Center at Chisholm and the Northeast Minnesota Historical Center in Duluth.

We did not ask to search people's attics. The main reason was we didn't have the time. But also discouraging us was the fact that family collections unfortunately tend to be an unidentified hodge-podge. It's up to all of us to get our own family pictures in order, labeled and stored in a safe place. More of that sermon later, at the end of the book.

**Who the photographers were.** Amateurs, mostly. They photographed the subjects we like most: Families, babies, houses, people experiencing the variety of seasons here. Many of the photos in this book are "just" snapshots, but they're zippy snapshots with technical mastery. You may notice some photographers' names several times in the credits under the pictures: Frank Wilson of Stillwater; John W.G. Dunn of St. Paul and Marine on St. Croix; Albert Munson of St. Paul, and Dr. Emil King of Fulda.

A few pictures in this book are studio shots, taken by professionals. The muted background, often a painted curtain, is a clue. We'll point some out to you.

Others were taken by newspaper photographers. I work for a newspaper, and I love the spontaneity of photojournalism. The photographers were where it was happening. One of our favorites was Myron Hall of St. Cloud, whose sense of whimsy we admire.

**Why so many of the photos are of children.** We like kids. We like kids' pictures. Often their photos are as unpretentious and as revealing of society as are the children themselves. Family pictures are especially fun to examine and to compare with our own.

**Why so many pictures are clumped around the turn of the century.** Again, the answer is subjective. Photos from the decades surrounding 1900 are the ones we really like. Before the 1880s, there were few non-stiff photos of regular-type folks. And after World War II, the photos didn't seem so different from today, except for varying lengths of hair, changes in clothing style and kinds of cars.

While we love contemporary photos of our friends and families and go bonkers over good photojournalism in today's newspapers, we like "old-old" historic photos, not the "new-old," like from the 1970s. To us, newer pictures are not as revealing as earlier ones. We've included a few of our favorites from the post-war era, and we think you'll understand why when you see them.

There's one more reason why there's a shortage of fantastic pictures since World War II. They're still in people's photo albums and shoe boxes. Photos from the 1950s are sparse in historical societies. From the '60s on, there are even fewer. And the color prints, slides and videos that people are shooting now will fade into nothingness before the good old black-and-white negatives of a century ago lose their vitality.

**Why few members of minority races are included.** The answer is not that only white people were in portraits and snapshots from the old days. It's known, for example, that many black families had cameras around the turn of the century. But historical societies and other institutions were geared to the white culture; they saved photos and other pieces of the history given to them as representative of the majority cultures. Most Native American and African-American people haven't felt comfortable in donating their treasures, partly because some photos of them were made as souvenirs or jokes and were demeaning. Some respectful photos that were passed down in families of color are making their way into public collections, which now value them highly, thank goodness.

**Why people don't smile in very old pictures.** Several reasons, all of them purely conjecture on the part of photography experts.

Very early forms of photography required a long exposure time — up to several minutes. The slightest movement ruined an image. That was no problem for photographers shooting landscapes, but it made taking pictures of breathing people difficult. People sitting for daguerreotype photos in the 1850s sat stiffly with their necks in tight-fitting braces. (In some photos from that period, you can see the head clamp.) Subjects couldn't possibly hold a smile precisely the same for minutes so they weren't encouraged to try.

Tradition dictated how formal photographs were to be taken. Lawyers stood in a certain way before the camera, preachers in another, writers were seated at their desks and many women were posed to look subservient to men. Each person had a conventional image to enact. None included frivolity.

Another explanation for the lack of smiles was that a visit to a photo studio was a special, formal occasion in the 1800s. It's true that photography was called "the great equalizer" because most people could afford a trip to the photo studio. Nonetheless, the tradition was that a somber expression was appropriate. It's as if you became very famous and hired a big-shot portrait painter to do you in oils. You would want to look important and fashionable. Ordinary people felt that way about photos back then. The custom of somber clothing and expressions lasted until after the turn of the century. No grins, no wild clothes, no clowning around. The key phrase was not, "Smile." It was as if the photographer sternly commanded, "Now be dignified."

One last reason for the smile shortage: Early dentistry was inadequate. Get the picture?

**When ordinary Minnesota people started having their photos taken.** By 1850, most American cities had photo studios where daguerreotype pictures were taken. (A daguerreotype was made on a piece of copper that was plated with silver.) St. Paul and Minneapolis were just beginning to be settled then, but St. Paul had a daguerreotype studio already in 1851. Even middle-class people could afford daguerreotypes. New settlers, mostly from the East Coast, also brought photos of loved ones with them; by now it can be difficult to determine if early photographs were actually shot here.

Photos called "cartes des visite" were immensely popular in the 1860s. The subjects' head and shoulders, and sometimes full portraits, were photographed in studios. Multiple images, like today's school photos, were printed on paper. The "Scientific American" commented on Aug. 9, 1862:

"The ease with which photographs are taken, and the cheapness at which they are sold, has reached its highest development in the carte de visite. A man can now have his likeness taken for a dime, and for three cents more he can send it across the plains, mountains, and rivers, over thousands of miles to his distant friends."

Photography changed radically in 1888 when Kodak made the snapshot possible. And by the 1890s hand-held cameras were easy to use by amateurs. In fact, serious photographers looked on the new devices scornfully and called those who used them mere "button-pushers."

Yet, the button-pushers took some remarkable photos that tell much about their times. By the turn of the century, regular people were shooting the "ordinary" but sublime parts of life: The general store, the new baby, the family reunion, the Sunday picnic, the kids at the beach, winter enthusiasts with skis. You get the idea.

**Why old letters and diaries are included in a photo book.** So many of the photographs are from the late 19th and early 20th centuries that I wanted to provide Minnesotans' words to tell more about the seasons over a larger part of Minnesota's history. I searched the writings of regular people and included pieces to give glimpses of Minnesota's seasons over time. I kept the writers' spelling and most of their punctuation.

**Why the photos are arranged by season.** Minnesotans arrange *everything* by season: Clothes closets, books, music collections, stuff that we carry around in our car trunks, memories. I once heard of a woman who arranged her kitchen spices by season; just how escapes me. But clearly, weather is a big deal here. We talk about it, take pictures of it, write in our journals about it. Whether gardening, proposing marriage, playing games or planning menus, we know that many aspects of our lives depend on which season it is.

Okay, okay, I admit I was imprecise about which photos and letters belong in which season, but if you've ever lived in Minnesota you know that makes sense. March and April are sometimes winter, sometimes spring. October is up for grabs. Most of November may officially be fall, but that's easy to forget during a fall blizzard. Some autumns seem to last a 60th of a second. A winter, though, can last several lifetimes. You may notice that we have more summer and winter photos than spring and fall.

I tried to get information on precisely the date or at least the season when the pictures were shot, but I didn't always succeed. Some I guessed on. The book's designer and I grouped the photos on particular topics. For example, we put all the school photos in the fall section and the dance recitals in spring.

**What I'm going to do with the photo information you send me.** If you can solve some of the mysteries we present, I'll pass on your information to the proper historical society. Please write to me at Neighbors Publishing, P.O. Box 15071, Minneapolis MN 55415. I'd love to hear from you.

**— Peg Meier**
**Minneapolis, Minn.**
**May 1993**

George Luxton photo,
Minnesota Historical
Society

***Coeds from a University of Minnesota swimming class toasted marshmallows at Lake Calhoun in Minneapolis after a swim workout in about 1910. Notice the outfits. They were oversized bathing suits of the popular sailor-suit style and probably were made of cotton — a big improvement over scratchy, woolen suits. These had bloomer legs and, for modesty's sake, skirts to attach when the wearer was out of the water.***

# Summer

Summer in Minnesota means lakes. Always has. Stretching back thousands of years, Indian bands settled on high ground overlooking lakes. The earliest attempts by whites to lure settlers to the region stressed the beauty of the waters almost as much as the richness of the farmland. An 1867 book called "Minnesota: Its Advantages to Settlers" gushed, "The State is encircled by lakes and rivers, like the Garden of Eden."

Even before the Civil War, Minnesota was popular as a tourist spot, especially among Southerners, who traveled up the Mississippi River by steamboat to find relief from their summer's heat. Those "miserable sunburned denizens of the torrid zone," as they were called by a Minnesota writer of that time, were urged to enjoy the lakeside advantages of the northern summer. "Come to Minnesota," urged a St. Paul editor, "all ye that are roasting and heavy laden and we will give you rest."

Early promoters stressed the region's clean air and water. They claimed Minnesota's weather cured about every disease and infirmity, and sick people flocked in to recuperate. In the summer of 1860, Thomas and Ellen Biscoe traveled to St. Paul from Massachusetts, where he was a Congregational minister. They came with hopes of regaining health and strength. In a letter home on July 21, 1860, she told of finding fish (good) and mosquitoes (really bad):

"I mentioned we were going a-fishing. . . . We took the horse and buggy and started for Bass Lake (Owasso). We had a delightful ride, when we had gone about three miles we came to Lake Como which we drove into, & through from one side to the other. . . .

"We came to a house where we left our horse, and got our fish poles and started for the lake. It was a long way, but we did not take the horse because of the musketoes. So you may imagine us starting off, each with a long pole following a cart path for about half a mile, then turning into the bushes and picking our way the best we could. Mrs. Stockton and I kept together, but Tho's [Thomas] went ahead, and we would learn his whereabouts by halloing back and forth. At last we came to the lake and the boat, the next thing to be done was to get our bait, so we all went in search of frogs.

"Presently I heard him calling, Ellen, Ellen. I went to him, and learned that he had knocked off his specticles in attempting to drive away the musketoes which were almost devouring him, such musketoes I think you never saw, so big, and so hungry."

There was a happy ending to this story. The Biscoes caught as many "pouts, perch and pickerels" (probably what we call catfish, walleyes and northerns) as they could carry home. But the pickerel that the writer swore was over a foot long got away. Some things never change.

The hype over Minnesota's lakes continued for decades. Lake Minnetonka, just to the west of the Twin Cities, got this favorable hometown review in an 1883 book called "Where to Recuperate During Summer Days: Information for the Pleasure Seeker, the Sportsman and the Invalid":

"The famed lakes of Scotland, the famous resorts of Italy, and the mountain lakes of the Pacific coast have all been lauded in song and story, and yet they are pronounced by tourists who have visited them all to be far less enjoyable than our own Minnetonka. Here the scenery lacks the rugged cliffs and bold peaks that make up a grand mountain scenery, but it also lacks the dangerous and precipitous pathways that can only be traveled by trained ponies and mules, and the wearisome climbing that mars the pleasure of the journey."

So much for mountains.

In the 1880s Lake Minnetonka had big, fashionable resorts that drew visitors from many states. Well-known resorts also had been established at White Bear, Lake Elmo, Prior Lake, the Dalles of the St. Croix, St. Croix Lake and Frontenac.

And, of course, generations of Minnesotans themselves have basked at the lakes and rivers. When we look at summer photographs in family albums and in historical collections, we can't help but notice the preponderance of photos shot at our waters: Families beaming beside lake cabins "up north"; lovers posing in front of Minnehaha Falls in Minneapolis; folks wading in streams to escape insufferable heat. The old albums

Hennepin History Museum

***The Lake Harriet Boating Club, sponsored by the Minneapolis YWCA, provided recreation and exercise for young women in about 1900. The hats perched on top of their heads, long-sleeved blouses and long, dark skirts were almost regulation apparel.***

show children swimming, rowing, paddling, splashing, diving, cooling off with the spray from garden hoses and, in recent decades, trying to stand up straight on water skis.

From the get-go, "the land of 10,000 lakes" (Minnesota's modest slogan; there are actually 15,291 lakes larger than 10 acres) has been praised in photograph, letter, diary, tourist brochure and newspaper article. Writers have reached for the poetry in their souls to describe summers here. They described glorious sunsets and pine wildernesses and lazy days. They told of weather so perfect you could almost hear the corn grow. They reveled in accounts of fabulous Fourth of July picnics and parades. They wrote of the summer's first berries and August's excess summer squash.

Settlers and visitors did remark on the beauty of the prairie as well as of the lakes. A man named Oliver Gibbs had this to say in his 1869 book, "Lake Pepin Fish-Chowder":

"Some days, when 'the signs' are not right for fishing, will be delightfully passed in driving about the country — especially when the prairies are dressed in their brilliant and varied garniture of wild flowers. If I were a fisherman taking my wife to Minnesota, I would never let her see the prairie flowers till the fishing was well-nigh done with. She would be bewitched with them at once, and give them her entire attention. In the latter part of June or early in July the prairies are perfectly gaudy, resplendent, and honey-scented with them. A half-hour's

ramble among them is sufficient to gather a bouquet that will put to blush the products of any conservatory. There are so many varieties that I once picked a bunch of them as large as a peck measure, tied them up just as they were gathered, promiscuously, and, on showing them to some ladies of fine floral taste, obtained credit for the artistic arrangement of the different colors."

Of course, summer in Minnesota also has meant hard work. Diary accounts prove it.

Philemon Tuttle, a farmer in southeastern Minnesota, kept a journal of his work in 1877. He finished stacking his barley on July 31 and began cutting wheat the next day. Day after wearying day, all he wrote was, "I cut wheat all day."

Lydia Woodward, an elderly homemaker living near Langdon in Washington County, kept track of summer duties in July of 1905: "Washing, Churning and so forth." "Canning Beans." "Pickling Beans." "Canning Raspberries." "Washing as usual." "Baking and drawing in Hay." "Canning peas and beans." "Feeding threshing crew." Her list of tasks was interspersed with mentions of visits from friends and family, descriptions of funerals, accounts of who preached at church and the simple notice that "58 years ago was my Wedding Day."

Diary-keepers and journalists have delighted in recording Minnesota's unpredictable weather — summer as well as winter. Try this one, from the Stillwater Gazette of June 7, 1876, when frigid

Myron Hall photo, Stearns County Historical Society

***Enough is enough. When a summer day is splendid and work is avoidable, it makes sense to head to the lake for a swim. Joe Lommel Jr. did on July 18, 1973. He was painting his parents' tavern in Luxemburg, 12 miles west of St. Cloud. His mom told him to use up the rest of the paint and then join her at nearby Beaver Lake. Use up the paint he did, but not quite the way she had in mind.***

winds from the north brought rain and cold:

"People who had put away their stoves and under-clothing, just because the almanac said it was the sunny month of June with its birds and flowers, wished they hadn't."

The same Stillwater newspaper moralized on May 17, 1882, on the destructiveness of what we now call a tornado:

"A school house near Lakefield, Minn., stood in the way of a cyclone not long ago, and was seized upon, torn into fragments and scattered broadcast over the adjacent prairie. The teacher and eleven children were in the building at the time. If it only had been a saloon filled with ungodly bummers, what a text would have been furnished for the temperance orators."

(Bummers; yes, the word used really was bummers. It meant bums.)

After automobiles came along shortly after the turn of the 20th century, summer in Minnesota meant motoring. Early road guides are a hoot because they offered extensive directions. An example comes from the 1912 "Minnesota Automobile Guide Book," published by the Automobile Club of St. Paul. It describes the 4½-mile route from Minnetonka Beach to Excelsior:

"You enter the village, Minnetonka Beach, on its east side over a long bridge; continue on main boulevard a few rods in straight direction, then turn left to the Lake, then right along bluff road (Lafayette Club on right), keeping always to left near lake (at the end of village a sign reading 'Excelsior 4 miles' will direct you). Continue a few hundred rods to cross roads; turn sharply to left here (good sign will direct) and proceed straight to ferry, which is a large flat boat, capable of holding four machines and perfectly safe, and easy to run on to without leaving machine. After crossing ferry (no charge), continue on main road which is quite winding, but level, bearing to right ¾ mile from ferry, (road to left leads to Tonka Bay), continue on main road across railway (be careful) past Wildhurst station, which is on the right; thence some distance on same road over R.R. tracks at Manitou Junction, to where it runs into an intersecting road; turn left, thence into village on Oak St., turn left on William St., one block; then right on George St., one block (conservatory on corner); turn left on Water St., and proceed across tracks to drug store, corner Main and 2nd St., which seems to be about the center of the village of Excelsior."

Imagine the length of directions to the Black Hills!

When cars first were first being introduced, families used to gather around a new auto and get someone to shoot a photograph. That's still a good tradition. Each summer gather the entire household, including the dog and the hamster, and take a photo with the car in the background. As the years go by, the procession of cars becomes as interesting —and memory-provoking—as seeing the kids grow up. Wow, look at that Olds 98!

***Two steamboats, the "Harriet" and the "Minnetonka," took tourists on outings on Lake Minnetonka in 1909. Built four years earlier and operated by the trolley company named Twin City Rapid Transit, the boats took up to 1,000 vacationers at a time to the Big Island Amusement Park. For those who had paid a 25-cent fare on a trolley from the Twin Cities, the steamboat ride was free. From downtown Minneapolis to Excelsior, where the boats docked, the 18-mile streetcar ride took 45 minutes.***

Louis D. Sweet photo, Minnesota Historical Society

Minnesota Historical Society

*Split Rock Lighthouse, on the north shore of Lake Superior above Two Harbors, already was a tourist attraction when this photo was taken in about 1925. Way back in 1854, a civil engineer, Thomas Clark, had mapped the coastline and found an ideal spot for a lighthouse on a high bluff on a dangerous stretch of the lake. But there was little demand for a lighthouse until 1905, when a November storm caused two major wrecks near there. The warning light, burning kerosene, shone for the first time in 1910, exactly where Clark had recommended. The light was visible for 22 miles, and sailors said it could sometimes be seen as far as Grand Marais, 60 miles away. At first the promontory was accessible only from the water. Tourists started coming when a trail was cut along the North Shore from Two Harbors to Beaver Bay in 1915. A paved highway followed in 1924.*

Otter Tail County Historical Society

***Fish and corn were bigger in the Olden Days. Okay, you're right; not this big. These photo hoaxes from Otter Tail County — and many like them showing chickens bigger than children and crops taller than grain elevators — reflected Midwesterners' love of exaggeration. Before the turn of the century, "Photos don't lie" was a standard maxim. Then photographers and darkroom whizzes learned how to stretch the truth, and a new postcard industry was born. The fish card, from Battle Lake in about 1906, shows Stanton Ogsbury, depot agent, on the left; Harry S. Everts, center, and Ambrose Everts. The two boys are unidentified. The corn photo with an unidentified farmer probably was taken later.***

DOES CORN GROW IN MINNESOTA?

Otter Tail County Historical Society

*A little girl exuded joy on a sandy beach in about 1940. Do you remember dotted-swiss dresses with smocking?*

Kenneth M. Wright photo, Minnesota Historical Society

Kenneth M. Wright photo, Minnesota Historical Society

Northeast Minnesota Historical Center

▲ *These bathing beauties, we would guess, were photographed in the 1940s. Any cleavage they had was carefully blocked by crossed arms.*

◀ *Hubba-hubba. They called it a "bathing costume" in about 1930. We'd call it ridiculous. The young woman wore high-heeled shoes and knee-high stockings, probably silk. The suit was a wool knit, clinging and sensual but also hot and irritating. The woman isn't as emaciated as today's models but isn't as voluptuous as women were in the 1880s, when roundness was really in.*

***See how people used to protect themselves from the sun? This was a bathing beach at Minneapolis' Lake Calhoun in about 1906. Dermatologists today would say these people had more sense than we do. Many of the men sported straw hats or bathing caps and long-sleeved shirts. True, some were in bathing suits, but not so abbreviated as today's. The women were in long sleeves and skirts. What was the occasion? Maybe that was a boat race out there in the water, or maybe it was just escape from a hot day in the city.***

C.J. Hibbard photo, Minnesota Historical Society

Revoir Historical Collection, Red Wing

***With cane poles, these boys, most likely from the Red Wing area, made the best possible use of a fine summer day. Judging from their clothing, the photo was probably taken in the early part of the 20th century, but perhaps as late as the 1930s.***

Minneapolis Public Library

***We don't know their names, but don't they appear to be well-off children? They were in a pretty wooden canoe on the pond of the W.D. Washburn Estate called "Fair Oaks," near where the Minneapolis Institute of Arts is today.***

Revoir Historical Collection, Red Wing

***"J.S. Excursion," a steamboat, was taking on passengers in Wabasha around the turn of the century. The pleasure boat was crammed, and the journey was blessedly uneventful. Unfortunately, the same could not be said for the river steamer "Sea Wing" on the evening of July 13, 1890. Overloaded with 215 passengers, it capsized in a squall in Lake Pepin, which is a wide part of the Mississippi River. Many passengers were trapped in the main cabin, and others were thrown into the water and drowned. In all, 98 passengers died. Capt. David Wethern survived, but he lost his wife and youngest son in the disaster and his license was suspended. Red Wing was in a panic; 77 of the dead were from the area. It was said that church bells tolled incessantly as funeral processions filled the streets for four days.***

*The man with the bowler hat is John H. Darling, a Duluth engineer who oversaw harbor improvements in Duluth and other ports on Lake Superior. He and family members, and perhaps some friends, were on board a boat named the Vidette in August 1908. The photo comes from his family album and is labeled "At Lilly Pond, Portage Lake." Do you suppose that's his child in the casual pose, a contrast to the nobility of the adults? And is the woman to the left doing needlepoint? What's the other woman reading? The photos you take may be studied carefully by future generations.*

Northeast Minnesota Historical Center

*Ah, front porches! For Minnesotans cooped up inside over long winters, summer porches have for generations provided pure pleasure, mosquitoes be darned! This is Henry and Lillian Hahn and their family on their front porch at 2421 Bryant Av. S., Minneapolis, in 1905. Henry was the president of Hahn and Harmon Co., a Minneapolis printing and bookbinding firm. The Hahns lived at this address from 1900 to 1942, and undoubtedly perfected the art of porch-sitting.*

H.L. Renne photo, Minnesota Historical Society

Minnesota Historical Society

▲ *William Schenk had a big laugh on his porch in 1912. The porch is big and gracious, and it seems odd that a child there would have on his lap a handbill reading "Socialism — mass meeting." With the aid of a magnifying glass on the original print, it's possible to read "Mozart Hall, Sunday, Oct. 13." There was a Mozart Hall in St. Paul, so maybe William was a St. Paul boy. Teddy bears such as the one next to him made their debut in 1903, when President Teddy Roosevelt refused to shoot a Louisiana black bear. About William's clothing: In those days, young boys wore dresses until they were about 6 years old.*

▶ *That's Harold Freligh and Philip Wilson on the Freleighs' porch at 663 S. Broadway, Stillwater, in about 1901, when, just as now, little boys reveled in getting dirty on perfect summer days. Almost invariably, young boys had their hair parted on the side, while girls' hair was parted in the middle. Someone must not have told Harold's mom.*

Frank T. Wilson photo, Minnesota Historical Society

*The same man who took the photo of the little boys on the preceding page shot this one of his parents, Chester Sumner Wilson and Ruth Moody Wilson, at their home at 654 S. Broadway in Stillwater in about 1898. Frank Wilson was a superintendent of schools and probate judge in Stillwater in the early 1900s. An amateur photographer, he lovingly documented his family over many years. He took pictures not only of the cute little kids but the old people too — a good idea for all of us.*

Frank T. Wilson photo, Minnesota Historical Society

St. Paul Dispatch photo, Minnesota Historical Society

Minnesota Historical Society

*▲ One drank iced tea or lemonade on the front porch. Not beer — at least not publicly. Especially not during Prohibition (1920 to 1933), when the manufacture and sale of alcoholic beverages were outlawed. Quite a few folks did make their own beer, though. This man took his home brew and cigar to the back stoop sometime in the 1920s. Do you suppose he was hoping his friends would join him or was he partying by himself?*

*◀ The good old garden sprinkler used to be the best way to cool down kids. This picture was shot in St. Paul during the torrid heat wave of July 1936, which still holds some records for high temperatures. The boys were, left to right, Willard Pelzer, Warren Pennig, Howard Pelzer and John Pelzer.*

Gilbert Ellestad photo, Minnesota Historical Society

***These Lanesboro fellows may have wanted to be out playing ball, but somebody made them get all gussied up in leggings, ties and caps for a Sunday photo in about 1910. That's Gerhard Ellestad, about 12 years old, holding the football. His dad took the picture.***

***Benedictine nuns were in the dugout to participate in the dedication of the new grandstand at the Cold Spring baseball park on June 30, 1950.***

Myron Hall photo, Stearns County Historical Society

Minneapolis Journal photo, Minnesota Historical Society

***This University of Minnesota pitcher and catcher warmed up at the Memorial Stadium gate in 1926. Records show the team was a bust that year: The boys couldn't bat.***

Minnesota Historical Society

***Little Theodore H. DeWitt posed in his baseball uniform. Judging from the background, he was photographed in a studio.***

Blue Earth County Historical Society

***This is the first baseball team in the Mankato area with a pitcher who could throw a curve. So said the Mankato newspaper. The team was called the Baltics, and the year was 1889. The pitcher was Billy Mead, front left, posing with catcher Harry Roberts. In the second row were George Peayer, Bill Schellbau, Manager Charley Griebel, Charles Roos and Chuck Wood. Third row, John Dachins, George Krost, George Roos and Albert Roos. Note the buttoned-up collars and variety of neckties. The photograph was taken at a studio with a backdrop. The guys probably would have looked happier on a ball field.***

Stearns County Historical Society

***Some girls got to play too. This was the Eden Valley Girls Baseball Team in about 1906. Baseball, the photo caption of the time said, not softball. Women in those days played in long skirts; it wasn't until the 1930s when they wore slacks for sports. These women wore upswept hair and most-attractive baseball gloves.***

***Recognize the man on the left? That's Babe Ruth. The Bambino was in Minneapolis in 1926 to fulfill a vaudeville engagement and stopped by the Catholic Orphan Boys' Home to show the kids how to clout the ball over the fence. The boys' team was the Casey Cubs.***

Minneapolis Public Library

Joseph Pavlicek photo, Minnesota Historical Society

◀ *Check out those mighty skyrockets! It was the Fourth of July, 1911, and the Hedlunds posed in front of Old Glory at their St. Paul home. This was no casual snapshot. The Hedlunds dressed up — notice those high collars on what may well have been a hot day — and they were carefully grouped on their porch at 410 Baker St. The man is Christian T. Hedlund, about 36, a native of Denmark, a naturalized United States citizen and a driver for a brewery. (So how did he afford such a nice house? We give up.) His 37-year-old wife, Anna, looking very pleased with life, was born in Illinois; her father was German and her mother Austrian. The children, all born in Minnesota, were Grace, about 12; Louis, 10, and George, 8. Just why the parents were showing off beer steins we don't know. Perhaps they were favorite possessions; perhaps the photo was to be sent to German relatives.*

Minnesota Historical Society

▲ *Back in 1916, when fireworks were manufactured, not banned, in Minnesota, this little man was all decked out for July 4th. He wore a handsome one-piece outfit that buttoned in the front and fortunately had a breast pocket, perfect for holding a flag.*

Clay County Historical Society

***Most of the businesses on the north side of Moorhead's Main Av. at the turn of the century were saloons. That made sense; North Dakota, just across the Red River, was dry. The flags may have indicated Fourth of July festivities, but more likely they were part of A.J. Rustad's advertising for his tavern. It's the center building with the peaked roof. Saloon owners of the period were flag wavers, sort of like car dealers today.***

◀ ***This was a foot race along a county road about 1900, before jogging outfits, before races were measured in kilometers, before runners raised money to fight diseases. It appears that the men got out of the water, kept on their one-piece wool bathing suits and took off running for the finish line. The women to the left wore fitted dark skirts and white blouses, typical of about 1890 to 1910.***

Louis D. Sweet photo, Minnesota Historical Society

Northeast Minnesota Historical Center

▶ ***The Oliver Iron Mining Co., the largest business on the Mesabi Iron Range and the company that introduced giant steam shovels to mining operations, held a big picnic every year for employees and their families. This was a sack race at the 1925 picnic. The mining companies prided themselves on their benevolence. Oliver had become a subsidiary of U.S. Steel in 1901.***

Minnesota Historical Society

***Exhausted from a day of singing and drinking beer, this unidentified reveler at the Concord Singing Society picnic in June of 1916 needed a nap. He was snoozing on a newspaper, his vest still buttoned. Sleep overtook him before he finished off the stein and glass.***

Minnesota Historical Society

*A family posed in front of Old Glory in about 1920. Notice the flower border and well-kept stucco house. Stucco (a combination of cement, sand and water) was used as the exterior wall covering for more than half of the Twin Cities single-family houses built in the first decades after 1900. Scandinavians and Germans had used it at home and made it popular here.*

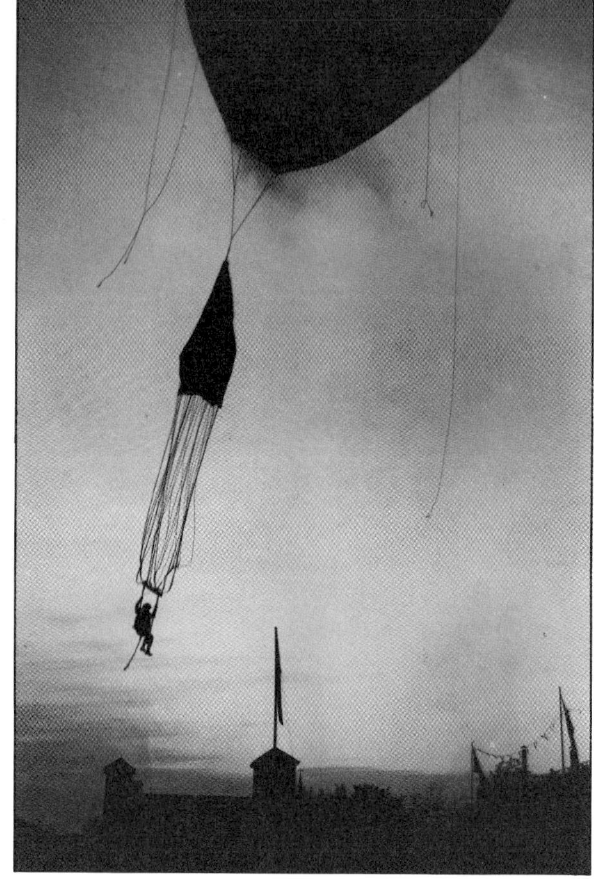

Minnesota Historical Society

***Up, up and away. A hot-air balloon ascended at a Red Wing street fair in 1898. Ballooning was a popular entertainment and sport in the late 1800s. Professional aeronauts, who preferred the honorary title "Professor," were showmen. They did a whopping business at carnivals and Fourth of July celebrations. The first aerial view of Minnesota was in 1857, when two men gazed down on the frontier town of St. Paul. They drifted close to Hastings — 45 miles in an hour and a half. The St. Paul Daily Minnesotan gasped, "Thirty miles an hour! Commend us to the balloon for fast traveling."***

John W.G. Dunn collection, Minnesota Historical Society

◀ *Jimmie Dunn of St. Paul posed with a roving photographer's goat cart in 1916. For 25 cents, the photographer shot the picture and provided two postcard-sized prints. Just before World War I was a time of heightened nationalism. "Made in America" was a message of patriotism, not protectionism.*

Otter Tail County Historical Society

▶ *Fergus Falls firemen had a huge water fight on the Fourth of July, 1911. They suspended a barrel from a line on the bridge and used streams of water from their hoses to push it toward their goals. Across the nation, the "glorious Fourth" was a favorite holiday and was filled with orations, band concerts, parades, cannon shootings and all-day feasts. To most people of the era, July 4th was a bigger celebration than Christmas.*

Minnesota Historical Society

*In 1942, a couple at a wedding shower got as excited about a new rolling pin as people do today about an automatic bread machine or even a Salad Shooter. Or perhaps this bride-to-be was pretending to bonk her man with a rolling pin, as was portrayed in cartoons of the time. The couple is Priscilla Mae Sculley and Jerome Francis Butler. She was from a prominent St. Paul family. He came from a less famous family in Duluth.*

Minnesota Historical Society

*The wedding photo of Henry Kroft and Mary Elizabeth Kroft on Dec. 12, 1888, shows them in the usual pose — the husband seated and the wife standing, with one hand on his shoulder. A bridal gown back then gave strong clues to a woman's economic class, religion and national origin. For example, many Northern Europeans wore a black gown, such as this one. It was likely to remain the woman's good dress for the rest of her life and for burial. The couple here must have liked flowers. Besides the bouquet, she also had blooms in her bodice and hair. The veil may have been a studio prop; in those years, photographers had a few around for those brides who didn't have one.*

Minnesota Historical Society

*This unidentified Duluth-area couple from about 1898 had a casual, even racy, pose. In most wedding portraits, the woman stood stiffly at the man's side. That was for two purposes: To show respect for him, and to show off her gown and figure to best advantage. The typical long, stiff corset would make sitting difficult.*

Minnesota Historical Society

*Huffy Charleston and his bride, whose given name has been lost over time, were from St. Paul and were very fashionably dressed in 1899.*

Minnesota Historical Society

*Talk about weddings! Charlotte Hill, the third daughter of railroad baron James J. Hill, was married to George Slade in 1901. Because she was Catholic and he Protestant, the ceremony was conducted at home, the Hills' stone mansion at 240 Summit Av. St. Paul. Charlotte, described as scholarly and not particularly sociable, chose a "simple" wedding. Archbishop John Ireland said he would not be able to officiate but changed his mind the night before the wedding. He and James J. Hill were close friends. The arrangement of the wedding party in this photo is interesting. The bride's mother, Mary Hill, was given the reverential spot — seated, in the middle of the photo. The man who footed the bill was at the right, peeking around the doorway.*

Matt Bue photo, Fillmore County Historical Society

***Believe it or not, this Preston "wedding party" in 1927 was composed entirely of men. So-called "womanless weddings" or "mock weddings" were a popular form of entertainment in the 1920s and were not considered strange. Many Minnesota county historical societies have such photos. Some pictures also exist of the less common "manless weddings," in which women took all the roles. Mock weddings were a form of theater, a chance to dress up (cross-dress-up?) and be silly. Usually the fattest men would play the pedal-flinging flower girls (guaranteed laughs) and the skinniest man would play the bride (he needed to fit into a wedding gown). The Preston group went further than most: There's a Charlie Chaplin imitator, several men in silk hose and others in black face. By today's standards, this event would be racist in addition to oddly sexist.***

Minnesota Historical Society

▲ *Mrs. R.A. Gray took a spin around the Minneapolis lakes in her Maxwell runabout in 1904. Note that windshields had not yet come into use. A society woman, Mrs. Gray didn't look like the type to chew gum, but many motorists in that era did. Two reasons: To relieve dryness in the mouth caused by the wind, and to patch leaks in the gas line. Almost from the beginning of automobiles, women drove.*

Otter Tail County Historical Society

◀ *This damaged photo shows a Brush auto from about 1910 with officers of the First State Bank of Battle Lake. W.L. Winslow was president and G.H. Hopkins, cashier. By then, Minnesota farm implement dealers were selling autos. The Brush auto was inexpensive and prone to break down on rough roads, which most roads were. Its unreliability had hecklers describing the Brush as "wooden body, wooden axles, wooden wheels, wooden run."*

***About 21 years after Mrs. Gray took her drive, three Minnesota "girls" in a small roadster were getting ready to head for California. Don't they look adventuresome? It's hard to imagine these flappers and all their bundled-up gear fitting into the little car; apparently they didn't have to make room for any men.***

Minneapolis Journal photo, Minnesota Historical Society

***Workers at the Ford Motor Co. in St. Paul polished vehicle bodies at the St. Paul assembly plant in 1935. The photographer kept the shutter open to show the motion of the men on the line.***

Norton and Peel photo, Minnesota Historical Society

William F. Koester photo, Minnesota Historical Society

***A photograper was standing on a bluff in West St. Paul at about 5 p.m. on July 13, 1890, when he saw a tornado on its way, about six miles from him. He shot this photo of what became known as the Lake Gervais Cyclone and made prints on 5x8-inch cardboard cards to sell commercially.***

Minnesota Historical Society

◀ *"I told you not to lean against that barn!" Actually this shows the damage caused by a tornado in Austin, probably the one in 1928. Many a tornado has caused death and hardship in Minnesota. In a typical year, one or two people are killed in the state by tornadoes. Prime tornado months are June, May and July, in that order. For generations Minnesotans have been wary on hot, stuffy summer days; tornadoes thrive on high humidity.*

▶ *Clarence Wilson held up a chicken killed and plucked by the winds of a tornado at Anoka on Sunday, June 18, 1939. He was carrying a box camera and ended up as a photo subject himself. The tornado made a 25-mile swath through Hennepin and Anoka Counties, and nine people were killed. Newspaper accounts of the storm delighted in recounting the oddities that the tornado performed: Ripped a wedding ring from the hand of a new bride and left her uninjured. Rolled a dog house for more than 50 feet and didn't scratch the dog inside. Picked up a glass bowl with two eggs from a kitchen cupboard, tossed it across the kitchen and left it right-side up; the eggs were uncracked even though the house was pulled 15 feet off its foundation and the roof was torn off. There were sworn, front-page affidavits to prove it. So there.*

Minneapolis Star photo, Minnesota Historical Society

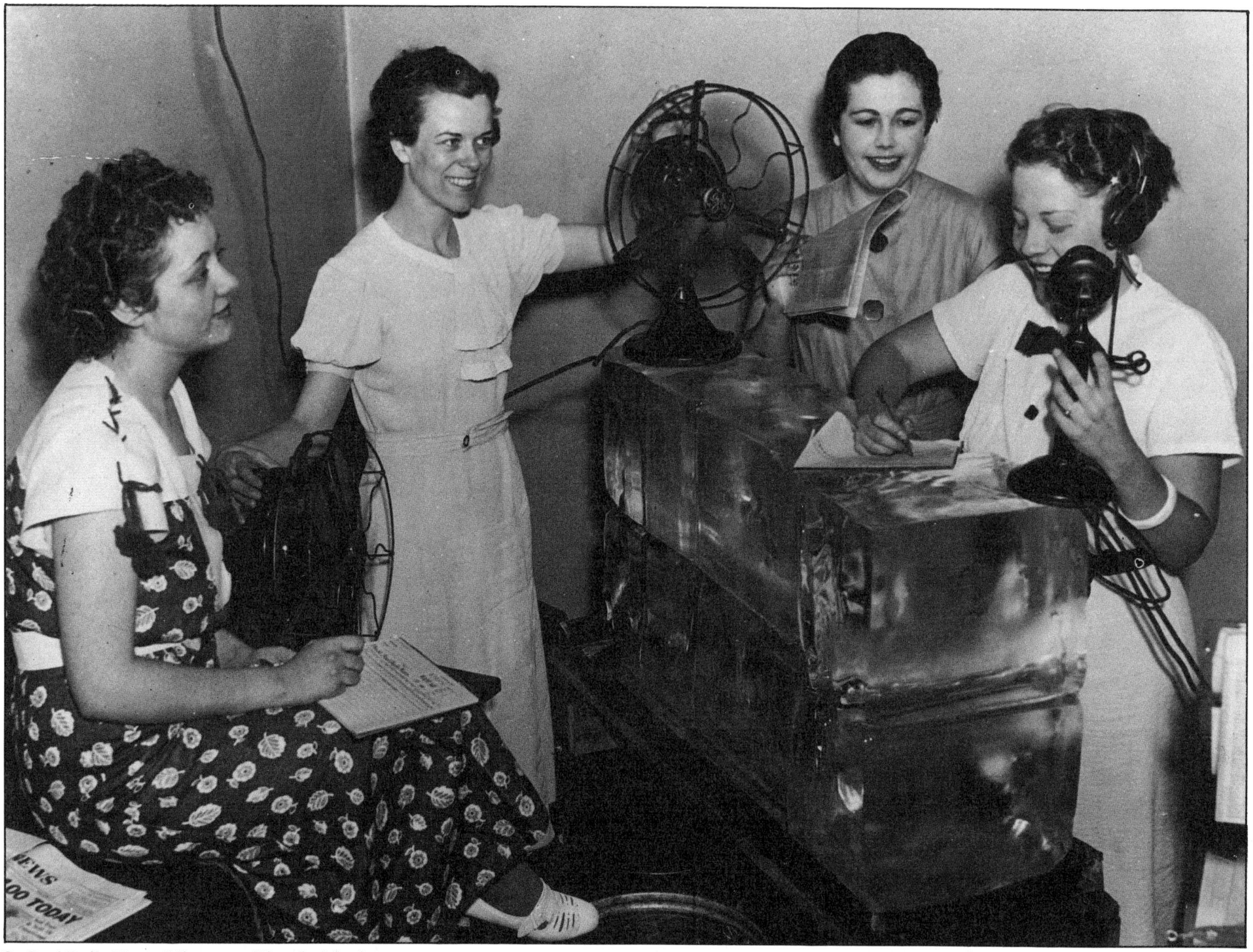

▶ *In 1949, when Gerber sold baby food in cans and Northland Ice Cream was big in Minneapolis, these kids played store near the Great Northern train depot in downtown Minneapolis. That's Edwina Zlonis in the chenille bathrobe; the other children are unidentified.*

St. Paul Daily News, Minnesota Historical Society

***How hot did it get? Hot enough that the newspaper's want-ad staff got 400 pounds of ice and two electric fans to cool the air, plus a big bucket to catch drips. "It's no wonder they're so cheery," the photo caption said. You betcha. The women were, left to right, Peggy O'Neill, Mary Ward, Ruby Brown and Marg Larson. The high-temperature records from this July 1936 heat wave have stood for decades: 106 on July 10, 11 and 12; 105 on July 13, 108 on July 15 and 99 on July 17. Yikes!***

Minnesota Historical Society

*The ultimate in low-tech, this Minneapolis macaroni factory in 1892 was staffed by girls who loaded macaroni into boxes labelled "Real Egg Macaroni." They look young; were they in their early teens? Especially young was the girl on the left, who wore a schoolgirl blouse rather than a fitted, corseted dress that young women wore. Child labor was common. Rapid industrialization came after 1870, and for the next 40 years child workers increased in numbers and as a percentage of the child population. This factory was pleasant compared to many; at least the window opened.*

Minnesota Historical Society

National Archives

▲ *Iron-ore miners were trapped in the Spruce Mine near Eveleth after a cloudburst flooded the underground workings on July 17, 1913. Ten were quickly rescued, but two immigrants from Austria and three from Croatia were more than a quarter-mile below the surface and were unable to move. They stood in shoulder-high water for 31 hours, rapping on pipes to let their colleagues know they were alive. They were saved. The photo may be of the rescue team rather than the trapped miners.*

◀ *In Factory M of the Red Wing Stoneware Co., Henry J. Tiedeman, left, and his colleagues made pottery sometimes between 1900 and 1918. They would, no doubt, be amazed that what was valued then for its practicality is now prized by collectors around the world.*

Revoir Historical Collection, Red Wing

Norton and Peel photo, Minnesota Historical Society

***This dignified man was without legs and had disabled hands. He was photographed at the Minneapolis Artificial Limb Company in June 1936. Was he an employee or a client? Sorry, we don't know. The city was a national center for the manufacture of artificial limbs, perhaps because of the many injuries in the flour-milling and logging industries that had been dominant here.***

Minnesota Historical Society

***A postal carrier on Holly Av. in St. Paul in about 1890 obviously had some friends on his route. The job of a mailman was considered a plum. Several Twin Cities mailmen of the era were black, as was this unidentified man. Does anyone recognize him?***

Alfred Miller photo, Minnesota Historical Society

***The employees of the Charles Holz & Co. Bake Shop at 383 University Av. in St. Paul in about 1910 turned out a good day's work. They had a wooden trough, on the left, for mixing the dough and a woven basket for carrying it. Note that the loaves were of various shapes and kinds.***

Brown County Historical Society

***This was the crew of the Empire Roller Mills of New Ulm in 1893. German settlers brought flour-milling skills with them from the old country, and milling remained the area's biggest industry until World War II.***

Minnesota Historical Society

◀ *Kids have loved toy balloons ever since the Chinese made them of paper centuries ago. Balloons as we know them came after vulcanization of rubber was invented in 1833. These children were delighted to meet up with a balloon man in St. Paul in the late 1920s or early 1930s.*

▶ *These unidentified women are a mystery. Could they be best friends? Sisters?*

Otter Tail County Historical Society

Minnesota Historical Society

◀ ***Women photographers gathered at a Minneapolis park (does anybody know which one?) in about 1905. By that time, many women were using the camera as an artistic outlet and as a means to document their homes and loved ones. Mrs. Charles M'Cutchen of New Jersey, an amateur photographer for more than a dozen years, wrote in 1898, "I call my photography my fancy work, and have never regretted that it took that form rather than crocheted mats and embroidered pillows. They would have worn out and faded long ago, whereas I have now in my series of negatives a sort of family history running through the [13] years from which I can print at any time."***

Truman Goresline photo, Northeast Minnesota Historical Center

***Don't you wish you could hear what they were playing? Four musicians jammed at the Merrihews' house at Colby Lake in the area of Aurora, a mining community. Those were saxophones to the right and left. The man with his knee up had a trumpet or cornet, and the woman had a slide trombone. The time was the late 1910s or early '20s.***

*On a high summer day in 1902, this group went for a carriage ride near Mankato. The foliage was thick, the horses fine and we hope there was a generous picnic stashed in the wagon. There might have been a few skinny-dippers to shock the ladies, though; the sign on the tree reads "No bathing allowed in this river."*

Albert Munson photo, Minnesota Historical Society

Hennepin History Museum

▲ *Lake Minnetonka was renowned for its extravagant resort hotels in the late 1800s, but the area also was enjoyed by people of moderate means, as proven by this Aug. 31, 1890, photo of tenting at Camp Orono on the lake. Tents were nothing new; they had been used extensively in the Civil War. Indians had long regarded Minnetonka as special and had several sacred sites there. For some decades, they kept it secret from whites by just not bothering to show it. That couldn't last, though. By 1867 the railroad reached Wayzata, and on the very first train were picnickers and excursionists. Summer traffic was heavy by the 1870s, and big resort hotels in the 1880s and 1890s served the wealthy, especially Southerners escaping the heat.*

Flaten/Wange Photo Collection, Clay County Historical Society

◄ *We call it a merry-go-round; they called it a carousel. The first one was made in Europe, probably France, in the late 1700s. This one was in Hawley in about the late 1910s, and, as you can see, pulled in the customers.*

Fillmore County Historical Society

***The Rev. DeVoe took his horse-pulled missionary wagon on the road in about the 1880s. He also was the pastor of the Methodist Church in Lanesboro.***

Fillmore County Historical Society

***Anna Neill was baptized in a river near Hamilton in Fillmore County about the turn of the century. She later was a mainstay of the Hamilton Baptist Church. A nurse, she assisted in operations by the Mayo brothers, who were attracting thousands of patients to the little town of Rochester by the 1920s.***

Brown County Historical Society

***On the day Mrs. Ted Lemke was buried in about 1890 in Sleepy Eye (nice name for a final resting place), the pallbearers probably dug her grave and then paused for a photo. Before 1900, funerals were most likely held in the deceased person's house, sometimes in the church and rarely in a funeral home. One of the undertaker's first tasks was to go to the house and cover the door bell or knocker with crepe to indicate a death. Black was considered the suitable color for the clothing of the bereaved, the hearse, the pall spread over the casket and even the horses in the funeral cortege. Survivors were expected to mourn publicly in many ways. It was the reverse of today, when society is embarrassed by public expression of grief and when people close to the deceased are expected to return to a normal life as soon as possible.***

Matt Bue photo, Minnesota Historical Society

*It was sweet-corn time in late summer at the Peter and Mathilda Abrahamson farm near Lanesboro in about 1919. The girl and two boys are their children — they're in other family shots — but there are others at the supper table. Could they be members of the threshing crew or other hired hands? Or neighbors? Notice the telephone on the wall, the dark shades and the pressed-back chairs, probably from a mail-order catalog. At the height of summer, many a supper on the farm and in town consisted solely of fresh corn and tomatoes.*

C.L. Merryman of Kerkhoven photo, Minnesota Historical Society

▲ ***This idyllic farm scene was probably from Swift County in about 1910. It included a fancy Victorian farmhouse, an elaborate windbreak and two barns, one likely for horses and cows and the other for hogs. People proud of their farms would hire a professional to shoot portraits of the land, buildings and special possessions hauled outside for the occasion, such as a sewing machine or washing machine. Some photographers made a good living by going from farm to farm, recording family homesteads.***

Palmquist Studio photo, Minnesota Historical Society

***In about 1915, the Milaca Farmers Cooperative Creamery was part of the movement of farmers forming co-ops as a way to get better prices for their products. These men were bringing milk to the creamery. Danish-Americans in Clark's Grove started a highly successful co-op creamery in 1890. By 1918 there were 630 in Minnesota.***

▶ ***These kids probably got dirty from work, not fun, in their World War I victory garden. The garden was labeled as a "vegetable patch" near the mining town of Soudan. It was a darn good-sized patch, we'd say. Oliver Iron Mine and other mining companies awarded prizes for the best gardens and yards. The companies regarded the towns, which they built as close to the mining sites as possible, as proof of corporate benevolence. But some reporters and social workers told of sanitation problems, exploited workers and low wages.***

Matt Bue photo, Fillmore County Historical Society

***Tena Larson, a Lanesboro resident most of her life, really knew how to grow glads. She was the sister-in-law of the photographer, who took this picture in about the 1920s. Mrs. Larson helped prove that gardening is good for body as well as soul; she lived to age 90.***

Iron Range Research Center

William Roleff photo, Minnesota Historical Society

***Lilly Therrien, a relative of the photographer's wife, picked blueberries north of Two Harbors at Brimson in 1916. Picking was good that day. Blueberries go way back in Minnesota history, with Indians enjoying them and fur traders making them into dried snacks. Railroad branch lines taking tourists to berry country were called "Blueberry Express." Also, there were skirmishes known as "Blueberry Wars." A well-known dispute was in 1872 in Brainerd, prime berry country. A white woman from Crow Wing went to pick berries and disappeared. Two Indian men were suspected of her murder. A whisky-frenzied mob of 300 or 400 whites broke open the Brainerd jail late at night and lynched the prisoners in front of the Last Turn Saloon. Four officers and 63 men of the First National Guard were sent to restore order. "All for Blueberries," observed the St. Paul Dispatch.***

John W.G. Dunn photo, Minnesota Historical Society

***In June 1912, Jack Dunn prepared the garden for planting in the back yard of the family home at 1033 Lincoln Av., St. Paul. Jack used the time-honored string method to get straight rows.***

Kenneth M. Wright photo, Minnesota Historical Society

***Harriet Johnson milked a cow on her farm at Kingston Township, Meeker County, in about 1923. Her husband, Magnus Johnson, was off at his other job — U.S. senator. A native of Sweden, he was best known for his earthy mannerisms and consistent support for farmers. During his years in Washington, his wife preferred to stay on the farm. Washington, she said, was lonely, and "you never get lonely on a farm."***

Hennepin History Museum

***It must have been late in the season. Look at all the watermelons. This was the Market Gardeners Association in Minneapolis in 1907. Farmers have been bringing their produce to the city market for generations.***

*Professor Albert W. Rankin, a University of Minnesota sociologist, and his family shared a meal at Clearwater Lake, Wright County, in about 1908. Doesn't the table look elegant and summery with nice china, flowers and plenty of food? The fifth setting is probably for the photographer, who may have been so pleased with the setting that he said, "Everybody, wait a minute. I have to get my camera."*

Chester S. Wilson photo, Minnesota Historical Society

*Mrs. Ross and her scabby-kneed child, Betsy, were baking a cake in their kitchen in about 1925. No, not the Betsy Ross of flag fame. Pay attention; this was 1925. The photo was taken for one of the Minneapolis newspapers, but we don't know the Rosses' claim to fame or why they were putting together a cake on the kitchen table instead of on the counter. But Mrs. Ross portrayed the new image of a mother as a trained homemaker.*

Minnesota Historical Society

Minnesota Historical Society

◀ *Longfellow described this scene in 1860 when he wrote, "Between the dark and the daylight,/ When the night is beginning to lower,/ Comes a pause in the day's occupations/ That is known as the Children's Hour." Mrs. W.P. Davidson, a St. Paul society woman, read to her children, Cynthia, Sally, Bob and Walter, in about 1905. We'd like to know which book captivated the children.*

Minnesota Historical Society

*Mom tucked the baby into the buggy and Dad watched. The date was roughly 1924, and that's all we know about this photo. If you can help identify these people, or any others in the book, please write. Take a guess: Do you suppose this father changed diapers? Most men of that era wouldn't think of it.*

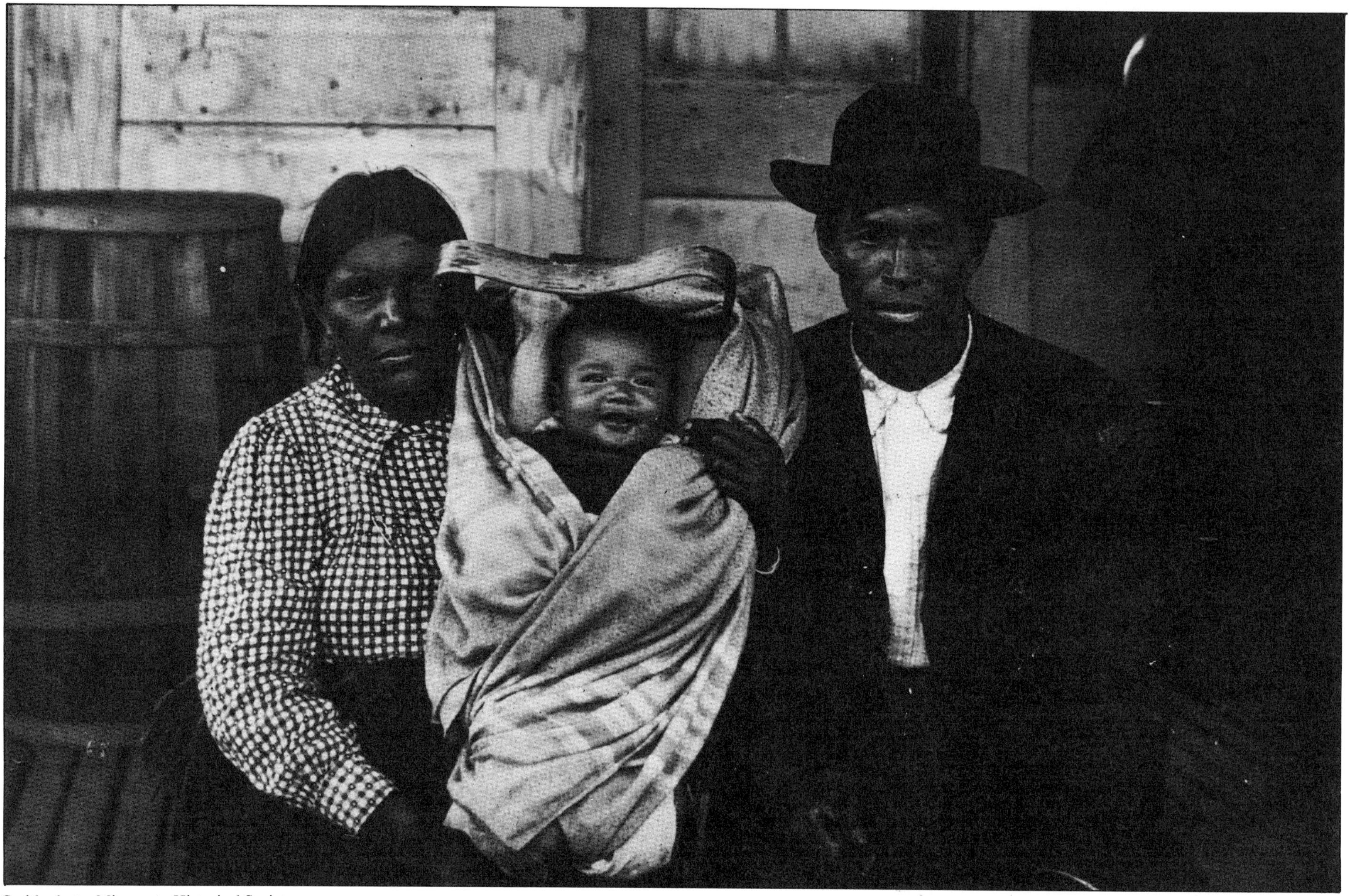

Smith photo, Minnesota Historical Society

***Sam and Mary Davis and their baby posed for a photograph made into tourist postcards in about 1910. In those days, roving and local photographers made postcards of Indian people who lived near resort communities. This one, in which the baby is incredibly cheerful but the parents look saddened by life's hardships, is sensitively done. Many other postcards of Indians were mocking and exploitative.***

Flaten/Wange Photo Collection, Clay County Historical Society

***The man, child and dog are all unknown. The date on the poster behind them is 1904, but, judging from the clothes, the picture may have been taken about 1915.***

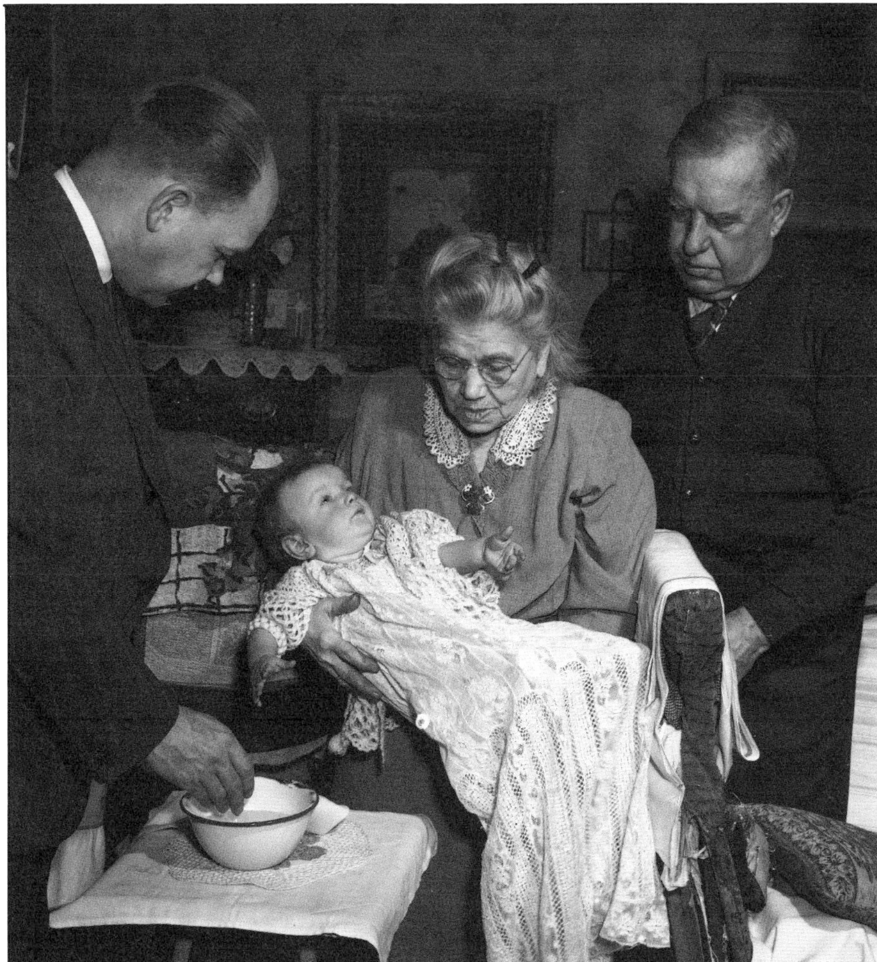

St. Paul Press photo, Minnesota Historical Society

***This 1948 photo shows Robert Martin Hummel, 10 months old, being baptized at home in St. Paul. The baby's godmother, Mrs. C.A. Finell, made the baby's baptismal gown from the wedding gown that she had worn 70 years before. The minister was the Rev. Joseph Simonson of Christ Lutheran Church of Capitol Hill, and the godfather was Francis Perusse.***

Northeast Minnesota Historical Center

***◀ A German family in Duluth used every inch of land for gardens in 1893. The lush vegetation indicates late summer. The home at 705 E. 2nd St. belonged to Franz Heinrich, a bartender at a saloon in the A. Fitger and Co. brewery, Duluth's longest continuously operating commercial enterprise until it went out of business in 1972.***

***▶ A miner with a wooden leg and his children were photographed in a typical iron-mining town on the Mesabi Range in about 1906. Note the tar-papered, tiny dwellings. One of the children carried a bucket, perhaps with water from a central well. The mines employed a massive work force of unskilled immigrant laborers, many of them Finnish, Italian or Slovenian. Mine accidents were not uncommon; there were numerous newspaper articles about miners being crushed to death or losing limbs. Animosity between the workers and management festered for decades, and there were strikes in 1907 and 1916.***

Library of Congress

*This couple, Mary and Charles Radeck, were married on Dec. 3, 1893. If this is their 50th wedding anniversary — a good guess, we think — the year was 1943. But her dress was summery, so our next guess is that the Radecks waited until the next summer to gather the family for a celebration.*

Flaten/Wange Photo Collection, Clay County Historical Society

Edmund A. Brush photo, Minnesota Historical Society

*About the turn of the century, a large group gathered at Long Lake, one of many Long Lakes in the state. When people had to name some 15,000 lakes in the state, some repetition was bound to occur. This Long Lake was probably the one in western Hennepin County because the commercial photographer who shot it was from Minneapolis. Whoever threw the party went to a lot of work. They brought tables, chairs, china and centerpieces. There were no children so the small table off to the left was for coffee and lemonade. With a magnifying glass on the original, we can see nice-looking strawberries. Never underestimate the fun of looking at old photos with a magnifier.*

Flaten/Wange Photo Collection,
Clay County Historical Society

▲ *Two children enjoyed a fancy tea party sometime in the early 1900s.*

◀ ***Donald and Ruth Wilson modeled with their parasols in about 1895. Clearly, the photograph was carefully arranged by the photographer, their adoring father. The parasols demonstrated the Japanese influence that was so marked at the time. To many Americans at the end of the 1800s and beginning of the 1900s, Japan represented a purer civilization, in touch with nature and free of the ravages of an industrialized society.***

Frank T. Wilson photo, Minnesota Historical Society

*Who are these great guys from about 1949? Sorry, the historical society doesn't know. If you do, write to us and we'll pass along the information to the society.*

Minnesota Historical Society

John Vachon photo, Library of Congress

▲ *Do you suppose these North Hibbing boys made any money? In August 1941, they were selling hunks of ore and other Iron Range souvenirs. This part of town was gradually being torn down as mining operations expanded.*

▶ *Shucks, it would be nice to know something about this little girl. Staff members at the historical society guess the picture was taken in about 1905, but they don't know her name, where she lived or what she named her doll. Does anybody out there in readerland know?*

Minnesota Historical Society

Minneapolis Tribune photo, Minneapolis Public Library

***These girls waited patiently, sort of, for the doll-buggy parade to begin in 1934. Notice the influence of the Red Cross on even children's play.***

Minnesota Historical Society

*Maude Misch, her pony Major and dog Ben Harrison (undoubtedly named for the former president) looked picturesque with a pony cart on an early September day in 1895. Maude wore her white gloves and fancy clothes to pose prettily for the photo.*

***A young boy named Louis, about 8 years old and dressed in a sailor suit, played outside with his toy soldiers and picture blocks in about 1910. For generations, little girls' dolls, tea sets and toy kitchens prepared them to be proper mothers and homemakers, while boys' adventure books, toy cars, trucks and trains, Erector sets, Lincoln Logs, guns and toy soldiers got them ready for careers outside the home.***

Minnesota Historical Society

# Summer letters and diaries

## Swaying pines

***Charles F. Johnson, 45, was active in the political and social life of Duluth. This journal item shows he loved nature and people.***

**Sunday, June 9, 1889.** Off on the N.P. [Northern Pacific railroad] to Sylvan Lake — a fishing resort about 10 miles beyond Brainerd. It was 9 p.m. and dark when we were left on an empty platform, and as it seemed nowhere in particular. O'Neil had in some way, however, appraised someone from somewhere of our coming so that when the train had left us and we had had time to doubt if we were really anywhere, there came from behind the shadows a horse with a comfortable Democrat [brand name] wagon in which we were rapidly wheeled along through what might be a pretty country by daylight for about a mile and a half and then came upon the shore of some water which we were informed was Sylvan lake and a little further on to a house which we got up into by a long flight of steps or if we did not exactly get into the house at first we got under a large breezy veranda which surrounded it. This with the cheerful welcome of a comely woman was enough.

All doubts were at once dissipated for with her cheery words we were made perfectly at home, and without being able to see very far, delighted with it, and, let me stop to remark right here, that a woman that can cause such an instantaneous reversal of feeling as we experienced — that is from a feeling of uncertainty and dread . . . to a feeling of contentment and home-like security — I say a woman like that who is able to do this in less than three seconds must have something awful good in her, that's all, and this is what Mrs. Nary of Sylvan Lake did for us.

But this feeling was not allowed to rest with its first infusion, for during our entire stay she proved herself so perfectly agreeable, homelike and indifferent to our going and doings that I must say once for all that she is a lady after my own heart. I know that a woman like that must have attracted a good husband. Although he was away at the time of our arrival — in the woods somewhere about his business, for he was a lumberman — but he returned before our departure and we found him quite as genuine, as great hearted, and, wholesouled, as his good wife. A splendid couple, and I was glad to find them quite well-to-do.

They had here a good sized farm and lands in all amounting to 700 acres on one of the prettyest of a chain of lakes and living in a comfortable and picturesque house . . . . The house occupies the base of a spur running out into the lake and as near the edge of it on one side that it suggests the idea of toppling into the water. All the trees available for shade have been left standing, tall pines on the spur carrying all the dignity of the forest in their tall tops and the birch and elm nestling so close to the house that they seem to hold it up . . . . To bed in a nice clean room with tall pines gently swaying over us, and with the birch tops looking through the windows.

Minnesota Historical Society, Charles F. Johnson Papers

~

## Northern lights

***Isabel Finnegan, a young woman of 19, spent the summer of 1936 at her father's resort, the Chase Resort Hotel on Leech Lake, in Walker. She wrote good, long letters to her friend Betty Walsh.***

**August 1, 1936**

Dear Betty,

As I sit here at my desk and look out over the lake, I wonder if it will rain tonight. The sky is becoming a violently dark blue and the water looks as soft as blue velvet. . . . Today was warm. My porch registered 88 degrees. My sitting room was several degrees lower. I have a new thermometer in the sitting room. It is a long deer's hoof and ankle (do deers have ankles?) taxidermied into a background for a glass tube and mercury . . . . Quite a decoration.

For a second just now I wondered whether or not I might have to continue by candle-light. The light flickered. At least once every summer the lights fail us because of storm damage down the line. Usually the occurrence happens on an evening when the hotel is filled. Quite a sight, that of seeing people wander down those long halls with flickering candles and if you could only see the dining room with a candle on each table and the girls rushing about. Those in the kitchen have quite a time. Poor chef! How he can see how he is filling orders I never know.

Speaking of kinds of light, I thoroughly enjoyed a magnificent performance one night this week. About one o'clock I was awake and watching the sky. The stars were brilliant and it somehow made me do a lot of thinking. Gradually the sky over the far end of the lake began to brighten with a white mist-appearing stuff. Then began the Northern Lights. They were really soul-stirring. The whole northern sky was lighted and spears of light shot up suddenly into tall Gothic spires, then gradually faded away. The whole thing was marvelous. How I did wish I had someone with me to enjoy the sight! Everyone around here was tucked in for the night. Too bad they missed such a soul-nourishing sight just for a few winks of sleep. We had enjoyed Northern Lights, pretty but not comparable, on two other occasions this summer. The next day I asked everyone if they had seen the "Lights" but no.

***We almost hate to mention this, but the reason Isabel was spending time at her dad's resort was that she was supposed to recuperate there. She had serious heart problems, and, in fact, died only six weeks after she wrote this to her friend.***

Minnesota Historical Society, Isabel K. Finnegan and Family Letters

~

## The Glorious Fourth in Bagley

***Maude Baumann, 15, was the daughter of Clearwater County homesteaders who emigrated from Mower County in 1900. She kept a journal to send back to relatives. Her description of the July Fourth festivities in Bagley reveals the racism expressed about Indians.***

**July 5, 1900.** Well we celebrated the Glorious Fourth of July in Bagley. We had a very nice time. Grace and I were in the parade. I marched with the girls. We came right behind the band. The name of the girl I marched with was Miss Swensen. Grace rode on the Liberty Wagon. Miss Bruster was the Goddess of Liberty. She has white hair & pink eyes. She is an albino. She is pretty tho. We saw those great fireworks. It was to represent the storming of the Fort at Manila. The men in the boat got their fireworks afire somehow. The boat looked almost exactly as tho it was blowing up. I don't think they wanted the fireworks to get a fire either. We heard a Negro Lawyer from Bemidji speak. I tell you he was smart alright. Miss Bruster and Miss Warren each sang a solo and one Lady spoke . . . . The Druggist read a piece and then the Band played. Pa said they had the nicest parade he ever saw, that is for a Fourth of July Parade. I am feeling pretty tired this morning. Only got about four hours sleep.

Ma is sick. I guess she is feeling easier now than she was . . . . I guess she will be all right in a day or two.

We saw the Chippawa Indian war dance. It was the funniest sight I ever saw. The squaws danced to. Of all the funniest dresses you ever saw, one old squaw had on two kinds of ribbon. My but she thought she was dressed up. She had one ribbon tied around her waist, and the other ribbon tied on to that. The Indians act as tho they enjoyed life. I believe they are the happiest race of people there is. Wasn't many drunk either.

Mr. Emerys, Mr. Thayers, his brother and nephew & Miss Peterson and Elmer & us folks took dinner together. There was seventeen of us. We had watermelon, bananas, oranges, candy, cookies, crackers, biscuit, bread & butter, chicken, bologna, lemonade, tea, cheese, pie & cake. Didn't we have a nice lunch. Well, by-by for now.

Minnesota Historical Society, Maude Baumann Arney Journal

~

## Of pants and pigs

***George Street Biscoe, a newly ordained Congregational minister in Cottage Grove and the son of the people who went fishing in Minnesota two summers before (page 3), wrote a letter home about the problems of being far from a store.***

Cottage Grove
Sat Eve
**June 21, 1862**

My dear Sister,

. . . I want to get some cotton cloth for lining to the pantaloons sent in the box. I had some cloth and there was some in the box but it was so thick and heavy that it would have made the pants about as warm as my winter ones. I alternate now between my thinnest-pair of winter ones and the white ones I got last summer. I have used up one pair of light black ones since I came here. So you may imagine I want to send to St. Paul. This is one of the disadvantages of living so far from any store. Mr. John Furber keeps a store as it is called here, but he hardly ever has anything I want. I have asked for rosin, cotton cloth, whiting and several other things that I thought he would have which he has not got.

To change the subject, I will tell you about our flowers. We have not been without a beautiful boquet in our room for many weeks. Mr. W. Watson brought Elisa a large one from his garden a few days ago. It had in it several different kinds of roses, dialetra, garden snap dragons, a white peony, and I do not know what else. It was very large and tastefully arranged. The children bring us wild flowers every day. I have a tumbler full of blush roses on my table now, the smell of which reminded me of the smell of those white roses that used to bloom at the upper corner of the grape-vine trellis and at the upper corner of the fruit yard by the elm tree. Are the roses I planted on the side of the front yard next to the lane doing anything this year?

**July 7th, 1863.** I did not tell you . . . of the way in which we spent the 4th of July. Elisa staid at home to tend the baby and I went down to the river to attend a picknic. It was very hot going but pleasant after we got there. This evening I have met with misfortune again. The pigs broke through the old fence and rooted up almost all the potatoes that remained from their last inroad. After all my hoeing it was rather discouraging to go in and see every row over-thrown . . . . Now there are not enough left to raise half a bushel. There are two rows of potatoes 15 rods long on the other side which have escaped entirely thus far and are doing well, but I do not flatter myself with the hope that they will escape all summer so that there will be any to dig in the fall.

Minnesota Historical Society, George Street Biscoe and Family Papers

~

## Disgusted in St. Paul

***Thomas Cahill of St. Louis, Mo., worked as a watchman aboard the steamboats "E.H. Fairchild" and "Home" in the spring of 1866. He arrived in St. Paul in May and stayed in Minnesota for a few months of summer.***

**Friday, June 20.** Went to the circus last night, it was tolerable, but there were no horse performances. A circus without horses is like a farm without a plough. Neither of them are worth the looking at.

**Thursday, July 5.** It was dreadful hot and sultry, but not as bad as yesterday was. It was 102 degrees in the shade most of the time and the celebration was postponed on account of the excessive heat. The rain of last night cooled the air.

**Saturday, July 14.** Spent all day loafing around town making calls upon some of my old friends. Two hours is all the time I want to spend in St. Paul at any time, it is insufferable dull and small and with it so proud and aristocratic. Ha.

**Tuesday, July 17.** Spent all day prospecting [for work] but St. Paul this season . . . is as dull as a small seaport on the African coast.

**Wednesday, July 18.** This day I also devoted to bumming but in vain. I am an outsider, the world is a closed circle. To me I cannot penetrate the ring, do what I will.

**Saturday, July 21.** This is my last day in St. Anthony. I am heartily disgusted with the rough set and poor accommodations that are here. None but a state of Maine man need apply here. [Many of the early settlers were from the east coast.] It is a miserable thieving hole full of the lowest grade of Yankees.

**Sunday, July 22.** Started for home again today and feel very much ashamed, and disappointed having spent twenty-five dollars and gained nothing, only to show everybody how unable I am to depend on my own exertions. It is very mortifying and humiliating, undurable.

***Cahill went on to work on a farm near Peoria, Ill., that fall.***

Minnesota Historical Society, Thomas Cahill Diary

~

## The good life

**Sunday, Aug. 3, 1952.** Gus & Kathryn here for supper. Brought the first cucumber. Also green beans.

**Wednesday, Aug. 6, 1952.** Louise Hughes came over & we had tea on the porch. A couple of hands of canasta.

**July 17, 1954.** Watched Aquatennial parade on television off & on because it lasted most of the A.M. Louise Higbee came early and saw it through.

**— Marion E. Crosby of Minneapolis**

Minnesota Historical Society, Francis Marion Crosby and Family Papers

~

## Record wheat yield

**July 9th, 1915.** On the face of things, it looks as though we would have another record breaker yield in both winter and spring wheat . . . . The crop needs more sunshine, more violet rays to bring out the substances that are to argue for good flour. If the rainfall would stop now, all would be thankful. If it does not stop, there is some question as to just what the quality of our grain will be. At present it looks well, and we are waiting to see it fill and mature.

**— Newsletter of the H. Poehler Co., Minneapolis, a wholesale grain and seed company**

Minnesota Historical Society, Emerson Cole and Family Papers

~

## So rare a day

**Monday, June 12, 1916.** I wish to remind myself in late years [when she expected to reread this childhood diary] that at this time a terrible war [World War I] is going on. I probably shall not forget that there was such a thing for I have read the newspapers, but it does not leave a very deep impression on my mind. Perchance I am too young or too light hearted; when nature is so wonderful one can not help but forget sometimes of the distress of others. "For what is so rare as a day in June!"

**— Abby Weed, age 14, St. Paul**

Minnesota Historical Society, Abby Weed Grey and Family Papers

~

## Worms and rafts

**Aug. 1, 1918.** Frederick [age 4] busy & dirty. Tries digging angle worms. Billy [12 months] feeds himself his cereal. Does very well. Quite a surprise for me . . . . Children go in swimming . . . . They find a raft by the shore & they have a great time pushing it about.

**— Dorothy Bridgman Atkinson of Minneapolis**

Minnesota Historical Society, Dorothy Atkinson Rood and Family Papers

~

## Afflictions and death

***Lydia Scott was a farm woman who lived near Lake Crystal in Blue Earth County in the late 1800s. She and her husband, Charles, had seven children. Her diary reveals a long problem with depression.***

**July 5, 1886.** The anniversary of our marriage [in 1852] & of Charlie's birth has come once more & he is 56 & I am 54 & no notice is taken of it except my own thoughts. I am reminded of flies, bugs, & insects for they seem to be always busy, doing their work I suppose, washing their faces, visiting, eating & sleeping & then die. Shall we be like them? Is there no future life to look after? O Charlie, Charlie, I am afraid you are not doing quite right neither by your children nor by the one you promised to love, nor by yourself, these future lives are all in your keeping to make or to mar, even my happiness.

**May 15th 1898.** 66 years ago a poor little crying baby was started upon her life journey, & many tears & much sorrow has been her lot through all those years, many troubles caused by errors in judgment & sometimes being sinned against more than sinning brought much unhapiness. Afflictions, sickness & death came & many loved ones were removed & some very near & dear, & yet some sunshiny days have made life bright & a great hope that reaches beyond the grave for I do believe in the dear Savior who died for poor unworthy mortals & because he so loved us. He will not refuse to bless — even me.

Minnesota Historical Society, Lydia M. Sprague Scott Diary

~

## The berries

**Aug. 1, 1951.** Picked 2 more crates raspberries. We are both very tired of berries.

**— Anna Kurtz, 50, who farmed with her husband, Frank, near Eden Prairie**

Minnesota Historical Society, Anna Mesenbrink Kurtz Diaries

~

## Hoping for the love bug

***Somebody named Ethel wrote this letter to her cousin about trying to get her man to propose. Her letter was preserved in her cousin's family papers, and no clue exists as to her identity.***

**June 9, 1938**
Dear Virginia:

. . . How are you two making out? I do hope that both of you have gotten positions by now. Things here are at a standstill and the ones that have not been laid off have taken a cut in salary. Lord only knows when this country will get out of this Depression.

How are you and the doctors getting along? Have any of them asked you to marry them as yet? My boy friend and I seem to quarrel all the time. I don't guess he will ever ask me to marry him and I do like him a great deal. I too am getting tired of working so wish the love bug would bite him so he would propose. I seem to have a terrible time with my men, especially if I like them, and I really do like this one as he takes me so many nice places and we both seem to like the same things. Say a little prayer for your old maid cousin that this "guy" will soon ask me to marry him for I think he makes enough so that we would not starve . . . .

It will soon be vacation time and I have decided to take another boat trip if it is not too expensive and I can get the time off. Hugh, my friend, wants to go along and we are trying to make up a party of friends to take the trip so that my Mother will not object to him going with me.

There isn't any news at this time so will sign off as I am writing this at the office and only have one eye on what I am doing. Say hello to Stanley for me and for Heaven sake write me a line for I want to know how you are. Also don't forget my little prayer above.

With love, Ethel

Minnesota Historical Society, Stan Asch and Family Papers

~

## Wildflower delight

Some days, when "the signs" are not right for fishing, will be delightfully passed in driving about the country — especially when the prairies are dressed in their brilliant and varied garniture of wild flowers. If I were a fisherman taking my wife to Minnesota, I would never let her see the prairie flowers till the fishing was well-nigh done with. She would be bewitched with them at once, and give them her entire attention. In the latter part of June or early in July the prairies are perfectly gaudy, resplendent, and honey-scented with them. A half-hour's ramble among them is sufficient to gather a bouquet that will put to blush the products of any conservatory. There are so many varieties that I once picked a bunch of them as large as a peck measure, tied them up just as they were gathered, promiscuously, and, on showing them to some ladies of fine floral taste, obtained credit for the artistic arrangement of the different colors.

**— "Lake Pepin Fish-Chowder," a book by Oliver Gibbs, published in 1869**

~

## Lump of sweetness

***George Brown, a 20-year-old Minnesotan working for the Chicago, Milwaukee & St. Paul Railway, wrote love letters to his 17-year-old sweetheart, Lillian Carver, in Des Moines, Iowa, the summer of 1888. These are excerpts from the mushy parts.***

**July 1.** My Own True Loved One, Oh Darling how happy I would be if you was only here to kiss me when I go out in the morning. I would be anxious to get back at night but as it is I don't car . . . . I am your Ever True Love. G.V.B.

**July 16.** Good night and sweet repose, half the bed & all the clothes [bedclothes, i.e. sheets]. Just wait a while & see who'l have the clothes.

**July 22.** I had a nice buggy ride this fore-noon . . . . Oh Darling if you was only here my face wouldn't have bin blistered. (But my lips would, I woudent mind that much tho.)

**July 25.** By, by, my Darling, Lump of Sweetness, from your Darling Lump of Sowerness.

**Aug. 9.** [Greatly missing ice cream] But I would give more to have just one kiss from you than all the ice cream they ever had in this town.

***In a letter Lillian wrote to George on July 23rd, she ended:***

Oh dear I was in such a hurry I didn't call you Darling once so you can scatter these around through the letter. Darling, Darling, Darling, Darling, Dearest, Dearest, Dear, Love, Sweetheart, Honey & everything else that is good. Goodbye from your Ever True Love, Lillian.

***They married, and by the time of the 1900 census lived in Owatonna with their three children, Mable, Floyd and Ozni.***

Minnesota Historical Society, Lillian Elizabeth Brown and Family Papers

## Hot air

A blast of hot air passed from south to north through portions of [New Ulm] and Renville county last Sunday evening. It lasted only a minute or two, but so intense was the heat that people rushed out of their houses believing them to be on fire.

**— Minneapolis Tribune, July 10, 1879**

## A perfect evening

**July 13, 1938.** Washed clothes. Vacuumed upstairs. In P.M. Oscar & I went for a walk around some of the fields. It was a perfect evening. The birds were singing in the trees by the Coulee [a small stream, usually flooded in spring, dry in summer]. Away off we could hear a train. The fields make us happy. Even the man in the moon came up with a cigar in his mouth. One of those rare perfect moments when everything is in harmony.

**— Maybelle Quarberg, who farmed with her husband, Oscar, near Crookston**

Minnesota Historical Society, Maybelle Jacobson Quarberg Brekken papers

## Summer treats

**Tuesday, July 10, 1945.** 47 degrees at 4 AM & 8" in hail in Cities, real cold, so Effie had Bee [probably quilting]. Furnace fire too & just right. Pot luck of course included ice cream, regardless of weather.

**Thursday, July 12.** A double-dip peach walk-a-way. Me for those nice treats. Strawberry pop.

**Tuesday, July 17.** Made nitie. These "short" war affairs [shortages created by World War II] & me don't like one another! But war being war & me not suffering 'cept for short nities. Miss elastic most. The 1929 drop in the market panic had nothing on the drop of my pants in 1945! Good thing my hips are bunchy enough to prevent 'em from making a complete embarrassment!

**— Myrtle Fortun, a telephone operator in Lyle**

Minnesota Historical Society, Myrtle E. Fortun Diary

## At the lighthouse

***Franklin J. Covell, the keeper of the Split Rock Light Station, kept a daily log. Here are two entries from 1936.***

**July 26.** Sunday. Only general duties at the station, weather cloudy, light rain most of day made everything look fresher, light northeast breeze, tempature 62-74, Barometer 29-28, 29-24. Keepers daughter Beulah returned from Bible Camp 7 PM.

**July 27.** Escorting visitors, painted No 1 Compressor, laborer worked in his dwelling forenoon, after noon went to Two Harbors to have finger prints taken. Weather clear all day until 5 PM, a thunderstorm passed east of us, edg strikeing here getting a heavy down pore and hail for about 15 minutes, hailstones lay thick for 2 hours, Changeable wind, tempature 58-70, Barometer 29-26, 29-18.

Minnesota Historical Society, Split Rock Lighthouse Logbooks and Diaries

## Overcoming depression

***Henry Nathan Herrick was a 40-year-old minister who in 1872 was worn down by bickering in his congregation, Free Will Baptist of Minneapolis, and plagued with bowel problems and nervous disorders. On leave from church duties, he recorded his recovery in his journal that August.***

Rented & moved out to an old home about Nov. 1st where I spent a winter of much suffering but usually able to get out to one service and during the latter part of the winter preached at St. Anthony or at Crystal Lake occasionally. With the warm weather my strength came back to me & thus far I have enjoyed a complete freedom from the old suffering. Rheumatism and some other minor ills have been interspersed with my happy days but have been able to labor with my hands till they are calloused & hard as any other laboring man's . . . . I have used my brain very little, been in the open air almost constantly. Eaten coarse food about twice a day. The Lord be praised for so much of health and strength.

Minnesota Historical Society, Henry Nathan Herrick and Family Papers

~

## Farming in 1877

***Philemon Montgomery Tuttle was a man of few words. He farmed near High Forest in Olmsted County. Typical of farm journals, his told about the weather, prices and farm work — breaking sod, killing hogs, threshing, planting corn, harvesting potatoes. He didn't emote and he didn't tell about family and friends. That doesn't mean he was cold-hearted; it just means his journal was intended as a brief business record.***

**Tuesday, July 31, 1877.** I finished stacking my barley. Nelse helped me.

**Wednesday, Aug. 1.** I commensed to cut my wheat.

**Thursday, Aug. 2.** I cut wheat all day.

**Friday, Aug. 3.** I cut wheat.

**Saturday, Aug. 4.** I cut wheat all day. Nelse worked half a day.

**Sunday, Aug. 5.** Went to church.

**Monday, Aug. 6.** Cut wheat.

**Tuesday, Aug. 7.** Cut wheat.

**Wednesday, Aug. 8.** I cut wheat all day.

**Thursday, Aug. 9.** I cut wheat all day.

**Friday, Aug. 10.** I cut wheat all day.

**Saturday, Aug. 11.** I cut wheat all day.

**Sunday, Aug. 12.** I staid at home. Nelse Monson went home.

**Monday, Aug. 13.** At noon Dan worked half a day.

**Tuesday, Aug. 14.** I cut wheat. Dan worked ¾ of a day.

**Wednesday, Aug. 15.** I finished cutting wheat at five o'clock and went to stacking wheat. Dan worked all day.

**Thursday, Aug. 16.** I stacked wheat all day.

***He stacked wheat until Friday, Aug. 24, when he wrote:***

Very warm and Dry we have not had any rain to speak of from the time we comensed to cut untill we got through stacking.

Minnesota Historical Society, Philemon M. Tuttle Papers

~

## Exploiting nature

***Oscar Hawkins, a teacher and principal in various Minnesota communities, joked in his journal in 1933 about the Depression, and was dead serious in 1936 about environmental damage.***

Isn't it a pity that the Depression had to come when there was so much unemployment? . . .

I am enclosing graph showing our "unusual" July heat record, and also Rain records comparatively. It is to be hoped that the period of drouth years will pass soon and that our permanent climate is not changing. Science seems to have evidence of previous drouth periods similar to this. But no "Dust Bowl" was present when the plains were sod-covered. Now it is up to man to undo as much as possible the mischief he ignorantly caused in his eagerness to exploit nature's resources (timber and soil). The big "timber belt" proposed two years ago is a fantastic and unsound proposition, I verily believe. But no doubt much of the plains region should be returned to sod — to cattle raising. And continuous reforestation will doubtless be a permanent policy. (Maybe a need of permanent CCC [Civilian Conservation Corps, a Depression-era reforestation program] setup!)

Minnesota Historical Society, Oscar Ferdinand Hawkins and Family Papers

~

## Pajama party

**June 11, 1908**
Gay broke her collar-bone. She fell off a tree while acting smart.

**June 13, 1908**
Mother & I went down town this morning and had lunch at Miss Mortons. It was great. I went over to Linda's to stay all night. We certainly did act up. After going to bed we of course got up & began to have some fun. First we had a cat fight — that is to say we spit & meowed something like cats until Mrs. McLain had to interfere. Linda then got on a feigned fit of grumpiness and wouldn't let me get into bed without tickling me out again so I played solitaire on the floor till she went to sleep.

**— Dorothy Walton, Minneapolis 14-year-old**

Minnesota Historical Society, Edmund George Walton and Family Papers

~

Bruce Sifford Studio photo, Minnesota Historical Society

*An apple for the teacher! At the Minnesota State Fair in 1953, one teacher from each of 77 counties attended the first Teachers' Recognition Day. Selection was based on length of service. Miss Helen Baker, 82, of Brownton, who taught in Glencoe, was honored for having put in the most years in Minnesota public schools — 60! We don't think she was in this photo, but we do believe she deserved at least two apples. The picture was taken in the days when ladies wore hats, even to the State Fair.*

# Fall

A 17-foot stalk of corn, a 28-pound cabbage and an 18-pound radish were displayed at the Minnesota fair long before chemical fertilizers were developed. The event was Minnesota's first territorial fair, held in Minneapolis on Oct. 17 and 18, 1855, three years before Minnesota became a state.

Farm men exhibited grain, vegetables and livestock, and their wives arranged displays of cheese and butter. The Rev. Gideon Pond, a well-known missionary to the Dakota Indians, showed three fine apples — apparently the only fruit shown at the fair — from a tree he planted in 1844 at his Oak Grove Mission (now in Bloomington).

Also exhibited were a few examples of hand-woven rugs and needlepoint, several early photographs by a St. Paul daguerreotypist and a blank book made by a pioneer bookbinder. The fair's highlight was a riding contest for the ladies. Four women were "elegantly costumed and mounted upon the most spirited horses in Minnesota," a newspaper reported. They put their steeds through various paces and exercises before an admiring audience. Mrs. Alvaren Allen of St. Anthony, "the lady in the black bodice and blue habit," won first prize.

That was it. No Pronto Pups, no Tilt-a-Whirls, no Princess Kay of the Milky Way carved in butter. No vegetable slicers, no encyclopedia salespeople, no giant hogs. The good old days weren't so commercial at State Fair time.

The date for the State Fair roamed around the calendar back then, and so did Thanksgiving. In the 1850s Thanksgiving was celebrated late in December. A New England man who happened to be in Excelsior for Thanksgiving Day on Dec. 21, 1854, wrote a letter to a Minneapolis newspaper called the North-Western Democrat, describing the bounty of food and hospitality. In the East, he wrote, only family and close friends are invited to expensive feasts. But he heard the Rev. Charles Galpin of Excelsior extend a public invitation to join in the Thanksgiving dinner at the Minnetonka House, run by a George Galpin. Some 80 or 90 people attended.

"Without exaggeration," wrote the New England man, whose name didn't appear in the newspaper, "no epicure seated himself to a more sumptuous feast. . . . Large plates of roast venison of the finest quality first met my eye, and in close proximity were several of the squealing, beastly tribe [pigs?], stretched at full length and stuffed with condiments that pamper the appetites of the most dainty. Next came the pheasant and chicken pies, with grouse, and the more honored of the feathered tribe [turkey], served up in every variety of style. The more common dishes, beef and pork, I need not mention. I came near losing myself in the countless variety of pastry of every description, and, yes, Mr. Editor, a school of good old New England pumpkin pies followed. Puddings and cakes brought up the rear in a deluge of luxuries."

The New Englander was lucky to get turkey for Thanksgiving. It was still a rarity in Minnesota. William Pitt Murray, an early settler of St. Paul, recorded that in 1850, the first official Thanksgiving in Minnesota, three local hotels "served up elaborate dinners of buffalo, bear and venison, placed on the table on great platters where everybody could help themselves," for "style and table waiters had not yet reached Minnesota."

However, on that same Thanksgiving, a very formal event was held at the Mazourka Hall in St. Paul. It was a magnificent ball, complete with chandeliers and exquisite paintings.

One thing missing from those early Thanksgivings was the sound of football games in the background. Football rules weren't formulated until the 1870s, and the game didn't come to Minnesota until late in the 19th century.

George E. Peterson wrote a letter to the editor of the Freeborn County Standard that ran on Dec. 30, 1891, about his new love of football. Peterson wrote his letter from Columbia College in Washington, D.C. Perhaps he was a young Minnesota man attending school there; we don't know for sure. But anyway, he heartily endorsed college football:

"The most popular sport of our eastern college is foot ball. As this is a game of which many of your readers are probably ignorant, and as it is likely in a few years to become as popular throughout the land as base ball, a short account of it may not be amiss.

"To begin with, the players, who are

Paul Hamilton photo, Minnesota Historical Society

*Prize-winning vegetables.*

*Fairs mean blue ribbons, and in 1926 Paul Hamilton roamed the Minnesota State Fair, taking pictures of people and their prize-winning entries. Minnesotans come in two kinds: Those who think of the State Fair happening in late summer, and those who associate it with early fall. For generations of both kinds of Minnesotans, the State Fair has ended the first or second week of September, and then children have gone back to school.*

Paul Hamilton photo, Minnesota Historical Society

*Prize-winning quilt.*

eleven in number on each side, are, or at least should be, an active, strong and enduring set of men. Since the game is a rough one in many respects, their knees, hips and shins are padded, and they also wear different contrivances to protect their teeth and noses. The field is 330 x 160 feet and is marked across at every five yards by parallel lines. At each end of the field equally distant from the side-bounds, are two upright posts 18½ feet apart having a cross-bar 10 feet from the ground, and over this the ball, which is melon-shaped and made of leather, is to be kicked.

"Let the reader understand that the sole object of each side is to force the ball so as to secure a goal, by kicking it over a cross-bar, or so as to touch it down beyond their opponents' goal-line, which is the line forming the end of the field."

Peterson went on at great length. He started winding down by writing, "Just as in base ball, team work, that is executive ability as a whole brought about by mental planning and secondary to which is physical effort, is the one potent factor and without which no college will ever see her college colors an emblem of glory and her college yell a cry of victory."

Much of what makes Minnesota autumns glorious is the spectacle of the golds and splashes of red in the trees. One writer in the last century described Indian summer as a "season worth a trip across the Atlantic to enjoy." The old black-and-white photos of people on fall expeditions

just don't do the season justice; color photographs are good for some things, even though the color fades in time. But journal-keepers and journalists wrote lasting accounts of wonderful trips to see the leaves and of lovely fall days. Here's what a writer for the Minneapolis Tribune had to say on Nov. 2, 1872:

"Minnesota is maintaining her reputation for getting up the most magnificent Autumnal weather that can be found on the continent of America. During the last ten days of the month of October, our eastern exchanges [newspapers with which the Tribune traded copies] from Illinois to New England were burdened with accounts of snow-storms, rain-storms, and cold, damp, lugubrious weather, while during the same period in Minnesota and northern Iowa we were enjoying the most beautiful Indian Summer weather."

Fall food has always been almost as fun to write about as to eat. In 1913, well before cholesterol was a dirty word, the Ladies Aid Society of the First Presbyterian Church of Stillwater published "Household Helps: A Family Cook Book" with recipes for such delights as Swedish coffee cake, lutefisk, cabbage pudding, fried chicken ("fry in deep fat"), mushrooms with cream, raised doughnuts, dumplings, Old Fashioned Southern Sausage, German chicken with paprika and, for dessert, German lebkuchen. The Ladies Aid Society said that meant "love cookies," but it was good old gingerbread.

This may have been slightly lighter fare than that featured in an 1886 cookbook

Paul Hamilton photo, Minnesota Historical Society

***Prize-winning doughnuts.***

Paul Hamilton photo, Minnesota Historical Society

***Prize-winning rabbit.***

written by a Mrs. Rorer of Philadelphia. Probably brought to Minnesota by a transplanted Pennsylvanian and now in the collections of the Minnesota Historical Society, the book features calf's head soup, potato omelets and boiled parsnips with cream sauce. You might also want to be informed of this 1924 advice from the "Home Comfort Cook Book": "Spinach may be the broom of the stomach, but Sauerkraut is the vacuum cleaner." Then again, maybe you didn't want to know that.

One of the more entertaining recipes was "How to Preserve a Husband," in the preserves-and-pickles section of a cookbook published in 1932 by the Ladies of Bethesda Lutheran Church in South St. Paul:

"Be careful in your selection; do not choose too young, and take only such as have been reared in a good moral atmosphere. Some insist on keeping them in a pickle, while others put them in hot water. This only makes them sour, hard and sometimes bitter. Even poor varieties may be made sweet, tender and good by garnishing them with patience, well sweetened with smiles and flavored with kisses to taste; then wrap them in a mantle of charity, keep warm with a steady fire of domestic devotion and serve with peaches and cream. When thus prepared they will keep for years."

While much of fall in Minnesota's early years was devoted to such tasks as candle-dipping, spinning, weaving, canning and making

dolls from cornhusks, some of the men went hunting for pleasure as well as for food.

An 1877 account tells of a hunting trip to Kandiyohi County. A party of four bagged 31 geese, five sandhill cranes, 14 prairie chickens, 17 canvasback ducks and 28 golden plover. That was when no limit was placed on the number of birds shot. Another record of hunting in the 1870s, preserved by the Minnesota Historical Society, described a Minnesota lake — we don't know which one — in the half hour between sunset and dark. Ducks were "falling like rain." One of the hunters wrote that "we shot and shot," and added that "it was not sport — there were too many ducks."

Minnesota was known across the country for its hunting and fishing, and railroads catered to the sportsmen's needs. In the 1870s, special coaches, fitted with bunks and cooking apparatus, could be chartered by hunting parties and run almost anywhere.

Probably the fanciest of these setups was one used by a group of 12 hunters from Worcester, Mass. They were bound for western Minnesota and the Dakotas to hunt upland game birds. Their private car, "The City of Worcester," was exhibited in St. Paul for a day in September 1878. Newspapers told of this "palatial home on wheels" being the "centre of an unusual degree of interest."

The car's exterior was a "lake color" and ornamented with gold leaf and silver moldings. The steps were mahogany, with brass treads. On the platform was a large refrigerator, a coal box and a water tank, and underneath were four lockers for ice, tools and vegetables. The interior was finished in black walnut, rosewood and mahogany. It contained a reading room, drawing room, and a dining room, with furniture upholstered in crimson plush, curtains of silk damask and Brussels carpets. The equipment included 12 double berths, silver-plated oil lamps, a kitchen and washrooms (probably with a drop-through toilet and a sink for washing).

"Hunting in the grand manner" was how this expedition was described. Accurately, we'd say.

Minnesota Historical Society

***Someone by the name of Edgar put up storm windows in about 1905.***

Carl Graff photo, Minnesota Historical Society

***A good-looking beef cow was the focus of attention at the Lac Qui Parle County Fair in about 1913. She wasn't the only one all cleaned up for the show; the men wore suits, ties and, in some cases, fur coats. They probably gave those mustaches a good brushing too. Ads for Saginaw Silos were on the posts.***

*A crowd lined up at the grandstand box office at the State Fair in about 1935. Grandstand seats were 80 cents. Ladies got in for 35 cents. For the few people with big bucks — remember, this was the Depression — there were boxes for $1.25. They may have been in line for tickets to horse races or auto races. Or it could have been Thrill Day, when autos smashed into each other, parachutes dropped, hot-air balloons ascended and Capt. F.F. Frakes, daredevil pilot, deliberately crashed his plane into a house constructed in front of the grandstand. He cut the motor at 2,000 feet, fell with the plane and walked away unscathed. It was a thrill, the newspapers reported.*

Minnesota Historical Society

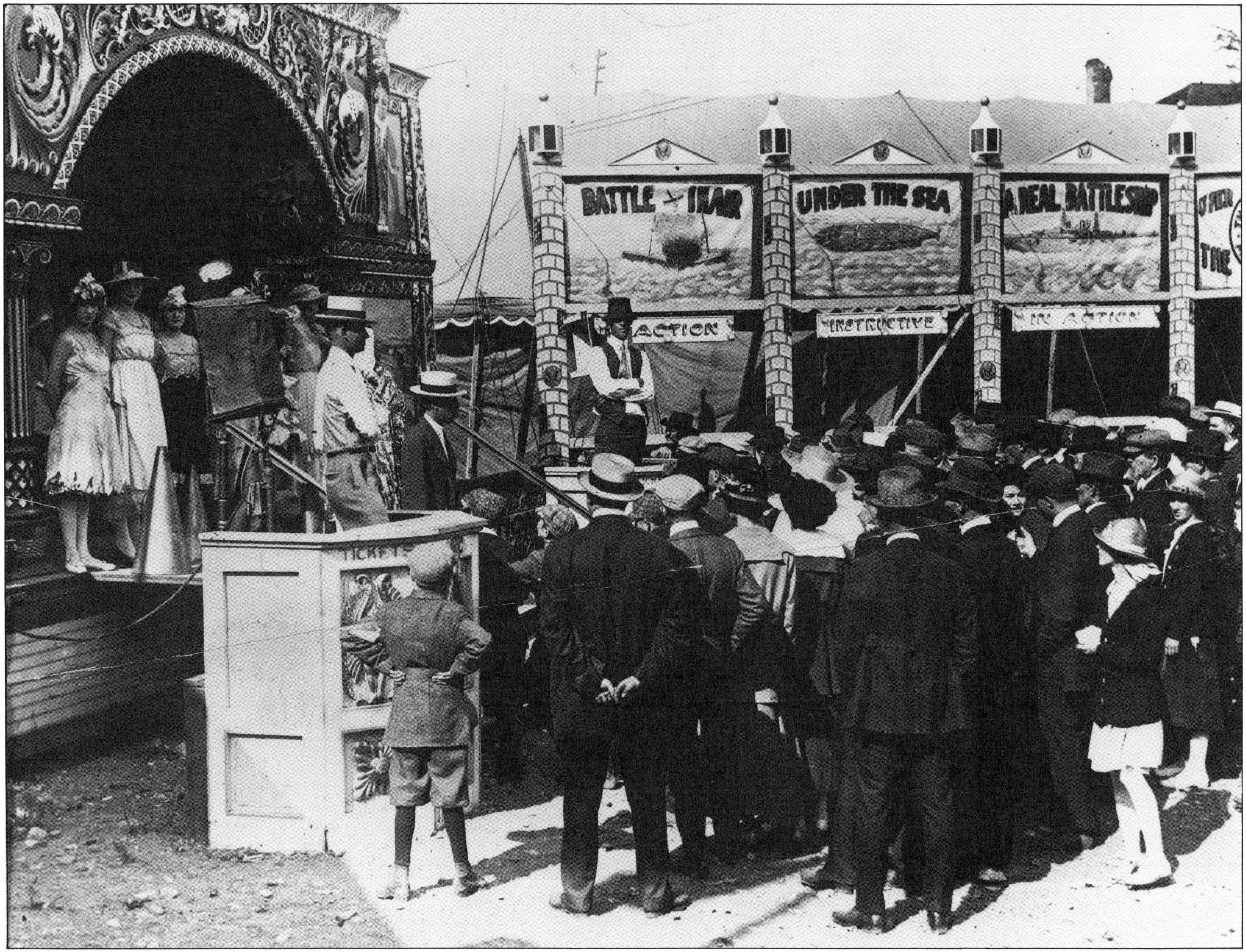

Minnesota Historical Society

◀ *Back in 1917, a crowd pressed to hear and see at a midway show at the State Fair. The United States had entered World War I by declaring war on Germany in April of that year, and signs in the background depicted war scenes. We haven't a clue about what the snazzily dressed young women on stage were up to.*

▶ *Talk about determination! This family rode to the State Fair in the back of a pickup truck in 1937. The folks were nicely dressed for the occasion. With a magnifying glass on the original print, you can see that the older boy wore a pennant reading "Babe Ruth."*

Minnesota Historical Society

*Looking hot and tired, George Gardner, a farmer near Clearwater, held a sheaf of the barley he grew in about 1955. Stearns County farmers then grew barley (harvested in summer and early fall), oats and corn. Soybeans became a major crop later.*

Myron Hall photo, Stearns County Historical Society

Fillmore County Historical Society

***A steam-thresher crew from Carimona Township in Fillmore County stopped work for a photo sometime in the late 1800s. The work was warm, dirty and scratchy; several of the men were wearing bandanas to pull up over their mouths to keep the dust out. This thresher was an early form of the technology that shakes grain from husks. The straw stack on the left would have been used for cattle bedding.***

Brooks photo, Little Falls, Minnesota Historical Society

*This farm scene from Morrison County at about the turn of the 20th century was not a typical photograph. Most farm families had their portraits taken to include their homes and barns. But these people posed in a field. Perhaps they were more proud of their land and crops than of their buildings. The woman in the center and the couple to the right might have been the landowners, or visitors from the city. So why the gun? It's difficult to tell about the man to the left; he's wearing a crisp white shirt but leaning against a farm tool. Another mystery is that there were no leaves on the trees, indicating autumn. But mowing meadow hay, which is what the activity seems to be, usually was done in June or July. Was this a second cutting? Can anybody out there clear this up?*

Northern Pacific Railroad photo, Minnesota Historical Society

*Ojibway Indians gathered wild rice in about 1925. High in nutritional value, it was a staple of the Ojibway diet for centuries. Ripe wild rice was — and is — harvested by "knocking" the stalks with sticks to dislodge the kernels into the canoe. Harvesters must be gentle so they do not break the stalks, which would rule out a second harvesting. The rice ripens over about 10 days.*

*Two St. Paul children, Jimmy Clark of 2127 Dayton Av. and Jeanne Hansel of 399 Dewey Av., were pleased with their jack-o'-lanterns in 1942. They look a little young to have been wielding knives. Maybe their job was to scoop out the seeds.*

Minnesota Historical Society

Edward A. Fairbrother photo, Minnesota Historical Society

*Then as now, pumpkins sometimes were planted as companion crops to corn; the pumpkin vines help to cool the corn's roots. "George, Edith and 'Grandpa' Fairbrother in the cornfield, Sept. 29, 1908," reads the caption in the family album, but we don't know where the photo was taken. We shouldn't complain, though. The information is a whole lot more than most family albums convey. The St. Paul Fairbrother family had a fine tradition; each year they took a picture of their Christmas tree, surrounded by opened gifts. Try it. It's sure to bring back memories someday.*

Minnesota Historical Society

*Fall has meant back-to-school for generations of Minnesotans. Here nursery-school children used their paint and best imaginations to come up with something beautiful in 1937. This was at Rice School and was part of the Works Projects Administration program during the Depression. The WPA was founded in 1935 to provide work for needy people on public works projects. In Minnesota, projects ranged from building an auditorium in Willmar to repairing a staircase at the state Capitol, from building a sewage disposal plant in Perham to making a ski jump at St. Paul's Battle Creek Park, from teaching canning and sewing to repairing library books.*

Minnesota Historical Society

*This photograph had been identified as children posing next to a horse-drawn school bus at Homecroft School at 2501 Edgcumbe Rd., St. Paul, in about 1914. But the historical society's photo experts now believe the vehicle was more likely one family's wagon. The kids look like siblings, but maybe that cap would have made even President Woodrow Wilson look like family.*

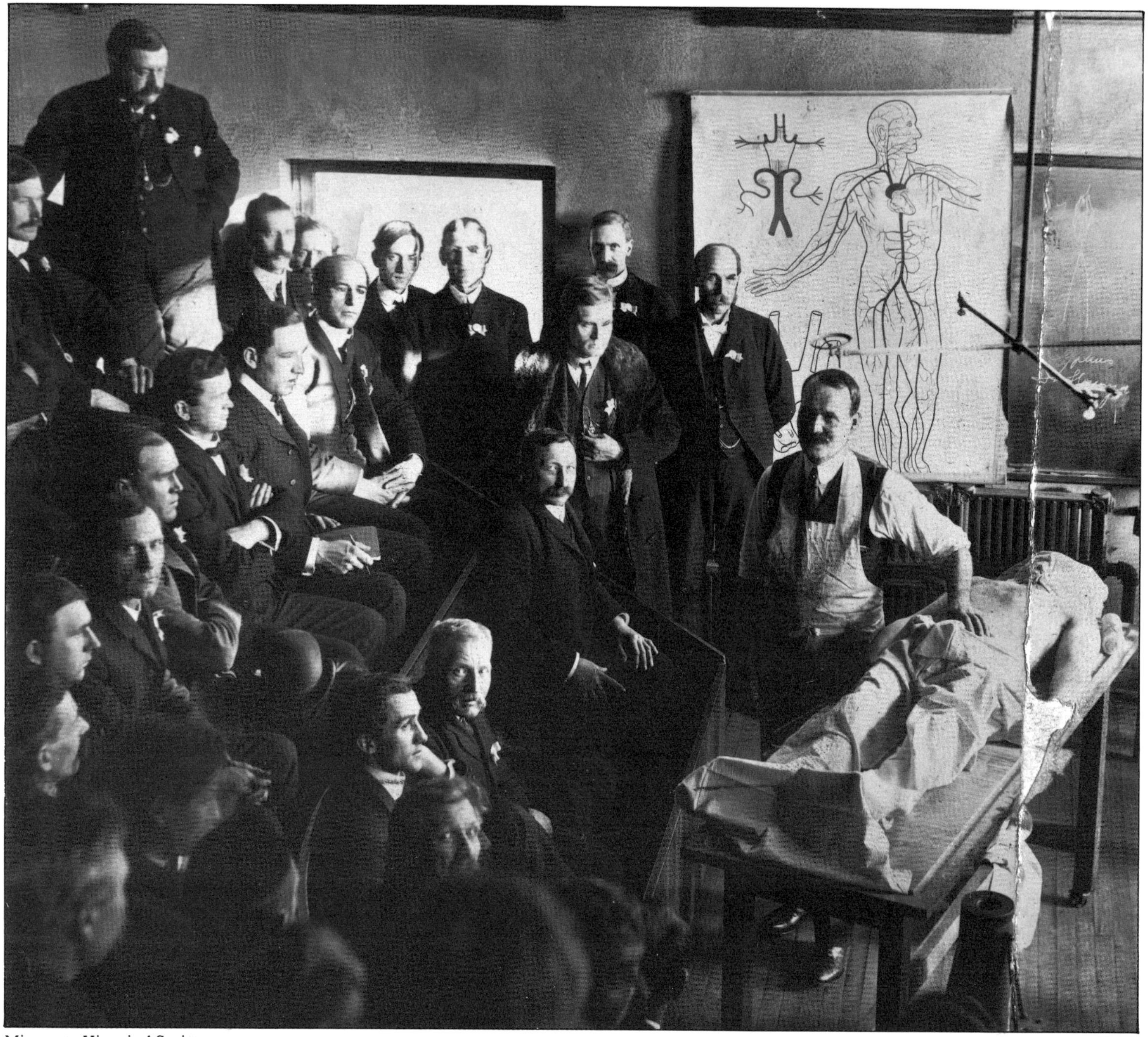

Minnesota Historical Society

◀ *Professor Clement Williams of the University of Minnesota lectured at what was probably an anatomy class, about 1905. One good clue was the cadaver on the table. The class looked older than average medical students. They might have been physicians at a seminar. No women were in the group, but there were female doctors by then. As early as 1883, Dr. Martha Ripley of Minneapolis specialized in obstetrics and children's diseases.*

▶ *In the days of starched uniforms and crisp caps, two students from the Fergus Falls State Hospital Training School for Nurses enjoyed each other's company. The photo was taken in a studio on Valentine's Day, 1918. The taller woman is Martha Noeth; the other's identity is lost. The striped uniforms and type of cap indicated student status.*

▶ ***Dressed in overalls but wearing dressy shoes, these University of Minnesota sorority sisters decorated for homecoming in about 1925. The house was Gamma Phi Beta at 311 10th Av. SE., Minneapolis.***

Otter Tail County Historical Society

Minnesota Historical Society

Minneapolis Star-Journal photo, Minnesota Historical Society

***Children lined up for the Good Teeth Demonstration at Rosedale School, Minneapolis, in about 1925. Can those be molar-shaped hats they're wearing? Sailor suits, knickers and cotton leggings were popular then among the elementary-school set. In the decades before fluoridated water, most kids had mouthfuls of cavities and fillings. Fluoridation appeared on the Twin Cities scene in the 1950s.***

*Never fear; the School Safety Patrol is here. Children learned traffic safety in Minneapolis beginning in about 1925. Across the river in St. Paul, the national school-patrol movement was started in 1921. Sister Carmela, principal of Cathedral School, feared that Model T Fords shooting down the Kellogg Blvd. hill from Summit Av. would hit her children. She asked responsible boys from the upper grades to help the little ones cross at Dayton and Summit Avs. A year later the St. Paul Police Department expanded the idea of her "school police" across the city. The American Legion took over sponsorship in the state in 1930, and soon the school patrol spread nationwide.*

Minneapolis Star-Journal photo, Minnesota Historical Society

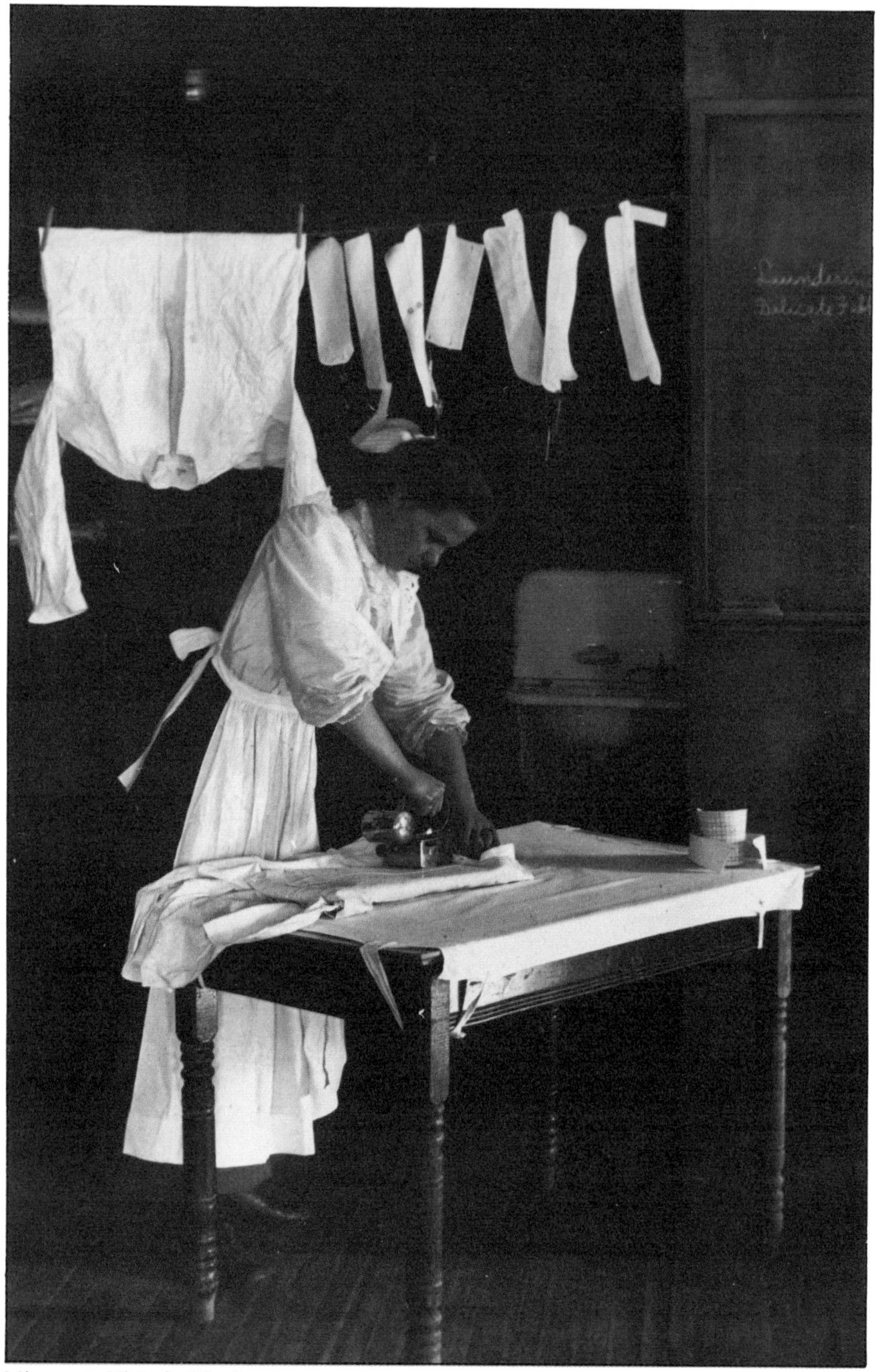

Minnesota Historical Society

John Vachon photo, Library of Congress

▲ *Elaine McCormick of Meeker County made beds one morning in 1942 before the school bus arrived. The wallpaper has come back into style.*

◀ *A student at the Minnesota School of Agriculture ironed clothes in about 1910. The school educated boys and girls for farming careers. Just why this young woman was using a table as an ironing board is open to question. Ironing boards had been around for decades, and the 1908 Sears catalogue had a nice folding model, adjustable to three heights, for 77 cents. Simple washing machines were available by then. Sears had the Superba Ball Bearing Washing Machine ($6.38), which was essentially a tub to which boiling water and soap were added. With someone rotating a handle, water was circulated through the fabrics. "In five to eight minutes the tubful of clothes is washed to snowy cleanness," Sears claimed. Guaranteed. Six months free trial. Even a child can run it. Order now.*

Frank T. Wilson photo, Minnesota Historical Society

***Amid the books and periodicals, Hamline University students studied in the Old Main Library sometime in the 1890s. Hamline, founded in 1854, is Minnesota's oldest university and one of the nation's first coeducational universities. The first two graduates, in 1859, were women.***

Minnesota Historical Society

◀ *At an early equivalent of a well-baby clinic, children were weighed at the Emmanuel Cohen Center in about 1925. Started on the north side of Minneapolis the year before, the center became a mainstay of the Jewish community, offering English classes, social clubs, a gym and swimming pool. In an attempt to diminish anti-Semitism, the center sponsored basketball and baseball teams that played against teams from Christian churches and settlement houses. The center was named for local Jewish lawyer and philanthropist Emmanuel Cohen and was a forerunner of the Jewish Community Center.*

Minnesota Historical Society

*Checking teeth at school, Dr. Ernest B. Hoag conducted a health survey at Central High School, Albert Lea, in the early 1900s.*

Eggan photo, Hennepin History Museum

***In 1907, when this photograph of an eighth-grade class was shot, many rural and urban students ended their formal education in their early teens. High school was available to the privileged and brainy. The rest went to work. This was the eighth grade of Jackson School, 15th Av. and 4th St. S., in Minneapolis. The nice clock and desks may have made their way to antique shops by now.***

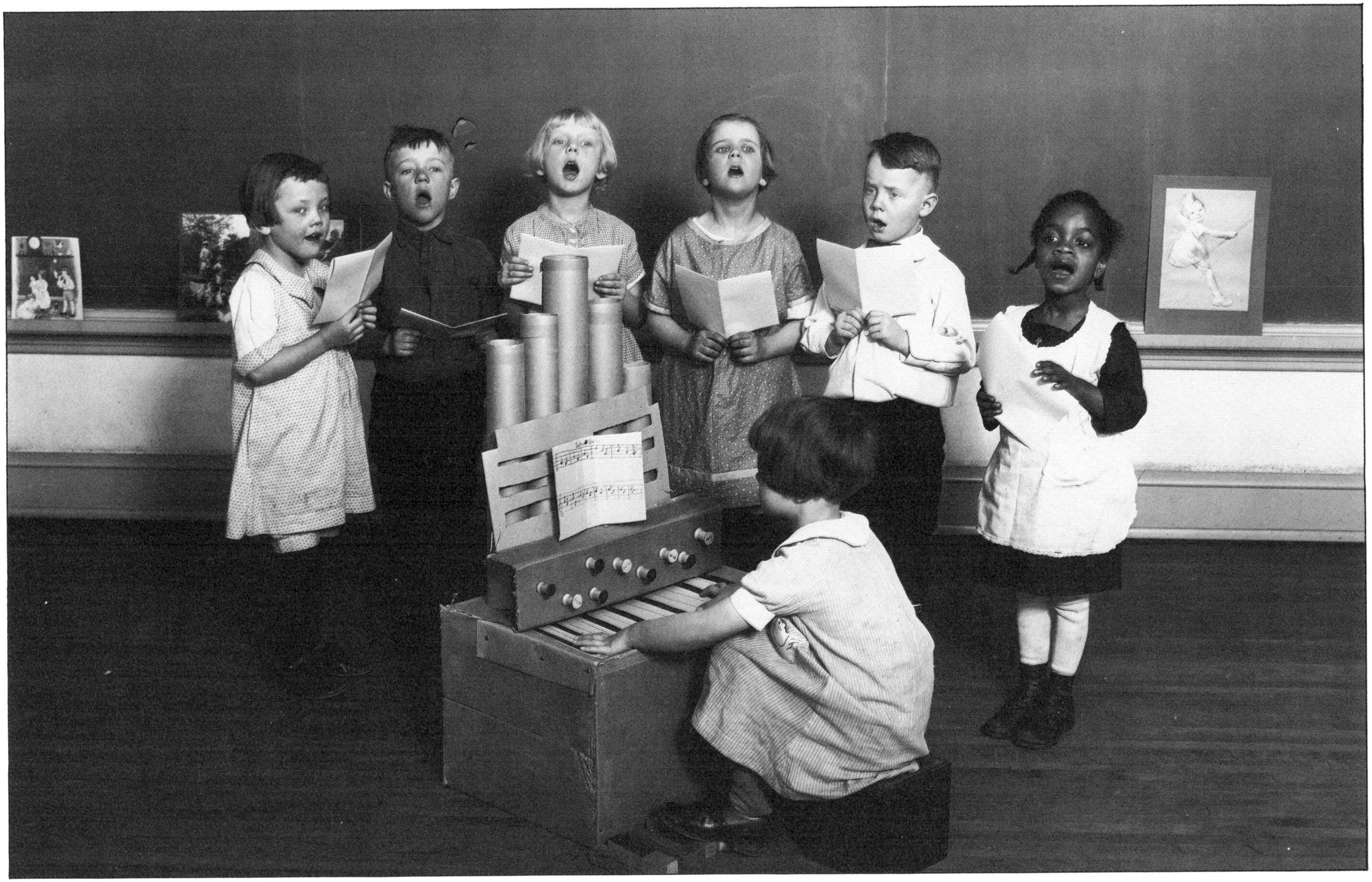

Minneapolis Star-Journal photo, Minnesota Historical Society

*The cardboard organ was only pretend, but these children at Whittier School in Minneapolis clearly believed they were making beautiful music, and they probably were. The photograph ran in the newspaper in about 1925. The only child whose name we know is the little girl on the right; she was Yvette Strader. If you're wondering, as we did, about the extent of racial integration in Minneapolis schools back then, you'll want to know that they were integrated — at least as much as the neighborhoods were. Rental and purchase agreements kept blacks out of many areas. Whittier School, at 2609 Blaisdell Av. S., was in a wealthy section of Minneapolis, where black people were employed in some of the mansions.*

Minnesota Historical Society

◀ *This must have been Bunny Day at Hallie Q. Brown nursery school, St. Paul, in 1938. The children were looking at picture books featuring Peter Rabbit and Barnyard Babies. They even had bunny furniture. Some of the knickknacks on the top of the book case appear African; the children may have been getting a lesson in their African roots.*

St. John's University Archives

*Not really in a planetarium, these student astronomers named Smith and Harrison at St. John's University in 1888 did their best to make a photography studio look scientific. The portrait on the wall behind them was of Father Peter Engel, the founder of the photo studio and later the prior of St. John's Abbey.*

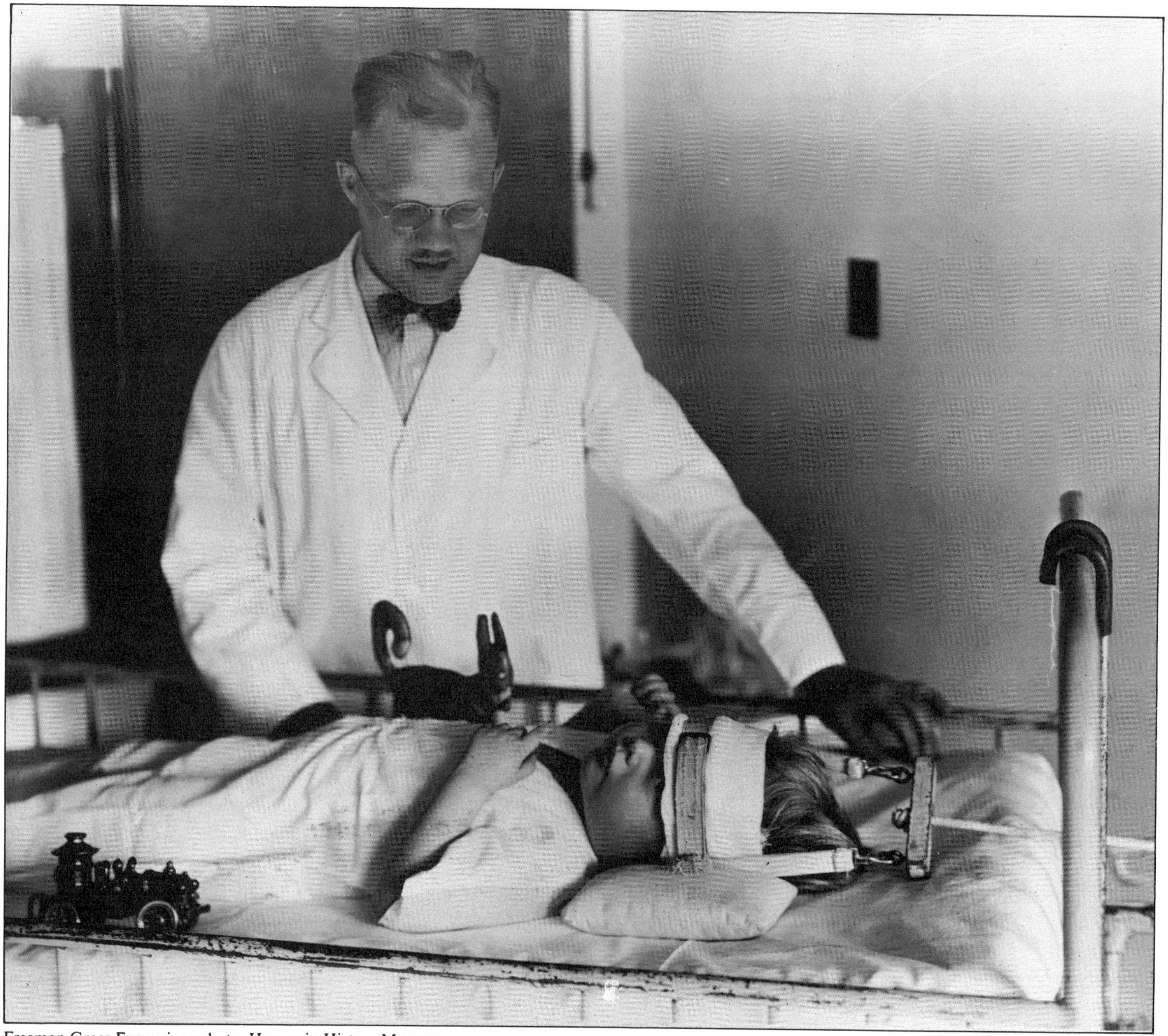

Freeman Gross Engravings photo, Hennepin History Museum

◀ *A child was treated for tuberculosis at Glen Lake Sanitorium in Minnetonka under the care of Dr. Charles K. Petter. We can't explain the head contraption, but lots of techniques, most of them unsuccessful, were tried on patients with the lung disease. As with AIDS later, TB was greatly feared and its victims shunned. But unlike AIDS, the TB virus was spread primarily through the air, on droplets from coughing, sneezing and even singing. Minnesota long had been considered a good place to recover from TB because the air was considered pure and healthy. When Glen Lake opened in 1916, treatment was limited to sunlight, bed rest and good, plentiful food. Patients stayed an average of 2½ years.*

▶ *After a long day's work in September 1937, the family of a Mexican sugar-beet worker had coffee in housing for migrant laborers near East Grand Forks.*

Russell Lee photo, Library of Congress

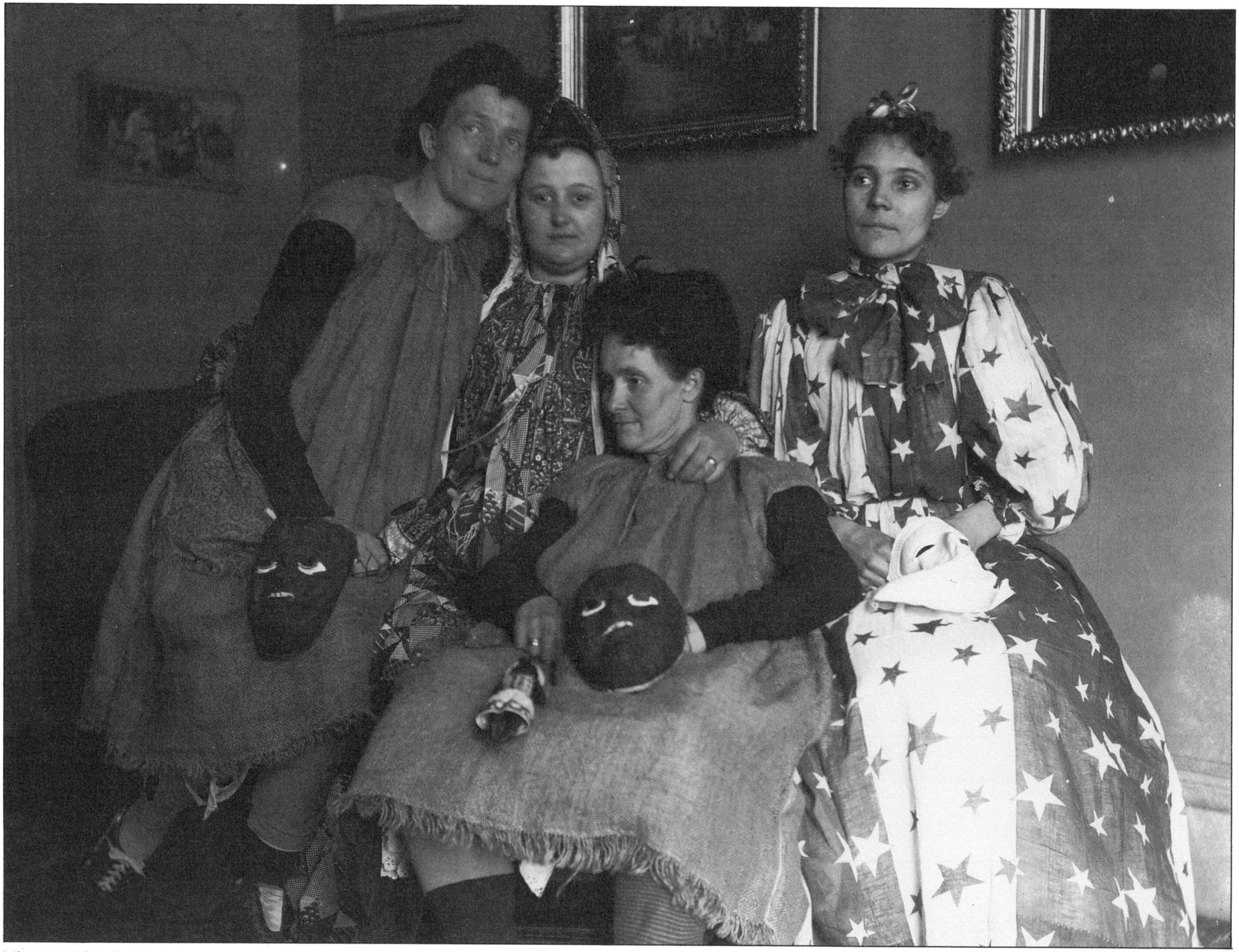

Minnesota Historical Society

◀ *Amateur theatricals used to be popular forms of entertainment, before television. Families and friends would write a little skit or find one in the library. In this photo, Sadie Mason Ray, seated, gathered family and masks and burlap costumes for some kind of production in about 1905. She was part of a St. Paul family living at 949 Laurel.*

▶ *A dancing team known as the Ward Sisters strutted in November of 1927. They lived at 4225 Bryant Av. S., Minneapolis. As far as we know, they never made it big in vaudeville, but this professional portrait resembles a publicity shot. Agnes L. Ward was listed in the 1927 city directory as a teacher, and Anne M. as a musician. Vaudeville was a form of stage entertainment consisting of a number of unrelated acts — usually songs, dances, animal shows, magic acts, comedy and dramatic sketches.*

Minnesota Historical Society

Minnesota Historical Society

*Here's the University of Minnesota football team in 1887. Names were written beneath the photo; we hope we're reading the handwriting properly. First row, Muds, fullback; Hoyt; Goode; Pillsbury, '90 captain; Corless, and Hayden, halfback. Back row, A.T. Mann; Willard; Fred Mann; Allen, manager; Heffelfinger; Watson and Morris. Pudge Heffelfinger stayed one year at Minnesota, then went to Yale, where he was an all-American guard. The guys had on the old version of letter jackets. During games, they wore something like our turtlenecks.*

St. Paul Pioneer Press photo, Minnesota Historical Society

◀ *This player was outfitted for the gridiron in about 1910. There must not have been a helmet rule.*

Minneapolis Journal photo, Minnesota Historical Society

*A University of Minnesota football player was practicing at the turn of the century.*

◀ *Students lingered at Northrop Field after a University of Minnesota football game in about 1910. The megaphones read "Rooters," which meant cheerleaders.*

H.D. Ayer photo, Minnesota Historical Society

▶ *Bobcats were so common in the Red Wing area in the 1890s that there was open season on them the year around. The hunters showing off their catch were, left to right, Mr. Dowel (his first name is lost); Dr. Arnold Lees, Red Wing's first veterinarian; Charles Crandall, and Bert Crandall.*

Goodhue County Historical Society

Norton and Peel photo, Minnesota Historical Society

***An experienced but unidentified hunter passed on his knowledge on Nov. 2, 1939. We meant the man, but maybe it's the dog who was the smart one on hunting.***

Hennepin History Museum

◀ *After a successful day of hunting in the 1880s, these men displayed their kill. It was common as early as the 1870s for railroads to run hunting and fishing excursions. In fact, some railroads owned resorts and organized tours that included fishing, boating and dinner. This railroad was the forerunner to the Milwaukee Road.*

▶ *John Hendricks posed with his deer for his brother's camera near Balsam in about 1915. Lots of hunting scenes have been shot in Minnesota in fall, but not many show a sportsman with a full three-piece suit and tie. Most pictures were shot at hunting shacks or back at the car.*

Jesse C. Hendricks photo, Minnesota Historical Society

*After a productive session with saw and ax in 1907, Albert Schafer had a less-than-cushy rest on his woodpile. A bachelor, he worked on the Albert Keye farm near Frontenac. Keye's wife and daughters are pictured on the cover of this book.*

Revoir Historical Collection, Red Wing

Minnesota Historical Society

*Lumberjack buddies looked their cleanest and sweetest for a studio shot in about 1900. The lumbermen were known for their heady aroma. They bathed in the springtime, whether they needed to or not.*

Brown County Historical Society

*New Ulm members of a German-American group known as the Turnvereine or Turners posed among their gymnastic equipment, fencing foils and bowling balls in about 1885. The Turners were dedicated to the principle of "a sound mind in a sound body," stressing gymnastics, dance and other physical activities. To strengthen their minds, these intellectuals valued education and culture, especially music and theater.*

Minnesota Historical Society

◀ *This self-assured child in the wonderful big hat probably was Anna M. Heilmaier of St. Paul, in about 1904. At least, it was she who later donated the photo to the historical society. Her father, likely the man in the picture, was a musician; her mother was a piano teacher. Both had come from Germany. They lived at 1799 Dayton Av., St. Paul. It's not known where the photo was taken, but note that the tended woods have little undergrowth. Tidy people, those Germans.*

Minnesota Historical Society

▲ *These little pilgrims, fresh from a Thanksgiving program in about 1935, were from St. Paul's Douglas School.*

▶ *When a fall nip is in the air, Minnesotans like to head for the woods, even a pine woods. The colors may not be as varied as in a deciduous forest, but the scent is superb. This 1920s auto was dwarfed by the pine trees. Even with chains on its tires, the car sank into the soft road.*

Minnesota Historical Society

Otter Tail County Historical Society

*Andrew Palmquist carried mail to rural Otter Tail County from Fergus Falls in about 1905. The names of the children and darling puppy aren't known. Mail delivery did a great deal to reduce the isolation of rural people. Before Rural Free Delivery, most went to town only about once a week for mail, supplies and conversation. Farmers' organizations were active in getting Congress to provide money for free delivery of mail to rural areas. In 1896 the first deliveries were made in West Virginia, and by 1917 the service was extended to most rural districts of the nation.*

*The crew of a Minneapolis streetcar showed off crisp uniforms and sparkling-clean car in about 1910. That was Herb Phillips on the left. Notice the ads for Campbell's Soup and other products. By that time, streetcar lines had gotten as far south as 50th St. on Bryant Av. S. They extended east on Lake St. over the new Mississippi River bridge to connect via Marshall Av. with St. Paul's Selby Av. line.*

F.P.D. Bruce photo, Minnesota Historical Society

Minneapolis Journal, Minnesota Historical Society

***Please, oh please, tell us who these women were. Judging from the clothing and the automobile, we guess the photograph was shot in the 1920s. But where? And what was the relationship between the women? Mother and daughter? It's an obvious guess, but we'd like to know for sure. The younger, artsy woman was carrying a suitcase and a music case, perhaps for an autoharp or zither. The other woman had welcoming arms and a hint of a smile. Our guess is that she was a Scandinavian thrilled about the visit. You know the joke about the Swedish man who loved his wife so much that he almost told her.***

John Vachon photo, Library of Congress

▲ *A woman stooped for her milk bottle, delivered to the back door of her St. Paul house in October 1940.*

▶ *Patrolman Hans Offerdahl and his look-alike assistant used a hand-controlled signal to direct traffic. It may not have had fancy electronics, but it did have an umbrella. At first we thought this was at Dayton's in downtown Minneapolis in the 1920s, but the building doesn't quite match up. Can you identify the site?*

Minnesota Historical Society

St. Paul Daily News photo, Minnesota Historical Society

***These Hamline University coeds were members of the Philo Browning Society, a literary group, in 1923. Their theme song was, "I want to be a Browning/ And with the Brownings stand/ A smile upon my features/ And an essay in my hand." Maybe that's what was in the suitcases.***

*This was the scene in front of the Northern Pacific Depot in Hinckley in about 1917. Then as now, the city was a stopping-off place for Duluth-Twin Cities travelers. On the left was Dr. Truman Stickney, a Hinckley dentist, and to the right was John T. Craig, owner of a Hinckley hotel and bar. The middle man is a mystery. The depot was a replacement for the one lost in the forest fires of 1894, which killed 418 people, 245 of them from the Hinckley area.*

Hinckley Fire Museum photo

Revoir Historical Collection, Red Wing

***A flat tire was no big deal to Model T owners. Spares were not routinely carried, but repair kits with rubber patches were. This photo was taken on Thanksgiving Day, 1917. That was August Prinz on the left, George Gross on the right. Gross was Prinz's father-in-law and also his boss at the Goodhue County Co-op in Red Wing. The Dahl Punctureless Tire Co. of Minneapolis was running ads in 1912 with comments from satisfied customers. One read, "They save me time, labor, money and profanity; they keep me from worry, accidents and delay."***

Russell Lee photo, Library of Congress

▲ *Mrs. Orville White, the female half of a farming couple near Northome, made pancakes on a wood-burning stove in September 1937. The geranium on the windowsill was planted in a coffee can covered with gift wrap.*

◀ *What appears at first glance to be a peaceful autumnal scene actually represents one of the worst chapters in Minnesota history. After the Dakota War of 1862, in which hundreds of Indians and whites were killed, Dakota people were imprisoned in this compound at Fort Snelling. Condemned Indian prisoners were taken to be hanged near Mankato, and other Dakota were forced that fall to make a long and miserable trip by wagon and foot to the fort. Even those Indians not involved in the conflict were spat upon, jeered and threatened. By the next summer, almost all Dakota were evicted from the state. Many died of starvation.*

Minnesota Historical Society

Minnesota Historical Society

◀ *Who would have thought Minnesotans needed to practice being friendly? Why, weren't they born smiling, and weren't their first words requests for coffee? Still, members of Unity Church in St. Paul decided in about 1958 that a big sign might motivate them to try even more fervently. That's Keene C. McCammon of St. Paul on the left, pouring for an unidentified woman.*

▶ *Unidentified Dakota women made lace at the Redwood Mission at Morton in 1897. Do you know their names? The mission was established by Henry Whipple, Minnesota's first Episcopal priest. The Dakota called him "Straight Tongue" in recognition of his integrity. Few whites were as dedicated to the cause of Indian rights as Whipple at a time when land-hungry settlers were moving in. His cousin, Mary Whipple, introduced lace-making as a cottage industry to supplement family incomes.*

Minnesota Historical Society

Minneapolis Tribune photo, Minnesota Historical Society

◀ *Martha Erickson carefully tended to her husband, Frank, at breakfast in Aitkin on a fall morning in 1950. Frank Erickson was featured in the newspaper because he had been a volunteer fireman for 50 years. He joined in 1900 as a schoolboy of 15, became chief in 1913 and missed only 10 fire calls in 50 years. He could explain why he couldn't show up on each of those occasions. For 1950s memories, notice the oilcloth on the table and the plastic see-through apron.*

▶ *In September of 1939, a farm woman in a familiar flowered apron showed off her well-stocked root cellar. It was chock-full of beans, corn, peas, cherries and maybe root beer and pickled eggs. The unidentified woman was a client of the Farm Security Administration, which taught struggling farm families to garden, sew, can, make mattresses and otherwise provide for their own needs.*

John Vachon photo, Library of Congress

Frank T. Wilson photos, Minnesota Historical Society

*These young Stillwater entrepreneurs opened a store to sell acorns in about 1899. They were four of the photographer's children with a cousin — Chester, Robert, Donald and Ruth Wilson and Madge Barclay. Some 15 years later, the same people gathered for another picture. This time they were sold out of acorns or, more likely, were not interested in the small profit margin in the acorn business. This before-and-after technique is fun; if you have a favorite photo of a small group of people, try to restage the shot after an appropriate length of time has passed.*

*The historical society knows nothing about this photo — not the names of the children, where they lived, what they were doing. This picture is in a lovely family album without identification. One good thing about it: The photos weren't pulled out of the album, as is sadly so often the case. Photo historians love albums. Albums tell a great deal about the compiler's creativity and also give a more complete look at a family than a few photos can. Moral of the story: Put together a photo album this year and put your name in it. And, please, don't rip apart old albums.*

Minnesota Historical Society

# Fall letters and diaries

## Homesick teacher

***Frances Liedl taught school near Fergus Falls in the late 1800s and recorded her impressions in a letter to a schoolteacher friend.***

**St. Lawrence, Minn.**
**Nov. 27, 1896**

Dear Matilda,

I know you are very provoked at me by this time for neglecting you so I have struggled O so hard to do my writing but I simply can't do it. There is nothing that costs me such an effort as to write a letter. It isn't to you alone I neglect, it is everyone, even at home. I can't write unless I have about three hours to do it in and I seldom have so much time at my command. After the scolding you gave me in your last letter I am afraid you won't answer this at all.

My enthusiasm over my school has not subsided in the least. But the school is getting smaller and smaller as it grows colder. To-day there has been a regular blizzard and only 7 children attended. The weather is fearful out here on the prairie. It is but a short distance from my boarding place to school but it is an impossibility to walk even that distance. All the people drive the children to school [presumably by horse and buggy] and come and get them evenings.

I have now become quite well acquainted with the neighborhood so I don't get quite so homesick but still I occasionally do have a blue spell.

The children's parents often come and get me evenings after school to spend the evening and stay over night and then take us back to school the next morning. In that way I have enjoyed quite a few evenings. Then down towards Perham there is a family that have an organ and are very anxious to have their little girl learn to play. So I have to go there occasionally, too. I have certainly come into a very queer neighborhood, in one respect. There are about 60 families living around here and they are all related to one another with the exception of but two families. Between 30 and 40 of these families are named Doll and it is almost impossible for a stranger to get any order out of such a chaos as there is with these names. . . .

I have made a few acquaintances among neighboring teachers and we have been discussing the advisability of forming a reading circle but will probably not begin work until the spring terms open. . . . Busy work [for the students] is not by any means the easiest thing to find. I have had less trouble that way through this term than my first one. They like to make pictures with

splints. I have two kinds, colored, and tooth-picks. Then putting cut up picture cards together. I also have a lot of boxes with the letters and numbers in and the children form words or examples with them. Then I take selections from the reading lessons, write them on slips of paper and one word or phrase on a slip, and give them to the children to assort and arrange as in the reading lesson. Then those little stories in the back of the Normal Instructor & Teachers World are nice for silent & supplimentary reading. . . . Here is one exercise that I like. Change "girl" to "bell." Thus, girl, gill, bill, bell, by changing one letter at a time in the word girl so that you will at last form bell. Other examples of this are "bear" to "salt": bear, beat, meat, melt, malt, salt; "dog" to "cat," "hope" to "rich," "time" to "late," etc, etc. I make out lists of questions for them to write the answers, like this:

1. What is the 4th day of the week? 2. Name 10 things sold in a grocery store. 3. Make a list of 20 words beginning with G. 4. Write 6 boys names. 5. Write XXVIII in figures. 6. Give full names of Tom, Ed, Joe, Mike, etc. 7. Write in full Jan., Feb., Sept. 8. If Tuesday is the 1st of Sept., make out a calendar for that month. 9. Name 5 kinds of fruits. 10. Write words meaning the opposite of good, little, long, high, rough, hard, etc. And all kinds of questions like that. Well, let that suffice for busy work.

I suppose by this time you feel quite at home as a "school ma'am." Is that what they call you? Out here anyway the older people call me "Miss Liedl" so I don't entirely forget what my real name is.

(I have been writing in a cold room and my hands are so cold I can scarcely write anymore. So you must excuse this scribbling.)

I now know more of the people in Perham and can have a better time when I go up on Saturdays or Sundays. They pay better wages around here than by Fergus [Falls]. There are two schools each about two miles from my school and one pays $50 a month and the other $45. They teach German in both. Both have gentlemen teachers

from St. Cloud. I have met one of them so far.

Do you get any chances to skate nowadays? I have only had one good skate so far, although the river is only a few steps from the house. It is so provoking to have such short days now. One can't do a thing after school hours but the sweeping. Don't you think teachers ought to be expert wielders of the broom?

Do you have any girls for company where you are, Matilda? I scarcely know what such a being is out here, they are so few and far between. . . . When does your school close? Mine closes at Christmas and opens again in April. It would not be possible to keep school during the winter months, it is so cold. Which classes do you like to teach best, the little ones or the big ones? I can't really tell which I like the best but sometimes think I prefer the little ones.

Did you go home Thanksgiving? It stormed so out here that I could not go away so I did not have such a very good time although I did have a very good dinner. . . .

And now, Matilda, I think I have surely made this letter long enough. So perhaps I'd better close so I will have something to say at some future date.

Please be so kind and answer me just this once and I'll try and try & try to be better. You will, won't you? So good-by.

From your Fond Friend,
Frances

Hereafter address me at Perham, Minn.

Otter Tail County Historical Society

~

## Go Gophers!

***The Rev. Joseph Simonson was a Lutheran minister who grew up in Lanesboro. In 1939, he and his family were about to move back to Minnesota from Chicago. He went on to serve as U.S. ambassador to Ethiopia from 1953 to 1957.***

**Saturday, Oct. 7, 1939.** The usual Saturday morning routine. After the confirmation class, I went out to get groceries. In the afternoon I worked in the study except that I took time out for listening to part of the Minnesota-Nebraska and Northwestern-Oklahoma football games. It is not going to be hard for me to whip up the usual Twin City interest in the Minnesota Gophers! No, I never had much of that spirit while an acual resident of Minnesota. I have gotten a great deal of it since.

Minnesota Historical Society, Joseph Simonson Diaries

~

## Redecorating fever

***Frances Linda James of Newport wrote a letter to "Auntie" (Helen Neil Haynes) on Oct. 18, 1890. The topic was home decorating, a fall tradition.***

We have had workmen here papering, painting, etc., for about two weeks. The new carpets for the children's room have not come yet so the rooms are in confusion and the house in not in a satisfactory condition. The children have just gone to dancing school, Margaret at the last minute forgetting shoes, tickets and I don't know what else and you can imagine the scurrying of the other children to help her get started . . . . Henry came home with Mr. Fitzgerald and they have gone hunting at Spring Lake, somewhere across the river. . . . Mother clutches eagerly for "David Copperfield" before she is fairly on the sofa and when she is through that she will select the heaviest one in the library to be its successor. . . .

The children's rooms will be lovely I think — Margaret's has a pale yellow paper, cream-colored frieze and ceiling with two soft brown lines on the ceiling, then a kind of yellow scrim [a sheer, loosely woven cloth] with a yellower figure on it for curtains, a little piece of lattice at the top of each window, small sash curtains below. Then her yellow toilet things are quite appropriate and I made a nice window seat for her and she is pleased with the result and studies in her own room. Cordelia's is in pink with the same ceiling and window arrangements in pink. Helen's is blue and the carpets are all the same colors so the upstairs as far as the back hall will be very nice. Little Henry's room also is papered a pale blue and is very comfortable. Then the hall to the billiard room and the room itself are beautifully papered in pale green and reddish brown. Henry [her husband] seems to like it but he considers it is driving him to the poor house. Then the two guest rooms in the third story are made lovely with greenish blue paper, and the green rug that was in the parlor all summer is in the same room Helen had this summer. It was almost threadbare but will do good service up there for some time.

Minnesota Historical Society, Frances Haynes James and Family Papers

~

## Arrested at the fair

***William Cummings, a St. Paul native, kept a diary beginning in 1933, when he was 15 or 16. He got into some scrapes as a teenager. His later diaries provide a day-by-day account of the lives of a working man and his family.***

**Friday, Sept. 7, 1934.** We went to the [state] fair today. Bob Jewell and I climbed over the fence. A cop caught us. I got Jewell out of it. But I got stuck in Jail at 10 A.M. I got out of jail at 6 P.M. I didn't eat during that time. I ate seven hamburgers for supper.

**Monday, Oct. 1.** Went downtown to the Court House. I was a witness at daddy & mother's divorce trial. I was sorry to have them divorced. It was very cold & raw today. I have a very bad cold.

Minnesota Historical Society, William M. Cummings Papers

~

## A moose on the mind

***Ernest L. Brown, a taxidermist from Warren, Minn., kept diaries of his hunting trips in northwestern Minnesota.***

**Friday, Oct. 4, 1889.** We went out through the spruce in the open brush country on other side I caught sight of a moose We tried to stalk him the wind was wrong he turned, War [Warren?] caught sight of him then he disappeared while we chased our shadows. After we tramped around a long time I worked back near the spruce and called I heard something coming thought it might be War, then caught glimpse of moose and heard the brush rattle on his horns had another glimpse of him and should have shot but waited for him to come past a bunch of brush where it was clear but he got my scent and did not come out he turned and slipped away and I never saw him again and so I went sadly back to camp and told my tale he looked very brown and I think was a young moose. It is too windy to call. War went down to Thief L and shot a white Goose and we tried to eat it but it was very tough.

**Sat. 5.** Cold and windy the team came up from the ranch and we went back I got out and took a long tramp around a tamarac swamp saw lots of moose track.

Minnesota Historical Society, Ernest L. Brown Papers

~

## Apple barrel

**To keep apples:** Take fine dry sawdust, preferably that made by a circular saw from well-seasoned hard wood, and place a thick layer on the bottom of a barrel. Then place a layer of apples, not close together and not close to staves of the barrel. Put sawdust liberally over and around, and proceed until a bushel and a half, or less, are so packed in each barrel. They are to be kept in a cool place.

**— "Ladies Own Home Cookbook," by Mrs. Jane Warren, 1891**

~

## Packing list

***Robert Mowry Bell, age 12 and living near Sauk Centre, wrote this list in his journal on Oct. 28, 1872. Guess what he was up to.***

1 can of corned beef
1 loaf bread
½ lb. butter
1 can peaches
Fishing tackle, trawling hooks and line, pole
1 knife
1 plate
1 spoon
Fish bucket
1 jar for butter
comfort. (bed-clothes)
flannel shirt
1 small amount of cash
1 doz. Eggs
Salt
Petroleum Stove, kerosene

Minnesota Historical Society, Robert M. Bell Papers

~

## Ground colors

***Bennie Bengtson, a farmer in Kittson County (the farthest northwest of Minnesota's counties), wrote about fall in the 1940s.***

Not all of the colorful leaves are in the treetops. The shrubs and smaller plants that grow closer to the ground have their share too. The highbush cranberries with their maple-like leaves and growing in the shade beneath taller trees acquire no ends of delicate tints. The red osier-dogwoods glow in purplish shades, and in soft salmon and mauve. The black haws show a sturdy silhouette of deep bronze-red, darker than any other in the woods. Still lower down are the wild currants and gooseberry, with patches of poison ivy in a dark red flecked with gold and brown. On the ground is a carpet of wild strawberries in various shades of red and russet, as if Nature had become an Oriental rug weaver.

Minnesota Historical Society, Bennie Bengtson Papers

~

## Naming the place

[The Minnesota territory's name comes from the Indian words] *mennah* and *shotah* (smoke), the former referring to the innumerable rivers, lakes, and streamlets that diversify the country, and the latter to the peculiar haziness of the atmosphere during the delightful period of the "Indian Summer" — a season when the fancy instinctively revels amidst bucolic scenes. Then nature seems to lapse into dreamy repose; the autumnal sunlight throws a mellow hue upon the prairies; the hum of the insect world is strangely audible; smoke floats lazily in the still air; and naught disturbs the placid surface of the lakes save the ripple of the birchen canoe, or the dip of the swallow as he skims the wave. The Indians' dream of the beatitude of the spirit land is here almost realized. What name so appropriate then as Minnesota?

***Most historians, nonetheless, say Minnesota translates as "sky-tinted waters" or "sky-blue waters."***

**— Harper's New Monthly Magazine, April 1859**

~

## Clean and bright

***Lillian Brown, age 80, of Austin Minn., delighted in fall cleaning.***

**Oct. 27, 1951.** 30 degrees. Cold but pleasant. Two [hired] girls came this morning and cleaned house. Washed the walls and ceiling, pictures, chairs, & washed the dishes. Did a fine job and were darling girls. They even took the drapes down, put them on the line and brushed them. It seems so good to have it clean. They also washed the windows. Wonderful!

Minnesota Historical Society, Lillian Elizabeth Brown and Family Papers

~

## Early couch potato

**Saturday, Nov. 25, 1950.** A warm day. Canned cranberries in morning. Went to Hopkins to look at television sets. Had a Philco sent out.

**Sunday, Nov. 26.** Stayed home in evening to watch television.

**— Anna Kurtz, 50, who farmed with her husband, Frank, near Eden Prairie**

Minnesota Historical Society, Anna Mesenbrink Kurtz Diaries

~

## Closing the cabin

**Nov. 24, 1942**

**A to-do list**

Take up dock boards and put them under house.
Put canoe in house.
Put row boat in garage.
Put all tools (axes, saws, shovels, etc.) in cellar and lock door.
DON'T lock ice-house.
Put outboard motor in house.
Take off screens and put them in cellar — laying them flat.
Lock front door and pull down all shades. Where there are no shades cover windows with paper or cloth.
Bolt side door.

Minnesota Historical Society, Abby Weed Grey and Family Papers

~

## From pigs to airships

**Sept. 3, 1908. Minnesota State Fair.** Mr. McLain took Linnie & I to the fair. We saw everything from *pigs* to *airships.* I had a *grand* time. We didn't get home till 10:30. I stayed all night at Linnie's.

**— Dorothy Walton, 14, Minneapolis**

Minnesota Historical Society, Edmund George Walton and Family Papers

~

## Snow in the bed

***Thomas Scantlebury was 21 when his family came from New York in 1856 to settle in New Auburn in Sibley County. He was with his brother, Edward, and his father, Samuel. The Quaker family was building a home and establishing a sawmill that chilly autumn.***

**Tenth month, 1856. 18th.** A very fine day. I shot a *large* duck, the first of the kind we have had and we had a very good dinner off of him and the prairie chicken.

**25th.** A cold day with a leaden sky. This is the sabbath but again we have not kept it but have been at work. . . . I hope ere long a sabbath [with] a morning of rest may come. It is time we begin to live a little like human beings again. It will be a blessing when we can sit down in clean clothes in a comfortable home and read and write to the absent ones.

**30th.** The wind blew a hurricane all last night and it was cold as Greenland this morning. . . . We have been fixing up and trying to make our place warmer. . . . The lake froze up for a great distance.

**Eleventh month. 1st.** A cold morning but pleasant day. . . . Our potato crop came home this afternoon. Our share is eleven bushels, the whole crop 16½, only double what we planted.

**4th.** A cold day with spits of snow. We have sent off three loads of lumber and have taken in over 94 dollars. We sawed bass wood all day.

**5th.** I made a large loaf of bread which was baked in the new stove.

**7th.** Last night it blew horribly and snowed a little. There was a drift in our bed in which George sat when he was undressed.

**8th.** The lake is now crossable for foot passengers, and it has been crossed. It is splendid skating.

**9th.** First day [Sunday] but of course we did not rest. It has been quite a mild day so we finished shingling our roof. My bowells have troubled me a good deal. We poked some victuals [food] down our throats and went to bed in very low spirits.

**10th.** Father has been poorly to day. I am better tonight.

**11th.** I hung and made two doors downstairs.

**12th.** A very beautiful warm day. We sawed to day. . . . I cut Edward's hair and have been playing on my accordion. I am sleepy.

**15th.** We cut hard wood to day and cut 1241 feet. The tax collector called on us and got nothing.

**17th.** [His mother arrived from the East.] Mother brought a thermometer but it is broken, like everything else.

**18th.** A very fine day. Edward and I put up some partitions and another window.

**19th.** A fine day with a strong southeast wind. We worked on our house all day. Edward and George got a load of hay before breakfast. We are getting a little more shipshape than we were though there is plenty to do yet.

Minnesota Historical Society, Thomas Scantlebury Journals

~

Minnesota Historical Society

*All dressed up and serious, these two men chose an odd spot to have their picture taken in about 1900. We don't know who or where they are, but we can guess it was not a spirit of fun and frivolity that motivated them to climb a pile of weird ice. Is that a Bible in hand? Were they clergymen? Mormon missionaries? Was the photo taken at Lake Superior, where the wind crashes ice into shore and smashes up the ice like this? If you readers can't tell us, we'll never know.*

# Winter

Almost as old as Minnesota's reputation for having lousy winters is Minnesotans' intense need to persuade the world that, honestly, it's not so bad here, despite the cold.

"Chilly, but healthful and exhilarating!" is what Minnesotans have bragged since before statehood in 1858. The first territorial governor had an assistant who spent a hunk of his work time denying that the region had long, frigid winters: "I can safely say that the atmosphere is more pure, pleasant and healthful than any I have ever breathed on the continents of North or South America. This is particularly the case in winter, the most buoyant, elastic and vigorous portion of the year."

He and other Minnesota promoters insisted that the bracing temperatures cured everything from head colds to malaria fevers to tuberculosis. TB in the 1800s was akin to what AIDS is today — highly feared and hard to treat. So the remarkable health claims were successful in drawing immigrants, first from the East and then from Europe. And perhaps the pure air and hard work did help some pioneers' lungs and muscles.

But with time, the boasting itself reached epidemic proportions. Take as an example the case of a New England woman who was so ill and weak that she couldn't even sweep her own room, according to a Nov. 29, 1873, report in the St. Paul Daily Pioneer. When she moved to Minnesota, miracles happened. After less than a year here, "She chased her husband a mile and a quarter with a pitchfork, and gave birth to a pair of twins the same afternoon."

For those not won over by the possibility of delivering twins or running the 1¼-mile pitchfork race while pregnant, an alcohol metaphor then in use might have worked. "The atmosphere in Minnesota in winter is like a wine, so exhilarating is its effects on the system," claimed an 1871 book with the catchy title of "Minnesota, Its Character and Climate, Likewise Sketches of Other Resorts Favorable to Invalids, Together with Copious Notes on Health; Also Hints to Tourists and Emigrants."

A famous visitor came here in 1861 to check out the healing climate, and the state's promoters have made much of the visit. Henry David Thoreau, the naturalist and writer, made a two-month journey to frontier Minnesota from his native Massachusetts in an attempt to regain his health. All winter he had suffered from a terrible cold and bronchitis, and then he developed tuberculosis. He thought of traveling to the West Indies but chose Minnesota instead. (Who wouldn't?) Actually, a deciding factor was that he wanted to further his studies of U.S. flora and fauna and American Indians.

Thoreau didn't get here until May, so he missed the exhilarating 50-below wind chills. He tramped around Minneapolis's Nicollet Island, visited a Dakota settlement at Redwood and found a plant specimen on the shore of Lake Calhoun that he was particularly eager to spot — a wild crab-apple tree.

Sadly, though, his health did not improve. He skedaddled on home, as fast as one could skedaddle by steamer in those days. What the boosters of Minnesota's healing air haven't emphasized about Thoreau's visit to the state was this: Within a year, he was dead.

Scoffers outside Minnesota didn't hesitate to object to exaggerated health claims and reports of mild weather. The Winnipeg Free Press on Oct. 23, 1875, reported with glee that while Manitoba was enjoying gorgeous weather, Minnesota had snowstorms. The Winnipeg paper said, "The newspapers of that state don't like to admit the fact of early snow falls, and speak of these circumstances as falls of so many inches of 'white rain.' "

Sometimes, though, the truth was told unadorned. Minnesota's weather could get bitter. A St. Paul man wrote a letter to the editor of the New York Tribune (reprinted in the St. Paul Daily Pioneer on July 30, 1871) in which he admitted that "once in a while here the wind draws itself across one's ears like a steel knife, but this seldom happens. On those days no sane person has any business out of house."

The cold was so severe in January 1872 that Fairmont people boasted, tongue in cheek, that dishwater tossed out the door froze before it hit the ground.

To this day, bragging about surviving winter is a vital part of Minnesota culture. More important than the size of the big fish is the size of the towering snowbanks. More interesting than how many snow forts the kids made is how many school days they joyfully missed because of

Minnesota Historical Society

***Three grandchildren of Alexander Ramsey, a prominent early Minnesotan, posed on a toboggan in about 1885. The photo was taken in a studio, in front of a painted winter scene. The illusion of falling snow was added by the photographer later. The children were Anita, Laura and Alexander Furness. Their grandpa had been governor of the territory and state of Minnesota and a U.S. senator. He lived until 1903.***

treacherous weather.

Journal-keepers tend to follow their forebears' practice of recording the weather each day. There is something satisfying in reading about how miserable it was. Blizzards are less fun when they're going on than later, when we know that once again we made it through the winter.

We do relish our blizzard stories. The Rev. Frank Peterson, a Baptist minister who was a newcomer to southwestern Minnesota in 1872, had a few good ones of his own, such as the time he trudged 30 miles in deep snow from Jackson to Worthington. But Peterson was especially chilled by a story about his brother that same year. Peterson didn't bother to give his brother's name, but he wrote the true tale in a book published in 1872 called "Early Days on the Minnesota Prairies":

"Walking up to the desk to register, upon his arrival [in Worthington], he was told there was no room. Insisting that he must have shelter for the night he asked permission to occupy a chair, but was told by this frontier landlord that he could 'go to hell.' Not caring to go there, he sought a shanty called a hotel, but found that packed like sardines in a box. There now remained to him the choice of one of two things: either to stay out of doors that cold February night, or seek the dugout of some homesteader on the prairie. He was told of one on the other side of Lake Ocheydan, some four miles away, and lost no time in making a beeline for it over the trackless prairie.

"Reaching the edge of a frozen lake he espied a mound which showed indications that it was the dugout of some settler. He went up to it and looked into the opening that served as a door, when out crawled a man who, black with soot and dirt, looked as though he had not washed since the lake had frozen over. He was friendly, however, and expressed his regret that he could not invite my brother to stay with him since there was not room in the dugout for two. This was found, upon inspection, to be true. He lived the same simple life as that of the gopher in his hole. My brother was told that if he intended to cross the lake he would better hasten since the skies boded the coming of a storm.

"This weather prognosticator was correct; when my brother got within forty rods of Mr. Swenson's home, the blizzard was on in all its fury and the blinding snow concealed every object before him. Happily the wind was in the direction of the house and he was driven on by its terrific force until he actually bumped against the wall. Feeling along the wall with his hands, he found the door which he lost no time in opening, and walked in on the astonished family. Mr. Swenson was moved to tears at the thought of the narrow escape my brother had had from such a storm, which lasted three days."

The good thing about bad weather is it brings out the Mr. Swensons. Minnesotans become a little more tender-hearted. Many of us have a story of a Good Samaritan — if not someone who saved a life, then someone who helped

Minnesota Historical Society

***Only in a land where winter is glorified would someone choose to pose in heavy coat and hat, holding oak firewood. This was a studio photo from about 1885, taken in front of a wintery backdrop. Most photographers' backdrops depicted summery gates, columns, archways, gardens and the interiors of picturesque cottages. This photographer and subject must have been proud of their frigid domain.***

push a car out of a ditch or walked a mile to a convenience store to get milk for the old lady down the block.

Our preoccupation with winter has been handed down from long-time resident to newcomer and from generation to generation. Here's advice from the Minneapolis Tribune of Jan. 27, 1893:

"Make mental notes of the temperatures these days, young man. If your luck is good you will be one of the oldest inhabitants 60 years hence, and you will have lots of fun telling the tenderfeet about the awful winter of 1892-3."

Yet if winter weather was uncharacteristically warm, Minnesotans gloated then too. The Stillwater Gazette reported on Dec. 26, 1877, "Frank Fisk celebrated Christmas day by plowing up a patch of land on his farm a few miles below the city. And this in Minnesota, just above latitude 45."

Minnesotans' photo albums and journals show that we have gloried in surviving the disasters of snow and cold, but we also have loved the positive aspects of deep winter — the coziness of a warm house, the glee of making snowmen and snow angels, the joy of being with our families and friends to celebrate winter holidays.

Records of holiday feasts are especially detailed. One St. Paul Christmas party in 1851 included turkeys, chickens, frosted hams, buffalo tongue, oyster soup, lobster soup, sardines, pastries, ice cream, jelly and "piquants of every description."

During the long winter evenings in the 1800s, families stretched to find enough entertainment to keep the children busy. By the end of the century, ready-made games had made their way into city homes, but it was not so in the country. Magazines and books made suggestions for activities that could be done by lamplight. One was to make a train from scraps of wood: Cut them into 6-inch pieces, decorate them with oil paints and use a sharp penknife to carve out windows. "Any boy of 10 can do this," it was believed in 1887.

Something else that got a lot of press in winters past was remedies on how to cure the common cold. Pick your favorite: At bedtime, eat a bowl of steaming hot gruel followed by a cup of hot lemonade (preferably laced with brandy), grab the hot-water bottle and sweat it out in bed. Or take a dose of goose oil. Or bathe the neck and shoulders with cold salt water each morning before dressing and rub with a coarse towel until the neck glows. Or roast a lemon and squeeze the juice through sugar; drink to relieve a cough. Or drink vast quantities of spearmint and a big dose of castor oil. Or drink rum.

Some people survived these remedies. The Minneapolis Tribune of Sept. 6, 1871, told about the oldest woman in northern Minnesota, Josephine Pegnard, dying at age 105. She died not of old age, it was said, but of too much food:

"A rich repast of potatoes and flap-jacks proved too much for her. This case of old age may be put down to the credit of our remarkably healthy climate."

***These women were having a rollicking good time in a cozy restaurant booth in about 1945. You can almost hear the winter wind whistling outside.***

Minnesota Historical Society

Northeast Minnesota Historical Center

◀ *Cold is cold! This ice-covered lake boat was photographed in the port of Duluth in about 1900. Until the 1960s, Great Lakes shipping didn't extend into January and February so this picture probably was taken on a chilly November or December day. The coldness of Lake Superior's waters was a curse to sailors here from the beginning. They suffered more than discomfort. (We can only hope these men had heavy wool coats and warm hats and gloves.) Even worse, the cold jeopardized lives when accidents happened. Imagine being shipwrecked in Superior's icy waters in the time when the north shore was virtually uninhabited.*

Minnesota Historical Society

◀ *A young man enjoyed a hearty winter dinner of thick-sliced bread (homemade?), meat and potatoes in about 1910. Maybe he had carrots or cabbage from a root cellar too. Note the European style of holding the utensils.*

Otter Tail County Historical Society

▶ *Coatless, hatless and using a fan to cool himself, here was a man proving how tough a Minnesotan could be when the temperature plummeted to 42 below in Otter Tail County. The date was Feb. 16, 1936. The advertising fan he carried said, in part, IBBON OODS. Our guess is Blue Ribbon Foods, but we can't find a record of a company named that. Is it familiar to you? Advertising fans were popular in this era. Entrepreneurs from undertakers to ice-cream producers used them to spread the good word about their businesses.*

Minnesota Historical Society

*This was the scene in Watkins during the Armistice Day Blizzard, a killer of a storm. We hope the man running for shelter found an unlocked door and a cup of piping hot coffee. The storm of Nov. 11, 1940, came with no warning. Temperatures in much of Minnesota were in the 60s in the morning and dropped to below zero the next day. In 24 hours, the storm dumped nearly 17 inches of snow on the Twin Cities and 26 inches on Collegeville. The weather service in Duluth recorded gale-force winds of 63 mph. The blizzard caused at least 48 deaths in Minnesota, mostly among hunters caught unprepared and far from shelter.*

Minneapolis Star Journal photo, Minnesota Historical Society

◀ *Two young women, Ruth Ollerman, 3212 E. Minnehaha Pkwy., and Lillian Hockinson, 5129 29th Av. S., found lodging during the Armistice Day Blizzard in the draft-board office in the Andrews Hotel in downtown Minneapolis. In the spirit of a pajama party, they seemed able to make the best of a bad situation. The Star Journal proclaimed the next day, "Storm Turns Loop into City's Dormitory." All the hotels were packed, and traffic was the worst in history up to that point. Most of Minnesota was bollixed up; 23 Minnesota cities were without telephone service the next day.*

Minneapolis Star Journal photo, Minnesota Historical Society

*Children watched the Armistice Day Blizzard through a window. This photo is something of a mystery. It was shot by a newspaper photographer but didn't make it into the paper. Judging from the lack of snow on the window ledge, the picture must have been taken when the rain had not yet turned to slush or snow.*

Minneapolis Star Journal photo, Minnesota Historical Society

Minnesota Historical Society

◀ *"Almost through" were welcome words near Sleepy Eye on Feb. 1, 1909. By the 1880s, railroads had rotary snowplows to clear the lines, but when the snow was deep — and this was deep — men were hired to shovel by hand too. The Sleepy Eye Herald Dispatch reported that it took the crew almost a full day to push through a mile-long drift between Revere and Walnut Grove. The plow got wedged in the packed snow, and workmen had to dig it out. Scenes such as this of Minnesota's brutal weather were made into postcards, which no doubt were sent to wimpy friends and relatives in Florida and California and other milder climes.*

◀ *Bernie Bierman said clear the field, so clear they did. What the U of M football coach said was law. The Gophers were scheduled to play Purdue the Saturday after the Armistice Day Blizzard (a Monday), and Bierman called in laborers to shovel. He also found a steam shovel to push out the snow. The Gophers won, 33 to 6. That big tarp was put down during driving rain the Saturday before, when Minnesota notched a 7 to 6 victory over Michigan.*

▶ *Ben Franklin, on a furlough from the Army to visit his family in Blue Earth, got caught in the blizzard of Feb. 14, 1866. He and another man were separated from their buddies and found themselves on a wind-swept strip of ice that turned out to be the Minnesota River. They followed the river to a camp of Indians, who took them in and cared for them as best they could, even though the men's arms and legs were frozen. On the seventh day after the storm started, the Indians took the two to Fort Ridgely. The other man died, and Franklin had to undergo surgery. The post surgeon amputated Franklin's arms and legs, and his survival was doubtful. But he lived, and the next summer he was taken to Europe and exhibited as a curiosity. For years the U.S. press allotted him considerable space as the only Civil War veteran to lose all his limbs.*

Brown County Historical Society

Minnesota Historical Society

Kenneth Wright photo, Minnesota Historical Society

▲ *The license plate on the Model T Ford reads 1925. That was before the days of Christmas-tree farms. Was the man who was piling trees on the car a tree salesman, or was he perhaps a family man so enthusiastic about the season that he took home multiple trees? Some households in the early 1900s proudly displayed several decorated trees. The photographer was from St. Paul, but the location of this shot is unknown.*

◀ *The main street in Redwood Falls was decorated for Christmas in about 1915. With quite a few cars, the town must have been hopping. The camera was pointed north on Washington St. from 3rd St., with Philbrick's department store on the left and the post office on the right.*

Minneapolis Times-Tribune photo, Minneapolis Public Library

*Shoppers sloshed along snowy sidewalks in downtown Minneapolis, at 5th St. and Nicollet Av. to be exact. The year was 1939, when women still wore galoshes that offered protection for shoes but little warmth.*

St. Paul Daily News photo, Minnesota Historical Society

*What's Christmas without lutefisk? No smart remarks please. Mrs. Andrew A. Olsen prepared the specialty at her home at 622 E. Magnolia St., St. Paul, on Dec. 23, 1936. For the uninitiated, it's best to explain that lutefisk is a Scandinavian delicacy. It's dried codfish, preserved in lye and prepared to this day in America but long abandoned in Scandinavia. It is reconstituted by soaking slabs in water; Mrs. Olsen used a sturdy galvanized bucket. Then the fish is boiled, drained and served all slippery and shimmering. Mrs. Olsen, born in Norway, served hers with cream gravy, she told a reporter. Mashed potatoes were a must with lutefisk.*

▶ *Herman ("Reindeer Man") Manheim was a hit in Hawley, even though his Santa tummy was as flat as the Depression-era economy. He was hired by Hawley merchants to draw shoppers to town in 1933 and 1935. Manheim lived up north in Ray. When he went on tour, he worked with a Native American man dressed as an Eskimo. They traveled with a dog sled, five huskies, a sleigh and, of course, real reindeer. One of the four reindeer was trained to climb stairs. His visit was such a big deal that Hawley schools called off afternoon classes, and the high school band played as Santa paraded the streets.*

Flaten/Wange Photo Collection,
Clay County Historical Society

*The Lutheran Sunday School in Hawley gave a Christmas program in about 1900. The photographer pulled the chandelier to the right to give you a good view. The pastor, S.G. Hauge, is sitting in the front pew on the right side. His wife, Anna, bedecked in a hat with plumes, is in front of the pulpit at the right. We can't be sure, but the program likely included Christmas hymns, Bible verses and other religious "pieces" that children memorized and recited. The tree is adorned with popcorn strings and paper chains.*

Flaten/Wange Photo Collection, Clay County Historical Society

Minnesota Historical Society

Minnesota Historical Society

***A boy with a hobby horse in about 1910 and a girl with a doll in about 1925 show how important children's toys can be. The girl was photographed at Rosedale Cottage, presumably a residence operated by a social-services agency.***

*In about 1904, the photographer of these children decorated the tree in a photo studio with candles, bags of candies, tinsel garlands, toys, mercury-glass ornaments, popcorn and cranberries.*

Minneapolis Public Library

***"We got our girl!" is the message of this photo. After seven sons (in descending order, Dan, Mike, Larry, Frank, Steve, Mark and Philip), Francis and Grayce Kortuem of Madison Lake had little Marie to put into dresses and hair ribbons. The photo ran in the Mankato Free Press in December 1954, along with a picture of another Madison Lake family that had seven girls followed by a boy. While all the Kortuem males looked directly into the camera, Mom was checking out the boys and the baby was checking out Mom. Do you suppose Mrs. Kortuem was worn to a frazzle by eight children? She didn't look it. Notice the wild wallpaper of the 1950s.***

Bill Altnow photo, Minneapolis Public Library

Minnesota Historical Society

▲ *Flinging aside the box and wrapping paper, 5-year-old Tom Coursolle obviously couldn't wait to try on the new Lone Ranger outfit that his mom, Melba, made. It was about 1953 at 3306 James Av. N., Minneapolis. The tinsel on the tree looked so good because it was the old-fashioned, leaded variety that was heavy. Unfortunately, it could poison children, and it's no longer sold. Today's fly-away, skimpy tinsel is safer.*

Minnesota Historical Society

◀ *This photograph was labeled "Harold's Christmas Tree." It's from Hibbing in 1900. We don't know Harold's full identity, but his folks must have been fairly affluent. They had a piano and lots of books under the tree and nice carpets. Harold, however, could have used a new suit. His arms had outgrown his sleeves, and he had gotten rather old for short pants.*

Minneapolis Journal photo, Minnesota Historical Society

***The tree was scrawny, the presents sparse and the mood somber for this Christmas photo at an orphanage. The picture was taken at the House of the Good Shepherd in St. Paul, on Blair Av. between Victoria and Milton Sts., in about 1900. Perhaps the holidays were stark reminders to the children of the loss of their families. In those days, of course, children didn't have the surfeit of presents that some kids do today. In many families, the girls shared one doll. Here the books, dolls and dollhouse furniture looked well-made, and the little girls are nicely dressed in pinafores, so not all was sad.***

John Runk photo, Minnesota Historical Society

***Can that be Rudolph? We're not sure. The historical society says this photo from about 1910 shows a reindeer, but sportsmen insist it's a white-tailed deer, dead and stuffed. Stillwater photographer John Runk unfortunately didn't leave notes on the family's identity. We presume the children aren't stuffed, unless with turkey and cookies and satisfaction about their toy soldiers and dolls.***

*Appearing content and prosperous, Edward and Ida Brewer relaxed near the Christmas tree at their home, 387 Pelham Blvd., St. Paul, in about 1950. He was a well-known Minnesota illustrator who created Cream of Wheat advertisements that ran in dozens of national magazines each month from 1911 to 1926. With a style as folksy as Norman Rockwell's, Brewer's work was immensely popular. It made Cream of Wheat, a Minneapolis company, famous. Notice in this photo the silver service on the game table, the electric lights on the tree and the carved mantle. There were children's toys under the tree, perhaps for grandchildren.*

Minnesota Historical Society

*Sarah Dougherty did her best to celebrate her 100th birthday on Dec. 23, 1921. She had been a longtime resident of Sauk Centre but at 100 was living with her granddaughter at White Earth. The Sauk Centre Herald reported that she "enjoyed exceptional health for a person of her advanced years." The dessert was shaped like the Scandinavians' "wreath cakes," composed of layers of cake rings. Usually they were not frosted. Maybe this woman, lacking modern dentistry, liked frosting for its softness as well as its sweetness. Her dress was typical of the 1890s.*

Minnesota Historical Society

*The tower of Minneapolis City Hall was the city's most recognized landmark when the building was completed in 1906. It offered a wonderful view of the burgeoning city. The tower, still standing, holds a carillon of bells and a giant clock, with each of four faces almost 25 feet in diameter. The minute hands, cast of solid copper, are 12 feet long. The city proudly proclaimed the clock to be the world's largest, bigger even than Big Ben in London.*

Minneapolis Public Library

St. Paul Daily News photo, Minnesota Historical Society

***Back when hefty was healthy and lots of bowlers were bruisers, this team proudly billed itself as the heaviest bowling team in America and sometimes even as the world's heaviest. The Seven Corners team of St. Paul was featured in a St. Paul newspaper in January 1911. Their story spotlighted a regional tournament of the International Bowling Association to be held at the West Side Club. The paper listed not only the big bowlers' names, but also their weights: Left to right, that's Fred Prieb, 265, and John Heidenreich, 270, in the back row, and seated in front were Sam Cross, 285, Joe Wagner, 340, and Bob Grady, 290, team captain.***

*This dining room in about 1914 had lots to be admired: Embroidered tablecloth, lovely dishes and artwork, beautiful woodwork, pretty rugs and curtains and a millinery or fashion book on the table. Nothing was very fancy but the room had a simple elegance. The small photograph on the back wall was wrapped in a dark ribbon; it was probably the portrait of a recently deceased woman.*

Minnesota Historical Society

Robert Hegre of Madison photo, Minnesota Historical Society

***Musicians Paul Ofstie, left, and Ingemar Hegre showed their skill with fiddle and guitar in about 1908. Neighboring farmers, they lived near Madison and frequently got together to make music. They were good, or so their descendants say. In the years when people made their own entertainment instead of relying on radio and television, they had a better chance to become proficient with an instrument. Ingemar wore a work shirt, vest and warm overalls and revealed a pale forehead, known disparagingly by city slickers for generations as a "farmer tan."***

***The Bald Headed Men's Club of St. Cloud installed Russell Ackerman, center, as president on Feb. 5, 1954. With a firm conviction that hair is an unnatural growth on the human head, the group had a theme song ("No Grass Grows on a Busy Street") and strict rules (any member who combed his hair over barren spaces was kicked out). Members gathered for lunch, prepared, of course, by bald cooks (no hair in the soup). They claimed the club was national, but the one and only chapter was in St. Cloud, founded in 1938. It enrolled as many as 40 members.***

Myron Hall photo, Stearns County Historical Society

Northeast Minnesota Historical Center

***Making sweaters for soldiers in World War I was the task of these boys in an unidentified school on the Iron Range. The boys look about ages 10 to 12, wouldn't you say? Even the youngest school children were involved in the war effort. In Duluth, for example, first-graders knitted squares for afghans and made envelopes for jokes, stories and paper dolls to be sent to the soldiers.***

*"Uncle Lambert and friends" hammed it up at the St. Paul Camera Club in about 1900. Was the game three-handed draw poker? The man on the right held a flush, so we wonder if this game was set up in the Wild West mode for the camera, complete with a pistol on the table. By the turn of the 20th century, amateurs could easily take pictures. George Eastman had introduced the Kodak camera, a small box camera, in 1888. It was sold loaded with film. When the last exposure was made, the owner mailed it back to Eastman's factory, where it was unloaded, reloaded and returned. The prints were mailed back to the customer in a few weeks.*

Minnesota Historical Society

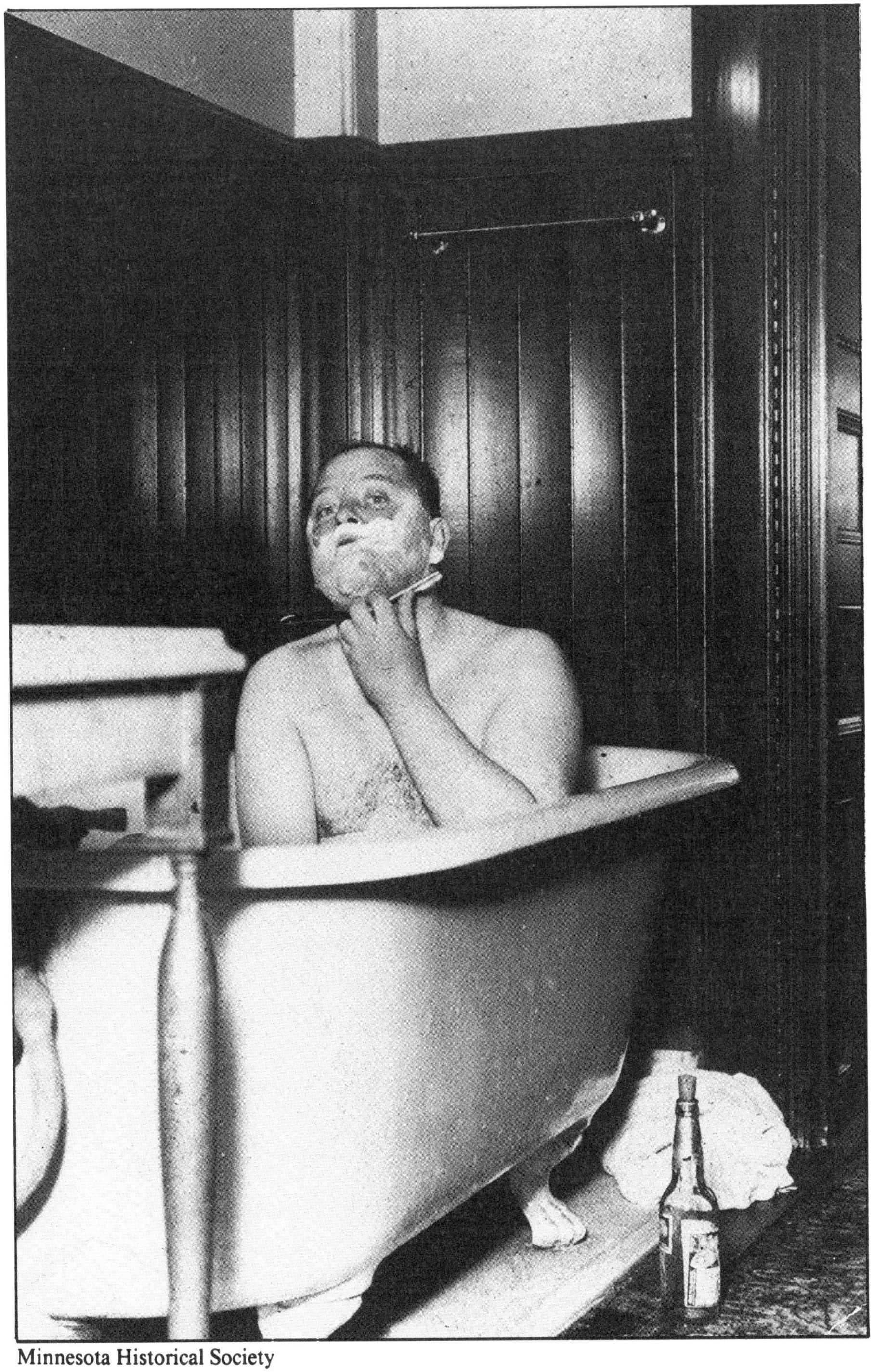

Minnesota Historical Society

YMCA Archives

***Sometimes nothing feels as good in winter as soaking in hot water. A man with a liquor bottle beside him used his straight razor in the bathtub in about 1915. Hubert Humphrey, then mayor of Minneapolis, asked for a towel at the Minneapolis YMCA shower room in about 1946.***

Minnesota Historical Society

◀ *With soft light from the piano lamp, Gertrude Chandler poured her soul into the music. She was from an affluent Minneapolis family; her father, Wallace, owned a business that sold railroad and steamship tickets. The photo was taken in about 1910, when she graduated from Smith College in Massachusetts and was exchanging letters with Harold Fisher, whom she later married. At the piano she wore a lovely long dress (maybe a graduation gown?), a pretty string of pearls, and bracelets pushed high up the arm, perhaps so as not to interfere with her music-making. Our guess is that's a big fat diamond on the left hand and a class ring on the right.*

▶ *Fred Pilakoff, a wrestler extraordinaire known as "the Finnish Lion," visited the Finnish-American community of New York Mills in 1905. Local lore goes that while at G.H. Kauppi's blacksmith shop, he twisted an iron bar around his arm for a souvenir. He probably got to keep it, don't you think?*

Otter Tail County Historical Society

▶ ***A different view of masculinity than the wrestler's was demonstrated by this man with a book in about 1905. He had either a toupee or a funny-looking haircut, which may account for why he's wearing his hat for this studio portrait. Do you suppose he was a short fellow, or did the camera angle distort his shape?***

C.L. Merryman photo, Kerkhoven, Minnesota Historical Society

Minnesota Historical Society

◀ ***Ah, the lure of a long winter's nap. This unidentified man settled down on a daybed in what looked to be a parlor in about 1910.***

▶ ***Ellen Flindt, 81, added wood to her P.D. Beckwith stove in January 1951. She lived five miles northeast of Kimball. Behind her is a photo of a young man in military uniform. Could he be a grandson who had served in World War II? Just a guess on our part.***

Myron Hall photo, Stearns County Historical Society

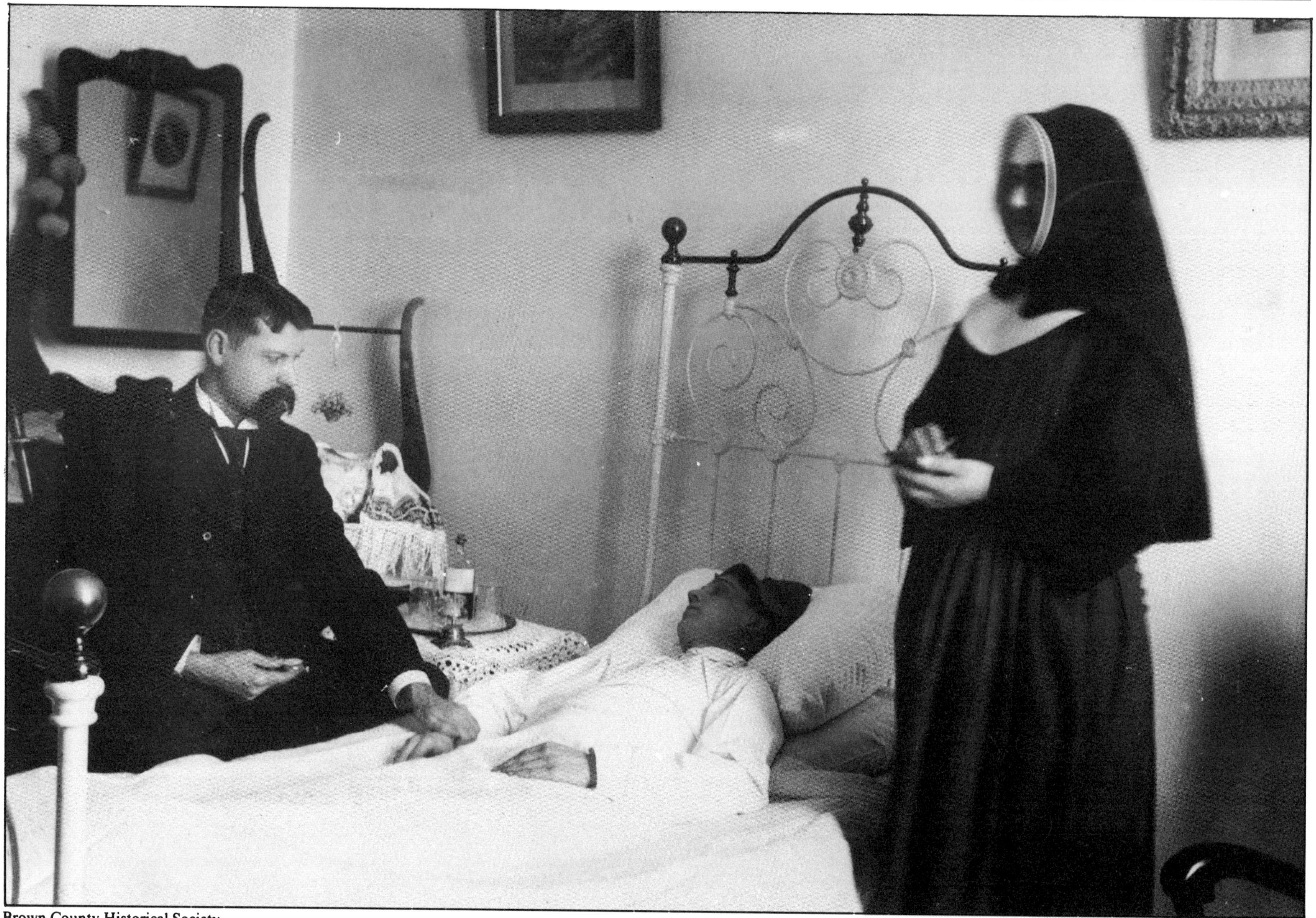

Brown County Historical Society

*Dr. L.A. Fritsche tended to a patient in Loretta Hospital in New Ulm in 1903. In those days, hospital rooms were more homelike, less institutional, than now. This hospital was staffed by the Poor Handmaids of Jesus Christ.*

Cokato Historical Society

***This photograph from the late 1800s shows a level of comfort with death that surprises us today. It surely was intended to be the last remembrance of all the children in a family. The little boy with his head on the pillow had died at age 3 or 4, probably at home surrounded by his family, and after his death his smiling siblings were posed with him. The family is unidentified, but a clue is that the photo was found in a farmhouse near Manannah. Often family members took pictures of a deceased person, both to remember the person and to finalize the death in their minds. In many cases, the death photo was the only picture ever taken of a person.***

Clay County Historical Society

***Frequently, photographs taken of deceased persons in their coffins were included in family albums. Identification of people in this picture is frustrating. When negatives shot at the funeral were donated to the Clay County Historical Society, someone had written "Nels Erickson funeral, June 1, 1916" on the envelope. But surely the month wasn't June; the mourners wore heavy coats. Several Nels Ericksons died in Clay County but none in 1916. The location probably was Hawley; the son of the Hawley undertaker recognized him in a picture. In those days children were exposed more directly to death than now, but nonetheless the little faces in the front row appear shocked or at least uncomfortable.***

*Such an idyllic scene. In 1889 Tallie Gotzian skated at Virginia Rink in a ritzy neighborhood of St. Paul — at Virginia and Laurel Avs., next to Neill School. Ice skating was especially popular for several decades after the Civil War. To quote Frank Leslie's Illustrated Weekly Newspaper, "Everybody skates, and it is about as much out of the way to confess that we do not skate, as it is to admit that we do not dance."*

Minnesota Historical Society

Charles J. Hibbard photo, Minnesota Historical Society

◀ *Ice skaters circled St. Paul's Van Cleve Park in 1912. It was this kind of image of health and peacefulness that Minnesota officials and authors promoted. In earlier decades, they used winter sporting scenes, along with free land, to lure prospective immigrants here from Europe and the eastern United States.*

▶ *Skaters Norma Jeanne Landry and Larraine Gellatly got their hockey and figure skates ready for skating at the rink in Duluth's Memorial Park, 602 Central Av. N., in 1944.*

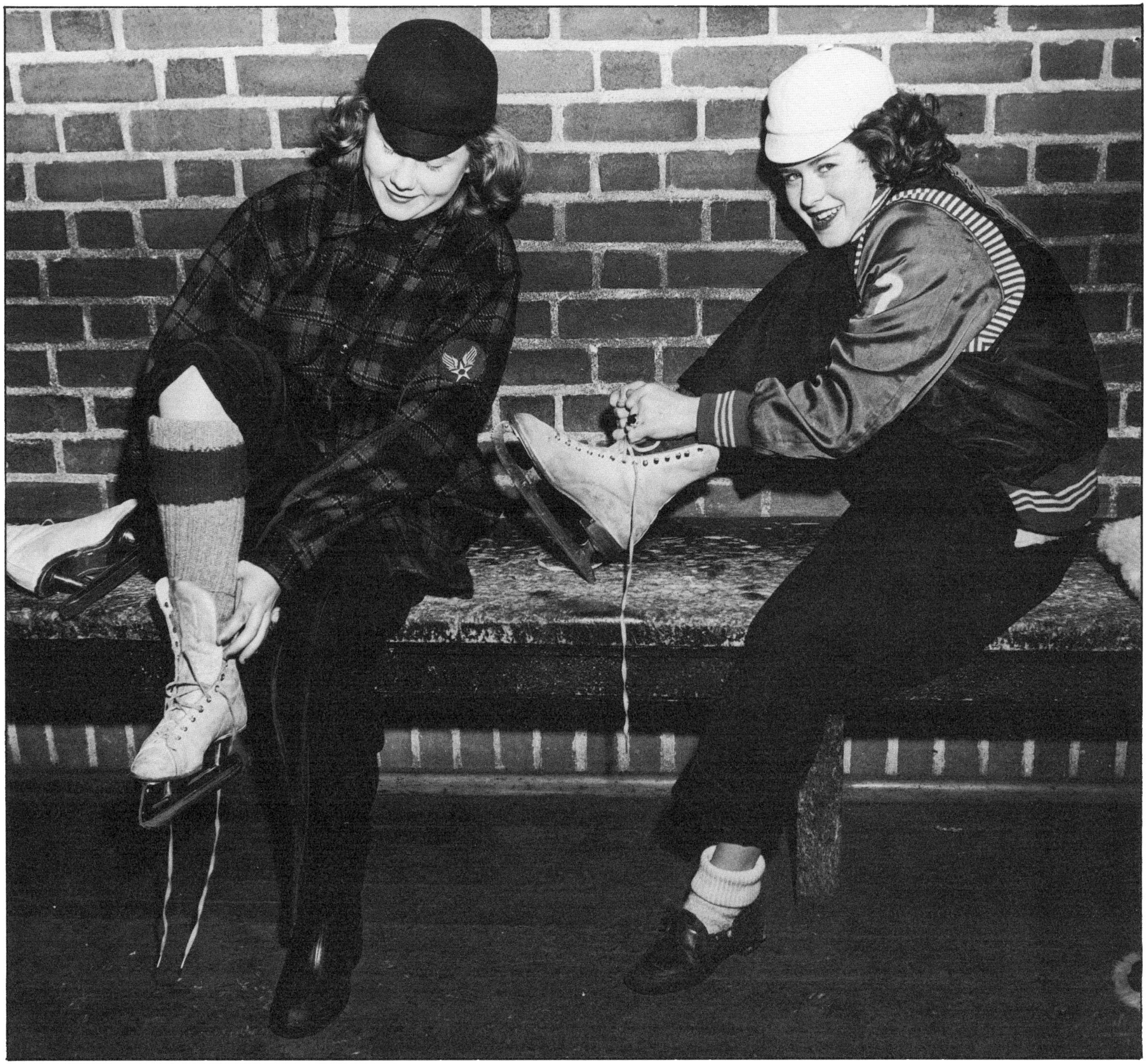

Northeast Minnesota Historical Center

Albert Munson photo, Minnesota Historical Society

*Eva, Chester and Raymond Munson built a snow fort in their St. Paul back yard in about 1903. The baby had mittens; the big kids had shed theirs. Their clothing looked like adult styles, but obviously it fit the children. The photographer was the children's father. Albert Munson was a machinist, a talented amateur photographer and, judging from his photos, a father delighted with his kids.*

Minnesota Historical Society

*Anna Hervin, a St. Paul widow who lived at 568 Sherburne, shoveled out on Dec. 29, 1940. She appeared to be using a coal shovel and probably used it at the furnace too. The neighborhood, originally home to French and German working-class people, was known as Frogtown. "Frog" was a belittling word for people of French descent; it referred to the French taste for frogs' legs. However, the "Frogtown" label was readily accepted by the neighborhood.*

John W.G. Dunn photo, Minnesota Historical Society

***St. Paul Boy Scouts were proud of the job they did clearing fire hydrants after a heavy snowfall in about 1924. The boy to the left was Dave McCloud; the other was unidentified. The photographer, a St. Paul insurance man, worked so long and hard with Boy Scouts that he was awarded one of scouting's highest honors, the Silver Beaver award, in 1934.***

Minnesota Historical Society

***Joe Wood, left, and Helen Bouton cleared a path through wet, heavy snow in Lake City in about 1885. The sidewalks still were made of boards.***

Minnesota Historical Society

Minnesota Historical Society

▲ *Staged in a studio with fake snow, this 1886 photo nonetheless showed the joys of winter. But come to think of it, the woman to the left looked a bit dubious. Maybe she was from Iowa or some other southern clime.*

◀ *In 1858 or 1859, a dog team, pulling a sled probably loaded with furs, had come south from the Canadian border and was photographed in St. Paul. The location was the intersection of Fort Rd. (now known as West 7th St.) and Walnut St. With the dogsled were the two drivers, named Tarbell and Campbell, plus a little boy who most likely was just hanging out with the visiting adventurers. The photo has deteriorated over time, but it does show an early view of the city. On the bluff in the background were six of the earliest houses built on what came to be St. Paul's prestigious Summit Av. In the 1850s there wasn't even a road there yet, and the isolated houses were virtually rural retreats of wealthy families. Most were torn down by the 1880s and replaced with even more luxurious homes.*

Goodhue County Historical Society

*◀ The members of the Aurora Ski Club in 1890 were ski jumpers. They were Paul Henningsted, Mikkel Hemmestvedt, Torger Hemmestvedt and B.T. Hjermstad — Norwegians all. Most winter sports photographs of the period were shot in photo studios. It wasn't that low temperatures outdoors harmed early cameras; photographers were able to shoot winter landscapes. The problem was that cameras were unable to capture speed. Mostly what these skiers would have wanted was a sharp picture showing them in their sporting regalia, and that they got.*

Minnesota Historical Society

*St. Paul curlers in 1891 were checking to be sure the Mississippi River ice was smooth, flat and strong. Curling was an old Scottish game (really old, like from the 1500s). It was played on ice with heavy "stones" of granite. Brooms traditionally were used to clear snow from the ice, but now it is known that sweeping ahead of the stones makes them go farther and straighter. Curlers played as early as 1865 on the river below the Wabasha Bridge. In 1885 the St. Paul Curling Club built a clubhouse on Raspberry Island, now called Navy Island, for indoor curling. The guys would flood the rink, open the windows and wait for the ice to form.*

Minnesota Historical Society

◀ *The St. Paul Winter Carnival, a highlight of Minnesotans' winters beginning in 1886, used to feature the blanket toss. Here a man was flipped high into the air from a sturdy blanket in 1887. Newspaper reports of the time told of the thrill of the toss and didn't mention injuries, so it might have been a safe sport. One of the better ice palaces in carnival history was behind him.*

Minnesota Historical Society

▲ *After being dormant for 20 years, the Winter Carnival was revived in 1916 by Louis Hill, son of the railroad builder J.J. Hill. To celebrate the revival, sponsors held a contest to depict the typical Carnival Girl. This young woman at the Town and Country Club struggled with a giant pushball.*

Ron Feldhaus photo collection

*This photo is from a scrapbook filled with Minneapolis snapshots from about the 1910s, so we can presume that this streetcar scene was shot in Minneapolis about then. This illustrates why scrapbooks should not be dismantled: So much can be told from the collection. The whole is worth more than the sum of the parts.*

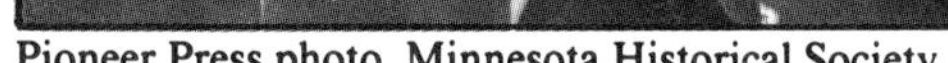
Pioneer Press photo, Minnesota Historical Society

Pioneer Press photo, Minnesota Historical Society

Minneapolis Star photo, Minnesota Historical Society

***Children love to frolic outside in winter, as these photos show. Young ice skaters braved the cold at Lake Como in 1954. They were, left to right, Fred Davis, 10, of 1150 Churchill; John Preda, 11, 1227 W. Como Blvd., and Tom Davis, 8, Fred's brother. An unidentified girl made an angel in the snow on Nov. 25, 1952. And David Tente, 2, of 84 S. Hamline and his dog, Chris, had fun in a snowstorm on Jan. 21, 1952, that kept most adults inside. Chris was in training for the Winter Carnival mutt races.***

Ron Feldhaus photo collection

*These people at Lake of the Isles in Minneapolis eagerly shared a letter on Jan. 14, 1894. It would be fun to know the contents of the letter that so captivated them. Hats perched on the backs of women's heads in this manner were fashionable in the 1890s.*

John Runk photo, Minnesota Historical Society

*This tremendous load of pine logs, 24 feet high, was pulled from the woods on March 17, 1909. The proud crew proclaimed it the largest load ever hauled on logging sleds in Wisconsin or Minnesota. The horses pulled it three or four miles near the St. Croix River. The teamster was Herman Siedenkrans; the top loader, George Villard; the foreman, Tom Boury; the logger, Lee Hammond, and the horses, Ballie, Nellie, Roudy and Dan. How's that for identifying a photo!*

▶ ***Logging the pine forests was a foremost industry in Minnesota from before the Civil War to the first few decades of the 1900s. It was extensively documented by photographers, partly because the isolated workers loved buying photos to send home. Here lumberjacks played cards at the Oliver Iron Mining Co. Camp #24 in 1916. Notice the pet dog, record player, rough-hewn furniture and snowshoes on the wall. Don't even think about the heady aroma in the lumber camp.***

William Rolleff photo, Minnesota Historical Society

Minnesota Historical Society

***Two cooks stood outside their lumber camp in northern Minnesota in about 1920. If this photo doesn't say Brrrrr!, nothing does.***

*Lumberjacks ate in the mess hall of the Scott & Graff Lumber Co., camp #1, near Ridge in 1913. They had a whole lot of food waiting for them; check out the plate of doughnuts in the foreground. Working outside in the winter could burn a lot of calories. The lumbermen didn't look particularly young. They may well have been farmers from farther south, who left their families behind during the long winters to work in the pineries of northern Minnesota.*

William Rolleff photo, Minnesota Historical Society

▶ *Who were these men eating baked beans in 1937, and why were they so silly about doing it? They apparently were the losers of a sales contest. Winners ate steak, losers ate beans. At least some of the men were district managers for the Minneapolis Star circulation department. We know a few names. That's Ken Jensen, standing to the right; Vince Enrooth, seated to the far left, and James Schnickel, seated second from the right.*

William Rolleff photo, Minnesota Historical Society

***This was the cook at the N.B. Shank Co., Camp #2, near Biwabik in 1913. See the hanging pig carcasses? Maybe they were early forms of frozen dinners; maybe they were freshly slaughtered. If fresh, this might help explain why people had more problems with food poisoning a few generations ago.***

Minneapolis Star Journal photo, Minnesota Historical Society

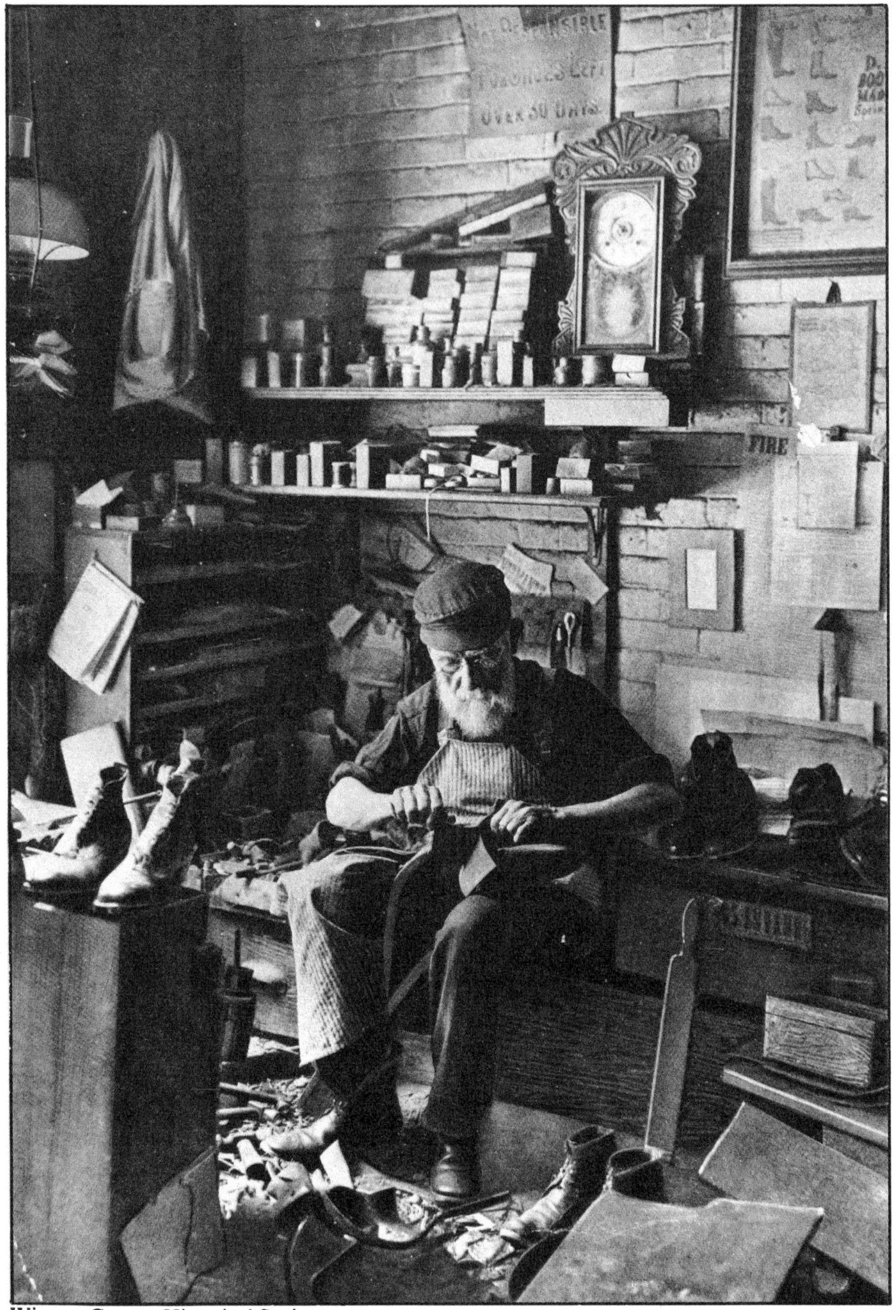

Winona County Historical Society

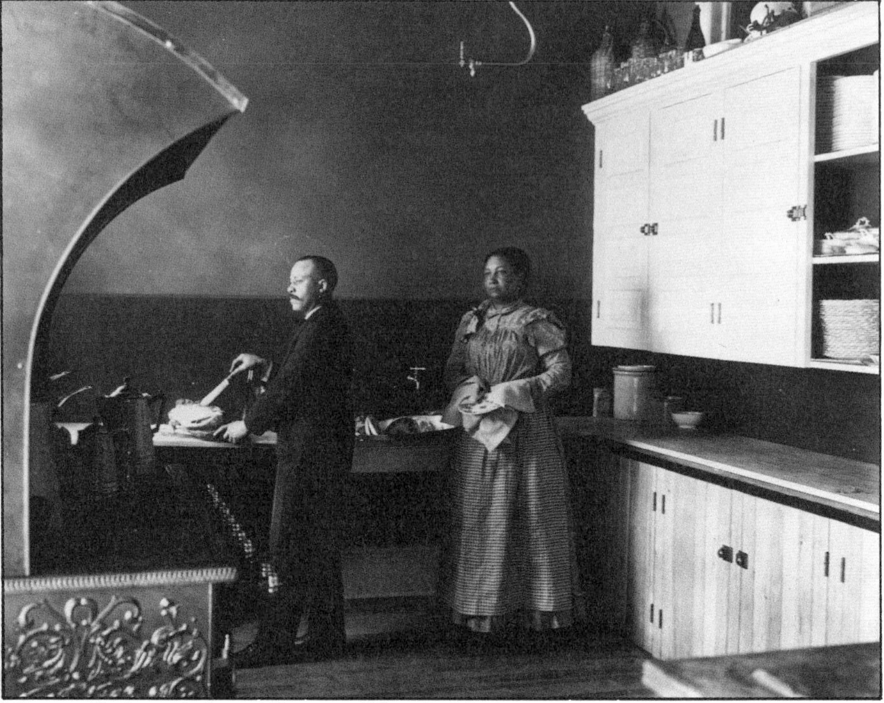

Minneapolis Journal photo, Minnesota Historical Society

▲ *This couple in the kitchen may be John A. Dickerson and his wife, who owned Dickerson's Restaurant at 208 Hennepin Av. S. in Minneapolis at the turn of the 20th century. That's the best guess at the historical society. From the size of the room, the number of plates and the big stove, this has got to be the kitchen of a restaurant or mansion. Does it look familiar to anyone?*

◀ *An unidentified cobbler was hard at work at his bench sometime after the turn of the 20th century. Many shoe repairers had been shoemakers in the old country. Because people had only a few pairs (if that) of boots and shoes, and could replace them only infrequently, it was essential to maintain them well. Few towns were without cobblers, and those who could repair speedily, well and inexpensively found themselves indispensable members of the community.*

*Anna Topness was on her way to milk the cows when her photo was taken in about 1910. We don't know where she lived. The weather probably was chilly. There was snow on the feed, and she wore a shawl over her apron and house dress.*

Minnesota Historical Society

Minneapolis Tribune photo by George Ryan, Minneapolis Public Library

◀ ***On a cold February day in 1936, a rail worker used a sled to haul wrenches and other heavy tools. The picture was taken at a Minneapolis siding, where smoke and steam drifted over long rows of freight cars and locomotives.***

▶ ***On the Northern Pacific Railway tracks, a switchman or brakeman with a lantern demonstrated the danger of insufficient clearance in about 1915. But judging from the wary expression on his face, the demonstration may have been more realistic than he wanted.***

Minnesota Historical Society

Hennepin History Museum

***◀ The boiler room crew of Donaldson's department store in downtown Minneapolis showed off the tools of the trade in this undated photo. Look how many workers it took to run a boiler room. They look like a bunch not to be messed with, don't they? We should all occasionally gather for a photograph with colleagues and symbols of our work.***

***▶ On the other end of the social scale, Mrs. William Webster stood beside a taxi at the St. Paul home of Mrs. Chauncey M. Griggs sometime in the mid 1920s. Cass Gilbert, who designed the State Capitol, was one of the architects of the house at 365 Summit Av., built in 1891. Chauncey Griggs was a merchant and lumberman. His brother Theodore lived in the house now known as the Burbank-Livingston-Griggs house, at 432 Summit Av. A William Webster was superintendent of Minneapolis schools at the time; perhaps it was his wife who was visiting across the river.***

Hennepin History Museum

Hennepin History Museum

◀ *Minnehaha Falls was one of the state's earliest tourist attractions, viewed by thousands of 19th-century travelers from the East long before Minnesota became a state. Thanks to Henry Wadsworth Longfellow's narrative poem, it later became known across the nation. "The Song of Hiawatha" was published in 1855, but Longfellow never saw the falls. He based his description on others' writings and an 1852 daguerreotype. Longfellow made up the story of the Indian maiden named Minnehaha, based loosely on legends from various tribes. By the time of the Civil War, the falls were famous. But they weren't as big a draw in winter.*

Minnesota Historical Society

***Cast members of an Anoka High School production posed for a publicity shot in about 1905. The plays were "Lend Me Five Shillings" and "A Likely Story." Don't they look grand!***

Minnesota Historical Society

◀ *At the Jewish Home for the Aged in St. Paul in about 1925, these elderly men were able to maintain their religious traditions. The home evolved into the Shalom Home.*

▶ *The crew from Minneapolis station house No. 22 showed its stuff in 1917. The station was at Oliver Av. and Kenwood Pkwy., and J.P. Henry was station captain. Fighting winter fires has long been a challenge up here in the northland.*

Hennepin History Museum

George Luxton photo, Minnesota Historical Society

◀ *For Valentine's Day in 1933, Judy Eggen and Arthur Haas exchanged ornate cards in the kindergarten class at Loring School in north Minneapolis. She's eager, he's not so sure. He's ready to take a card but not quite ready to give. They wore white cotton stockings, probably held up by garters and worn over long underwear. Remember when girls wore dresses to school, no matter the weather, and little boys wore short pants?*

▶ *On a cleaning spree, these ladies swept off their elephant in about 1925. You're right; they weren't the usual elephant caretakers. These society women, fashionably dressed, were involved in some kind of charitable activity with the Shrine circus.*

Minnesota Historical Society

# Winter letters and diaries

## A mother's pride

***Dorothy Atkinson of Minneapolis kept a journal when she was 28. She was the mother of three young children and the wife of Frederick Atkinson, the wealthy owner of the Atkinson Milling Co. Her father, George H. Bridgman, had been the president of Hamline University in St. Paul for 29 years, from 1883 to 1912. She started her diary with a new year.***

**Tuesday, Jan. 1, 1918.** I am going to keep a diary of the children and for the children — that I may be better able to look back upon our happy days of babyhood and childhood and that they, when they grow older, may recall many things otherwise forgotten.

Mary is nearing 6, in the first grade of school. She loves her work and is much interested in it. Learning to read and to write. In writing they start right out on words, rather than beginning with letters. Her first word was Halloween, next Thanksgiving, followed by Christmas and Santa Claus. She is doing very well. Of course some in the class do better than she, but they are considerably older.

**Jan. 3.** Frederick started in to kindergarten last fall when we came in from the lake. I found that it interfered with his sleep a little, that he would not go to sleep after going to bed, until nearly 9 o'clock. So we stopped kindergarten for a while. Also stopped our nap at noon — only let him rest for a short while. He was given a medicine by Dr. Schlutz. As a result he goes to sleep immediately on going to bed and has resumed kindergarten, but he sleeps late in the morning and we do not waken him. A boy full of go and spirit. Quite a tease, with a considerable sense of humor. Really very appealing. Quite affectionate at times.

Both Mary and Frederick are devoted to their baby brother Billy. Mary just loves to be with him, is very sweet and gentle to him. Always running to him on hearing him cry, calling him her little "sweetheart Billy." Says when she is old enough she is going to take all the care of him. She has a great deal of the Mother instinct. Plays continually with her dolls. I wonder if it will stay with her. She really is very sweet, wanting to do what I want her to do. A darling little companion. And so is Frederick. They are truly devoted to each other which will continue, I hope.

Billy is a dear, dear baby. Really the happiest and best I have had, perhaps because I have taken almost entire care of him. Miss Rood left and consequently he has not had so much attention & is happy to lie by himself, kicking, talking & smiling, for he smiles nearly all the time. We have Billy sleep in a little porch off our bedroom, so we see a great deal of him. His father loves his smiles too. He is very strong. Just 6 months old this January 12th. Weighs about 16¼ pounds. Does not roll over, but seems to exert his effort in trying to raise himself. Already loves to be held up on his feet, which of course we cannot do very often.

**Monday, Jan. 7.** School started after the Christmas holidays. Both Mary and Frederick glad to go back. Mary came home quite excited because they were going to start a knitting club to knit 6 in. squares for the soldiers [fighting World War I]. Nearly all the little girls know how to knit, after a fashion. Frederick says he would like to "swash" the Germans.

**Wednesday, January 9.** I visited school for a little while this morning & was really very much pleased when Miss Roemer . . . told all about Frd'k that A.M. A little girl from 1st grade came across to get some water for the bird which Miss Hill has brought to the 1st grade room. It was Miss Hills' Xmas present & she knew the little girls would love it, which they do. Frd'k was standing watching some other boys play & the little girl got the water in her dish & started for the door. No one was talking. He immediately went to the door & opened it for the little girl to go out & then closed it. Pretty nice for 3½ years.

**Thursday, Jan. 10.** I took Mary and Frederick over to Clinton Morrison's to play. It was quite cold, 5 below zero, but they slid down the hill for ¾ of an hour any way. A nice hill in the Morrison back yard. Clinton is fine little boy, just a year younger than Frederick. Very sturdy. Frd'k rather amusing in his care of Clinton.

**Sunday, Jan. 13.** A nice restful Sunday with weather a little warmer after the 24 degrees below we have had. Able to open the window on Billy's porch again. He takes a fine nap after his bath, sleeps a good 3 hours nearly every day. After dinner I take Mary & Frederick out for a walk. Take one sled & they took turns pulling each other. They have great fun, rolling off & laughing. After we came home they built towers & buildings and read in our Hiawatha Primer. The northern lights were of great interest. Father & I put them to bed. Frederick insisting on undressing himself entirely. Even the buttons he manages now. They listened delighted while "Fathie" (as Frd'k sometimes calls him) told stories of his boyhood, hunting hickory nuts & falling from the tree, sliding down hills & going over the wall & losing his breath, Minnie & Dicky lost & found again. Frederick almost in tears.

***Dorothy Atkinson became active in the Minnesota Birth Control League and was its president in the 1930s. It advocated a "happier family life" by determining the number of children.***

Minnesota Historical Society, Dorothy Atkinson Rood and Family Papers

~

## Really cold

**Jan. 29, 1882.** 18 below zero. Got up late. Began to wear under clothing.

**— L.J.G. Archer-Burton, proprietor of a Fairmont saloon**

Minnesota Historical Society, L.J.G. Archer-Burton Papers

~

## His little sick girl

***Miner Ball, a mill operator in Delano, started keeping a journal on New Year's Day of 1876, two weeks after his 34-year-old wife, Katie, died of typhoid fever. She had been ill four weeks. Her obituary reported that she left five children, "the eldest not yet 12," and was buried next to "a little daughter, gone before." These snippets from his journal tell of his 6-year-old daughter and others who had typhoid.***

**1/1.** The Glorious new year ushered in by firing of Guns and a General Jubelie. As for my self, I passed the day only as I have past the last months, stayed home all day taking care of my little sick girl Ruth who thank God is improving.

**1/5.** Ruthey very restless during night but better during day . . . . Henry Ball taken wors today. Miney Chanc quite sick. Lacey Bourk Better. Mrs. Chance Better.

**1/6.** Ruthey resten better.

**1/7.** A butiful day clear & warm. Took Ruth out riding in morning to Aunt Calley and Aunt Mary's. Winy Ball not so well.

**1/10.** Rose 5 o'clock morning clear & cold. Ruthey rested varey well. Worked on my [accounting] books all day. Mellvill Powers & wife visited and our little boys had a splendid visit. Ruthey growing better very slow.

**1/14.** This day one of God's Butiful Mornings. clear and Comfortably warm. Took Little Girl out walking 5 o'clock in morning.

**1/18.** Atended Lodge for first time in 3 months. Ruthey travels around the House alone. Winey is improving very rapidly.

**1/20.** Ruthey quite a considerible wors.

**1/21.** Ruthey quite bad during day. Had Doctor. Quite high feaver.

**1/22.** Ruth great deal wors. Stayed in hous all day, no bissness. Children varey noysey.

**1/30.** Ruthey geting better walked around house som . . . . Caley Ball [his sister-in-law] sick. Elley staying there.

**1/31.** Ruthey rather poorley all day. Caley Ball quite sick.

**2/2.** Ruthey not improving much.

**2/6.** Caley Ball a great deal worse, was during day crasey she thinks she is in purgatory poor girl. stayed with her most of day, got better about 6 P.M. Got her right mind. Mary Olsen taken vary sick, choking, got realeaf in about ½ hour.

**2/12.** Set up at night with Calley Ball. George LaClair got scarlet. Lon taken sick. Ruth Young sick.

**2/15.** Calley Ball to all apearance better. about 12 o'clock took wors and now I have no hopes of recovry. continued to grow wors all day.

**2/16.** Cally Ball died at 1 o'clock in an incontious state died peasfully. yesterday she called all of her friends around her and gave them good advice. spent the most of the day trying to sing God Bless Her. She has gon to rest with Jeasus. O what a blessing to have Jeasus with you when you cross over.

**2/18.** Up at 6 in morning quite cold but varey pleasent run mill untill noon shut down for funeral. A vary large atendance. 31 [horse] teams went to grounds. More persons than could get in House. Everything went off varey butifuly.

Minnesota Historical Society, Miner Ball Papers

## 27 below and falling

***Nathan Jarvis was a U.S. Army surgeon stationed from 1833 to 1836 at Fort Snelling, near what is now the Twin Cities. He wrote to his family in New York on Jan. 2, 1834, about the bitter cold.***

We have at last winter in earnest, the thermometer only 27 below zero at 7 o'clock this morning and a prospect of its being colder tomorrow!! Think of that and blow your fingers. I never knew what cold weather was before. The highest the thermometer has been the whole day was 12 below zero. Out at the Fort the thermometer sunk as low as 32 below zero!!! at 7 A.M. Everything cracks & snaps with the cold. Thanks to our stoves & plenty of wood we defy Jack Frost. The snow is now 18 inches deep. The officers all dined yesterday with Major Bliss who on the occasion of the New Year gave us an excellent dinner and good wine. This together with some good Irish whiskey punch constituted our enjoyments of the day, which neither in variety or extent, of course, cannot equal those with you on that day . . . .

Our express [mail] did not, as you see, start today, it goes tomorrow. The thermometer in the Garrison, where it is warmer than outside, was at 9 o'clock A.M. 29 below zero, at 2 o'clock and at 9 P.M. 24 below zero and falling rapidly!!! In going a mile or two today I nearly froze my nose and ears.

The New York Academy of Medicine Library, New York City

## Newsprint works

Cold feet are the precursors of consumption. To escape them, warm your feet well in the morning, and covering the sole with a piece of common paper, carefully draw on the sock, and then the boot or shoe.

**— "Ladies Own Home Cookbook," by Mrs. Jane Warren, 1891**

## Full stomachs

***Marjorie Bullard kept a diary when she was a girl in St. Paul. Here she described Christmas Eve day in 1897.***

**Dec. 24.** This morning we did up our presents and got things all ready for to-morrow. To-night we (Polly, Betty and I) went down to the church to an entertainment we were going to have . . . . We went right down to our Sunday-school room, and the girls had brought our present to Mrs. Sanford in a box. When she came, she of course opened it and found a bust of Beethoven. She was very much delighted with it and invited us to her house Friday afternoon and she wants each one to tell something about Beethoven.

By-and-by when the children were all in the Sunday-school room, Mr. Dyer called the name of each class and they passed up into the church one by one. We sat near the back of the room and Mr. Bigelow's class was behind us. The carols were sung and when it came the time to take up the contributions all of our class went up. We had to sing something so went right into the choir-loft. Pretty soon Lilias Joy got up and spoke her piece. At the end of each verse the rest of the class sang "Glory to God in the highest, on earth peace, goodwill to man." We were supposed to sound like the angels which the shepherd boy heard. After that we went down and pretty soon Mother Goose came running down one of the aisles. She was Louise Jewett all dressed up. She said some funny things and the children were almost crazy. She gave each one of the primary department a cradle to the girls, and a shed of candy to the boys. And the rest were given a box of candy. It was soon over and we went home. We hung up our stockings, filled them with presents and soon went to bed very sleepy.

**Dec. 25.** Under my stocking was a big book filled with 19 of Mozart's Sonatas from Papa, "The Last Days of Pompei" from Polly and a picture with a large frame from Kate. Also there was some blue flannel for a dressing-jacket from Mamma, and in my stocking was a little glove-buttoner from Betty. Mamma thought the irons which I gave her were fine, and she says she shall want to use them right away. The bag that Polly and I gave Betty she likes very much and goes around carrying it on her arm all the time . . . . About twelve o'clock Betty and I walked up to Grandma's . . . . Dana [a cousin] is getting just as cunning now, and he can walk quite well. When we were all up there, dinner was ready. The goose was very good except that there was no gravy. The plum-pudding came and we had great fun about Uncle. Before he had said that his stomach was full but afterwards he said it was all right.

We had the tree right after dinner and it was lovely. We all had lovely presents and especially Grandma. Her lap was full and she kept saying, "I have so many more presents that the rest of you." Not very long after we went home and it seemed as it always does, very lonesome to get home with the house all dark. It has been altogether a very happy Christmas day.

Minnesota Historical Society, Marjorie L. Bullard Papers

~

## Christmas pressures in 1910

***Lillian Brown of Owatonna received a letter dated Dec. 22, 1910, from her brother, Edward A. Carver. He told how busy and broke he was.***

It seems our lives are crowded so full of affairs these days, we are not living; just flying here and there, hardly taking time to eat or sleep. But when we get on the other side of life we will not have to give any thought of what we shall eat or wear so we will have rest along that line any way.

Christmas finds us wishing we were financially able to do something for each one of those who are near and dear to us, but we can at least send words of cheer and sincere wishes, and that we do to you and yours at this time.

Minnesota Historical Society, Lillian Elizabeth Brown Papers

~

## An oyster meal

**Christmas, Tuesday, Dec. 25, 1866.** Clear, Cool, Beautiful. 28 degrees. A very quiet day. Spent most of it outdoors at work. Most of the family made us a brief visit. Uncle J's family are at our house. Had an oyster dinner; the oysters fresh & excellent. [The oysters may have come from Lake Pepin, or perhaps from the South by railroad.] In the evening we also had a pleasant little candy party, and had quite a pleasant evening of it, and all the candy we could dispose of. Received a nice little Christmas Gift from Mr. J.

**— John W. Murray, a farmer living near Excelsior**

Minnesota Historical Society, John W. Murray Papers

~

## A remarkable Christmas

***Catharine Goddard owned and operated Winona's first boarding house and was the hostess for the town's first big Christmas party. That was remarkable, considering how her year had gone. But before we get to that, here's her cheery description of the Christmas of 1852, written in a letter to her sister, Lucretia:***

This Christmas dinner was given in the upper story of the Winona House on Water street, in which Edwin Hamilton was keeping what was called Bachelors' Hall. The young men set up stoves and Mrs. "Elder" Hamilton and myself looked after the culinary part of the dinner. In the absence of the bird that usually graces the Christmas dinner [a turkey], we were obliged to use coon, or rather several coons, with entrees of venison and wild goose. At the request of the young men, who said it would not be a Christmas feast without them, we fried enough nuts [doughnuts] in coon's fat, and they were much relished.

By 11 o'clock, every resident of Winona, old and young, big and little, except Mr. and Mrs. Henry Gere and Mr. and Mrs. Thompson, some thirty in all, were present. In addition to these were several from Minnesota City, besides some St. Paul men who were hauling goods on the ice from LaCrosse to St. Paul and who shortly before noon broke through the ice on the river opposite the business part of the town. These men were assisted in rescuing their teams and goods by our townsmen and invited to share the hospitalities of our Christmas dinner.

It is needless to say that our guests were surprised at their reception. One of them in a short speech said that their knowledge of Winona was obtained from the St. Paul paper which usually referred to our little town as desolate Wabasha Prairie. He also expressed his intention of seeing hereafter the town at which they partook of a public Christmas dinner and which included in its menu five kinds of cake, three kinds of pies and plenty of coon and venison.

The remnants of this dinner furnished us with a bountiful supper, of which all partook except one man who had gone over the lake in search of fish. While we were at supper this man came back and excitedly asked for a team and sled with which to haul his catch.

It turned out that this man found an air hole in the ice on the lake and he had but to dip into the water to get all the fish he wanted. This find proved to be of nearly as much benefit to the "Wabashaites" as it did the quails to the children of Israel when in the wilderness — and was the beginning of many fishing trips.

***She did hint of sorrow:***

I had hoped to write you sooner but could not because I was tired after the Christmas dinner. It was a great success, but as you know, the preparations take much time and energy. Although I had not thought I would overcome my sorrow at the loss of our dear ones since our arrival here in the spring, I felt that I was being a good Christian to do my part. Also, even though it was so close to the loss of dear Abner in September, I felt that he would have wanted me to help.

***Here's what had happened: Catharine had been born in Pennsylvania in 1812 and married Abner Goddard in 1833. Tragedy struck in 1842. All four of their children died of scarlet fever within two weeks. They were three boys and a girl, aged 7 to a baby. Catharine and Abner moved around the country; he taught school and she ran boarding houses. In 1852 they moved from LaCrosse, Wis., to Winona. By then they had three more children. Their home became a stopping place for people new to the area, so Catharine opened a boarding house. In August 1852, Abner was appointed Winona's first postmaster and a notary public.***

***More loss befell them. In early September, Abner and two children contracted a malarial-type fever. He died Sept. 11, and the children, Lucretia and William, soon after. (Charles was their only child who survived to adulthood; he served in the Civil War but died of an illness at age 24.) Just three months after the deaths of her husband and two children, Catharine was cooking the Christmas dinner about which she so enthusiastically wrote.***

***She continued to operate her boarding house after Abner's death. In August 1853, she married Alexander Boyd Smith, a former lumberman and river pilot. They had one child, Orrin Smith. Shortly after Alexander built a hotel called the Wabasha Prairie House in 1855, he left the building one evening and was never seen again. He often had carried large amounts of money, and it was assumed that he met with foul play. Catharine retired from the hotel business in 1860 but continued to run her private boarding house for years. She lived with Orrin, the only child of her eight who outlived her, and died in Winona on June 2, 1888.***

Minnesota Historical Society, Orrin Fruit Smith and Family Papers, and the Winona County Historical Society

~

## A lutefisk and flathead supper

***Maybelle Jacobson of Crookston was about 9 years old during the winter holidays of 1911.***

**Week before Xmas.** Sun. went over to Marie's for lutefisk and flathead supper after which we had a Xmas tree.

**New Year's.** Sunday eve. went to church basement to watch Old Year Out and New Year In. Very large crowd. Ladies Aid served refreshments. Ladies Quartet (Lillie & Geneva Stenshoel, Louise and Clara Hanson) sang. Emil Sabreson and Male Choir sang. Played Going to Jerusalem. I nearly sat on Salmer Haugen's lap. Both on same chair. Played ring on the string and then Wink Em. Went home about one o'clock. Salmer Haugen walked home with us.

***By 1916, Maybelle was more cynical:***

If a man steals a ride on the train, he is sent to a penitentiary. If he steals the whole train, he is sent to the Legislature. It's funny, funny, funny. But it's money, money, money.

Minnesota Historical Society, Maybelle Jacobson Quarberg Brekken papers

## More fun than picnics

***Abby Weed started keeping diaries as a little girl and continued after she married Benjamin Grey, an Army officer, and throughout her life. She was from a wealthy St. Paul family (her grandfather, A.B. Stickney, founded the Great Western Railroad), attended a private girls' school and did her socializing at the Minikahda Country Club. She was 14 when she wrote this in 1917.***

**New Year's Day.** Every single one in the family went over to the golf links where the toboggan slide use[d] to be and watched the carnival men. There were just lots of people wearing carnival suits of every description. They had a push-ball, some were behind horses on skis, others had skis and still others had toboggans and sleds. The movie man was cranking his machine for all his might and the police-men were ordering people around as if they were the whole cheese. It was a splendid sight to see all the clubs march around the king and his court. My feet were nearly frozen so I came home and I really think I froze my big toe.

**Thurs. Jan. 18th.** Today I started to come down with a cold so Mother put me to bed at five, gave my feet some hot mustard and my mouth some eurotrophine. I think it probably did some good.

**Sat. Jan. 20th.** Today has been eventful, too. Louise and Eddie Ritchie came out to spend the day. They went out sliding while I was inside studying. Not very long after they had gone Sunnie came running home and said that Eddie was hurt awfully and for Mother to come right over to the C.C. [country club]. We went over there and a little while afterwards Dr. Ritchie came. Eddie has been unconscious and had blood all over his face from a big cut. He was taken right down to the hospital where he had an exray taken but nothing was broken and I guess he'll be all right. This afternoon we had lots of fun making pop-corn and malasses candy on the stove.

**Tuesday, Jan. 23rd.** Maybe I'm a scardy cat; I don't know. Today there was a great big pagent at the C.C. A whole lot of the girls scipped school. Some were caught in the act and some went at recess through the furnace-room and up the cellar-door. Some who were goody goodies and some who were afraid of their parents staid at school. I was the latter but Dad said he wouldn't care and gave me permission to go to the next one. The first chance I have I'm going to take advantage of the offer.

**Monday, Feb. 12th.** Today is Lincoln's birthday and a holiday. I have had more fun than picnics. . . . This morning and this afternoon both I went skiing. In some places there is a crust but in others there isn't, and if you are not on skis you sink to your knees in snow but if you have skies you only sink a few inches or so. I skied in the fields at the side of our house. There were some foot-prints which zig-zagged all over and which I tried to follow and succeeded but could make nothing out of them.

**Saturday, Feb 24.** I couldn't find anything to do all morning except to study.

**Friday, March 16th.** There was the peachiest blizzard out today. The snow and wind were just something awful! Ma Backus [Carrie H. Backus, principal] let us out a half hour early. The street-cars weren't running so I went to Aunt Carrie's for lunch. We (Eliz. & I) started the "Marble Fawn" by Hawthorne, which we have to read. At about 4 o'clock, we came out on the street-car and Sibley is going to stay all night.

**Saturday, March 17th.** My, I've had fun today! The drifts were just grand. Sibley and I put our skirts inside our tights, put on our mackinaws [heavy wool jackets] and went out. We were soon joined by Daisy and together we dug a narrow path to the road. It was ***some*** work, and when we were thru we had to go in and change, the snow was so wet. . . . First we fried some sausages, ate them and bread-and-butter, drank some cocoa and started to fry pan-cakes. I say started because it must have taken at least half an hour to flip six pan-cakes. I ate two, carefully flipping them for myself, but Sibley and Paul ate, hum, about eight; then we stuffed down some cream puffs! It's been a glorious day!

**Sunday, March 18th.** Lovely weather out. Not too melty. This morning I read Hawthorne's "Marble Fawn" and think it's just awful. I don't see what they make little girls read it for.

Minnesota Historical Society, Abby Weed Grey and Family Papers

~

## Fish in trouble

It is feared that the fish in many of the lakes will perish before spring. It is stated that on most lakes the ice is over 30 inches thick, and covered with snow at various depths, completely shutting out the air, and the fish perish from suffocation. The same thing happened two years ago, large numbers of dead fish appearing when the ice went out. Numbers are now taken out of holes out through the ice, and spring may find the waters depopulated.

**— Daily Minneapolis Tribune, Feb. 3, 1883**

~

## Dreaming of Florida

***Lucy Lusk had enough of winter in the north woods. She wrote to her cousin, Abby Weed Grey.***

**Deer River, Jan. 30, 1945**

My dear Abby,

Have thot of you so often and wondered if you both were well. We certainly miss you both. Tell you frankly I don't like Minn. winters, especially in the woods or at the Lake. We can't get out and do little but sit, read, housework. We have been fairly comfortable but 28 degrees below in a cottage isn't all it should be. A dear little cottage, bright & clean, but very much alone. I am not saying this to people here but trust next year we can be in the South.

We see the Warners seldom. The roads are so slippery & we are afraid to venture out. For two weeks Will has been fighting a painful boil in his nose. He looked more like a clown, nose swollen twice its normal size. It finally burst & is draining nicely, but can't get out in the cold. . . .

The men have been working cutting & storing ice since before Xmas. . . . You should know what a joy your fur coat is to me. Don't think I could go to the Cities, D.R. [Deer River] or G.R. [Grand Rapids] unless I had it. I am perfectly warm & I bless you every time I put it on. Hope some day I can give as much pleasure to some one. Tell the Col. he misses nothing eating the fish out of the ice. Mr. Hanson brot us some & we could hardly eat them. The men got 45 crappies in 40 minutes. Murder I should say. Not out of Deer Lake, thank goodness.

With love,
Lucy

Minnesota Historical Society, Abby Weed Grey and Family Papers

~

## A good jail cell

***William Cummings at 16 had a tough winter in St. Paul.***

**Monday, Dec. 10, 1934.** Went to school today. Got caught [by] special dicks [detectives] for lifting [stealing] overcoats. Got expelled from school. I got put in jail (East Side Jail, Minneapolis) at 2:30 P.M. Didn't have a good supper. Called up Mother to tell her where I am.

**Tuesday, Dec. 11.** The cops took [me] in a police patrol car to the Hennepin County Jail at nine a.m. I stayed there until 5:30 p.m. Then two St. Paul police came to get me. They took [me] to the St. Paul Jail. Had a good cell.

**Wednesday, Dec. 12.** Sat around all day in my cell with Bruce Crosby, a 17 year old "gangster." We just talked & read. Hedsnicker & his assistant took me around to get all the overcoats I sold. The food is rotten here.

**Thursday, Dec. 15.** Hedsnicker & his assistant took [me] around to get some more coats. In the afternoon they took me to the court house. Hedstrom my probation officer took me home.

**Christmas.** Received presents from:
Grandma Gold — shirt, socks, hankie, diary & key case.
Grandpa Cummings — handkerchief.
Lola Jean — fish.
Ann — snail.
Art Oltman — socks.
Daddy — skys [skis?].
Mother — pen.
Jimmy Hadlow — tie.
Jeanette Cummings — tie clasp.
Jeanete Joachum — tie.
Aunt Peg — handkerchiefs.

Minnesota Historical Society, William M. Cummings Papers

~

## Thanks anyway, dad

***James Gray, a writer with the St. Paul Pioneer Press and the St. Paul Dispatch and the father of three children, told in a letter about the tribulations of getting Christmas toys ready.***

**Jan. 2, 1930.** The holidays, conducted with a proper Rooseveltian strenuousness, end as always with the feeling that there is something rather wrong with sentiment in general or with the native interpretation of it. I am feeling particularly thwarted because the doll house which I, with unaccustomed patience, devoted the evenings of several weeks just before Christmas to making for the children has already been removed to the attic in such a state of ruin as never befell a French farm house during the war. I had completed it in a high state of ecstasy, amazed that I had actually done it and feeling that at last I had found my creative level. The children immediately fell upon it with what seemed to me an especially revolting imitation of German Kultur and ripped apart the enchanting pieces of early American furniture that I had made out of the cardboard that comes in shirts from the laundry. I suffered in silence because after all I had theoretically been working for their pleasure and amusement. But yesterday the end came and in high dudgeon I carried it away to the attic where I shall probably retire from time to time to play with it quite peacefully and nicely by myself.

Minnesota Historical Society, James Gray and Family Papers

~

## First snowfalls

The following is a statement of the first snowfall in Minnesota for nine successive years, commencing in 1871: 1871, Oct. 14; 1872, Nov. 4; 1873, Oct. 22; 1874, Oct. 30; 1875, Oct. 10; 1876, Nov. 18; 1877, Nov. 16; 1878, Oct. 27; 1879, Nov. 1.

**— St. Paul Globe, Nov. 3, 1879**

~

## Frozen ink and ears

***J.W. Rodgers of Duluth wrote this letter on Dec. 25, 1872, to his father, the Rev. George Rodgers in England. It later was printed in a Duluth newspaper.***

You ask me about the weather; let me tell you what I have experienced so far. I arrived in Duluth on the 4th of November; a gentle rain was falling which continued with little interruption for three days. After that we had, until about the 15th, some truly delightful Indian Summer weather — sharp nights followed by mild sunshiny days. Somewhere about this time we had another slight shower, but since then not one drop has fallen. A snow storm (I ought to say snowfall, for it was very light) followed upon this fine spell, and since then the ground has worn a robe of white, most delightful to the eye, pleasant to the feet, and an immense help to all heavy-removing work [pulling felled trees from the forests]. Two horses go on a brisk run with a load which they can with difficulty move at a walking pace when the snow is absent. We have had about four falls of snow. It is now about eight inches deep.

Since writing the early part of this note, I have been out for about two miles' walk, and was surprised to find it so mild and pleasant. Yet the thermometor is 6 degrees below zero. I have walked leisurely to and from church without an overcoat, enjoying the bracing weather, while it has been two or three degrees below. Thanksgiving Day it stood at 18 degrees below, yet I attended a service at church at which half of the congregation were ladies, and they were not more muffled up than those are at Lancashire.

Yesterday the mercury got down to 24 degrees below, yet people were out on business and pleasure. The most enjoyable feature I have seen so far is the delightful moonlight nights. Just picture the effect. Duluth built on the side of a hill — a background of dark pines crowning the summit — a glassy lake of vast size at our feet — glimpses of the dark and richly-lined shores stretching away on either side — and a moon of wondrous beauty bathing everything in a most exquisite light! You can't understand it. No one can who does not stand near the summit, as I do every night, and look down on the town of snow-white houses.

Yet let every one who comes out here expect to feel immense cold. This morning when I attempted to write, the ink froze on my pen, and I had to desist. People sometimes get an ear or perhaps a finger or two frozen, but they soon come right again. Keep the extremities well protected, and all is pleasant.

**— The Duluth Minnesotian, March 1, 1873**

~

## Used-auto blues

**Feb'y. 6/16**

My Dear Elva,

The Overland people have a second hand 1915 model, original price $1075 which they took in at $600, have repainted it and want $631 for it. I went to see the Ford people yesterday . . . . We talked over the car business for an hour, he says he has a second Ford for $340 and will cost $85 to install the self starter & electric lights which would make $425 . . . . He says (and I rather agree with him) don't buy until you get home, that the Auto business will begin to be more lively in about 6 weeks, and that he will keep a look out for second hand cars, any make of car you may designate. . . .

Lovingly, Daddy

***Sorry, we don't know who Elva was or which car she bought.***

Minnesota Historical Society, Sue Dickey Hough Papers

~

## Top this list

***Margaret Turner Holyoke, apparently a teenager, kept a list of the books she read — 288 books from 1907 to 1912. Here's a sampling.***

**Books I Have Read**
Begun Nov. 1907

"David Copperfield" by Charles Dickens. Liked it quite well, especially when read aloud, but think I will like it better when I am older. Read once.

"Bleak House" by Charles Dickens. Liked this pretty well but don't care much about it. I don't like the story. Read once.

"Rob Roy" by Sir Walter Scott. Liked it very much.

"Standish of Standish" by Jane G. Austin. Liked it very much indeed. Read twice.

"Little Women" by Louisa M. Alcott. Of course I love this. I have read it so many times that I've lost count of them.

"Rose in Bloom" by Louisa M. Alcott. This is another satisfactory ending. Have read it twelve or fifteen times.

"The Bird's Xmas Carol" by Kate Douglas Wiggin. Liked it very much and laughed and cried over it.

"Rebecca of Sunnybrook Farm" by Kate Douglas Wiggin. This is a dear book. Rebecca is so quaint and funny. Read three times.

"Wide Wide World" by Susan Warner. Did not like it at *all.* Ellen was a goody-goody. I don't think *any* girl of fourteen would think so much about religion or be so good. Any *sensible* person would hate God if they thought He did what Ellen thought He did to her.

"Black Beauty" by Anna Sewell. Liked it very much. Read twice.

Minnesota Historical Society, William H. Holyoke Papers

~

## A quick wedding

***Abbie Griffin Dike, 34, was a Minneapolis seamstress.***

**Monday, Jan. 26, 1885.** I have determined to write a Journal once more to record many transactions. Last Tuesday night at 11:50 P.M. we had a very interesting ceremony here. For two weeks, mother had been very low and in that night we gave up all hope of her and feeling that her end was approaching she felt as if she would like to see me married. Clint went directly up to get cousin Ed and they went together to get a lisence came back hunted a minister and were ready. I had only a common dress and it was a dark grey trimmed with pipings of crimson. Just a full skirt & slashed basque [a closely fitted bodice]. The Rev. Archibald Hadden transformed me from Miss G. to Mrs. S.C. Dike. Mother has been very low and is so still. Last night was the first night for eighteen nights that I could sleep all night. Nettie Silliman wrote us a letter today and I received one from Poughkeepsie.

**Tuesday, Feb. 10.** Since I last wrote have passed through a very trying time. Jan. 29 I just gave out & had to go to bed & have the doctor. My hands & limbs swelled to an immense size & I had a good prospect of inflammatory rheumatism but with a good girl in the kitchen [&] good care I am at last up again. Dear Little Mum has gone through [died] & I am so lonely without her. She went to Father [God] last Thursday morning Feb. 5 at 3:45 A.M. and went triumphantly. I was able to see her but not able to sit up on Saturday at the funeral or to see her but once after she died.

***By spring Abbie was in better health. "How can I help getting well in such a lovely day? All nature seems to rejoice after the rain," she wrote on May 25.***

Minnesota Historical Society, Abbie T. Griffin Diary

~

## A woman's work

***Anna Skott of Stratford, S.D., and later Minneapolis kept a record of her housework each day, detailing such tasks as cleaning the refrigerator, hanging out clothes, starching curtains, mending small rugs and working at her husband's restaurant. Often the list was concluded with the words, "besides doing the usual work." Occasionally she gave details of her troubled marriage.***

**March 10, 1958.** i wash dishes, wait on customers, cook, mend, August still mad at me on account i don't like to see his false teeth and to make matters worse i didn't let him sleep on my Pillow, i will hunt him Another on account he has an itch mite eating a bald spot on the back of his head, i don't want to catch it, he says i have so many things the matter with me, i might just as well have a few more.

***August died in November 1959.***

Minnesota Historical Society, Anna Skott Diary

~

## Frozen stiff

***Irene Krumpelmann wrote about doing the family's laundry as a child in Duluth and Two Harbors. Her mother continued to do the wash this way as the family grew to seven children in Clear Lake, Wis., in the 1920s.***

After rubbing clothes on a washboard, we put them through a hand-wringer and two tubs of rinse water, one with blueing. All this water had been carried from the outside windmill. Pillow cases and socks must be turned inside-out to rinse, and white linens boiled with a bit of lye on top of the stove in a copper boiler, and hung outside summer or winter. Unwieldy frozen shapes were plucked in to wilt by the kitchen stove.

***By 1927 Irene was an elementary-school teacher in Clayton, Wis., and came to Minneapolis for her first permanent.***

The twisting and twining of the strands of hair on dozens of rods, soaking with solution, plugging each into the prongs of the heating unit, and hand-fanning the hot spots were ordeals lasting 4 or 5 hours by the time the hair was shampooed, set and dried. That I could easily cope with. I was perturbed with the mediocre results and the operator's indifferent, condescending manner. "Really, they have electricity in the country?" City dude!

Minnesota Historical Society, Irene Krumpelmann Papers

~

## Before baby aspirin

**Nov. 8, 1891.** [Pre-schooler] Ray's nose is stopped up with a cold. He said, "My nose won't go."

**Jan. 1, 1892.** The children enjoyed Christmas. Santa Claus brought them lots of presents. Ray was so proud of his hobby horse & fire engine and Hazel of her stove and wash-set.

**— Mrs. Frank Purcell, wife of a St. Paul photographer**

Minnesota Historical Society, Mrs. Frank W. Purcell Diary

~

John W.G. Dunn photo,
Minnesota Historical Society

***What a kid-like thing to do! Swinging on the gate looks delightful, as good as playing in the sandbox the first time in spring or picking the blooms off the neighbors' tulips. That's neighbor Dolly Geer on the left, Jack Dunn in the rompers on the right. They were at 1033 Lincoln Av. in St. Paul, Jack's house, in 1906. His father shot the picture.***

# Spring

Spring in Minnesota is a tease, a quick tease. After cold months colored in white and gray, the first little purple crocus or patch of green grass is well documented by almost everyone with a journal or camera. Generations of Minnesotans have posed their children with symbols of spring's rebirth — tulips, bunnies, marshmallow chicks, Easter dinners, Passover Seders, bicycles, baseball uniforms and dance-recital costumes.

The burst of spring must be recorded immediately, because it's likely to be followed the next day by either a snowstorm or a heat wave. There's no luxuriating in spring here. Hurry! Pack a supper and some baseball gloves and rush to the park. Play hooky from work for a few hours. Cram in some pleasures. Let spring tickle the senses. Once we're middle-aged, we know that spring, like life, is fleeting.

Bennie Bengtson loved spring in Minnesota — the sounds of running water, the frog choruses, the feel of the wet earth, the sighting of the first trilliums and showy ladyslippers.

He was born in 1907, spent his life on his farm in Kittson County in the northwest corner of Minnesota and wrote extensively about nature. Reading his essays about spring, written in the 1940s and now preserved at the Minnesota Historical Society, we can imagine him crouching down to get a handful of wet black earth and cocking his head to hear the songs of returning birds. More than that, we can picture Minnesota farmers and nature-lovers before him — and after him — doing the same things. Bengtson wrote:

"March is the month when spring first puts in an appearance. And how welcome it is, after the long, cold, icy monotony of winter! The first day with the real feel of spring in it usually comes late in the month. It may be the day when I hear the first meadowlark. A mild morning with a light southeasterly breeze — I listen intently as I step out of the house and there it comes. Clean cut and penetrating as an arrow, there is no more inspiring sound in all of nature. . . .

"That first spring day! It may not look like spring, for much of the landscape is covered with snow, but it feels like spring, and it smells like spring. The breeze is mild, the sun's rays are warm and in the air there is that indescribable aroma of spring."

To Bengtson, March was not a beautiful month. It had nothing to compare with the fresh green of June, or the autumnal hues of September or October.

"Even December with its hoar-frost-covered trees and brilliantly starlit nights has more to offer in beauty. In March the snow has a worn, dirty, bedraggled look, and the entire countryside appears bleak, windswept and cheerless. But in spite of this rather dismal aspect there is that in March which gladdens the heart. The snow melts and the streams begin to flow; we hear again the sound of running water. The little rills whisper and tinkle on their way to the creeks, and the larger streams purl and laugh."

But so often, March in Minnesota is still the dead of winter. Even better than March, Bengtson wrote, is April, the time of new beginnings, especially to a farmer. "It's the beginning of another crop year, which he always hopes will be better than the last one. April 1st would be a better New Year's Day for a farmer than January 1st."

With Minnesota winters as hard as they are, Minnesota springs have forever been blissful. Spring brings eternal hope, prospects for bumper crops, kites, marbles, doll buggies, young love and old love too. The cynical would also say spring means gray snow (with yellow highlights provided by the animal population), an inch of muck over everything outside the house and a layer or two of grit over everything inside. It means rivers and streams flooding, snow on the tulips and mud on the snowpants.

But who cares? The worst is over. Summer is almost here.

Spring also has meant housecleaning. The March winds, dust and dirt that make us — well, some of us — want to clean house brought out the same feelings in our Minnesota forebears.

"Cherish the broom and duster as your chief friends," urged one chirpy book about housekeeping. Called "The Home: How to Make and Keep It" by Mrs. Henry Ward Beecher, it was published in Minneapolis in 1883.

Spring house-cleaning, Mrs. Beecher recognized, was a pain. To prove it, she quoted a letter from a young wife, one who obviously had money:

"Last year I thought house-cleaning would be 'real fun'; I had never before taken the entire charge of such extensive operations, and thought, in my simplicity, that I would show the old ladies how a smart young housekeeper would walk through the fiery furnace with not even the smell of fire upon her garments. But I little dreamed what I had undertaken. I found out, however. . . . Now, in this my second year of housekeeping, I look forward to the 'spring cleaning' with the greatest repugnance, gladly enduring all the cold, the winds and storms of early spring, because they postponed the evil day. But now milder weather and warmer suns are upon us, and this great nuisance may be no longer deferred. How I dread it! No regularity; all rules abolished; servants rebellious; husband — to put the finest point upon it —uncomfortable; baby cross, and I — the crossest of all! Oh, dear! What shall I do?"

To which Mrs. Beecher responded soothingly:

"Take it easy. *Patience*, my child. . . . Give each hour its own work; do not permit yourself to groan over that which belongs to the next, and you will find the heaviest and most disagreeable labors, if arranged and performed systematically, glide smoothly through your hands."

In other words, lady, cool it and get organized.

Start in the cellar, Mrs. Beecher advised the frazzled woman. Have your coal bin filled first; coal usually is cheaper in spring than fall. Then have your men remove ashes and clean the furnace. Sweep the cellar floor if it's dirt; if it is stone or cement, scrub it clean. (A good housekeeper would have had that done each week all winter, Mrs. Beecher wrote, a bit snidely, but . . . .) Then tackle the attic; whitewash the walls, polish the windows, don't allow the attic to become the "catch-all for all kinds of useless trash."

Next, if you can afford it, hire four good housecleaners. Keep up a "quiet but vigilant superintendence." Be sure they get clean the corners of rugs where moths love to congregate. Have the servants untack and remove most carpeting, but not the good Brussels rugs, which are so firmly textured that dust cannot easily penetrate them and therefore need to be removed only every three years.

And then get the work-crew busy: Shine those windows with warm, sudsy water, fortified with spirits of ammonia. Starch that lace. Shake the family's winter garments and use a stiff whisk-broom on them. Pack away the clothes in spare trunks with pepper, camphor, cedar chips, sandalwood and/or moth powder. Dust the walls with a long-handled feather duster, then with a clean, dry cloth pinned smoothly over a clean broom. Wash the chimneys and shades from the gas-lamps. Make the marble shine. Look for clues that mice or rats have invaded. Meticulously clean the chairs and sofas, down to using a furniture-button brush. And give the beds a special cleaning, although, tsk-tsk, they should have been stripped to the bedsteads once a week all winter to remove dust and lint.

Zowie! All in the days before vacuum cleaners, not to mention indoor plumbing. But that's another matter.

Of course, not everyone had a team of servants to do the spring housecleaning. Most housewives did have some help, though — their husbands. M.C. Russell, a Minnesota humorist who also edited a Wabasha newspaper, wrote in his 1882 book called "Odd Hours":

"When the lady of the house intimates that a thirty-yard carpet must be taken up, pounded, and then put down again, all in the same day, the man of the house has been struck with one of the greatest calamities of his life."

Somehow, Russell wrote, the man yanks the carpet out into the yard, manages to get it on the washline, beats the heck out of it for an hour or two and fills the neighborhood with a cloud of dust and gravel. The task gets worse when he tries to tack the carpet back into the room. It won't stretch back to its pre-cleaning rectangular shape. He lies in 50 different agonizing positions so as not to be lying on the very width he is trying to tighten. Inevitably he reclines squarely in the plate of tacks. The only solution is to call in a strong, cheap boy. Russell concluded, "No man who is not a natural born lunatic ever puts down more than one carpet. Very few live through a second job of that

*Before the trees leafed out in spring, two women and a dog went for an outing, probably in Fillmore County. The date was about 1900.*

Minnesota Historical Society

kind anyway."

Maybe Russell cheered up with a nice bike ride. Already in the 1880s, April and May meant pulling bicycles out of storage. In the September 1885 issue of "The Minnesota Wheelman," George S. Hull urged his fellow physicians to go about their rounds on bikes:

"Bicycling, until lately, has been looked upon by many as a sport for the youth, or as a 'craze,' soon to pass out of fashion; but slowly and surely it has been dawning upon the public mind that this great invention is really a vehicle that is destined to supplant, in many instances, the horse and buggy. . . . To say that it is hard to learn to ride the bicycle is an exaggeration, and arises mainly from the fact that the pride of some who are graceful riders makes them magnify their own accomplishments by alarming, unnecessarily, those who are anxious to learn. A few lessons and a little determination, and, before one is aware of it, the art is acquired. Certainly it is easier to learn than skating, and I might say, from my own experience, not as difficult as horseback-riding."

For its body-strengthening possibilities, Hull recommended bicycling "in nearly all cases where horseback-riding is indicated, the exceptions being ladies and very old or crippled men."

Excuse his antiquated thinking. Biking actually played a big part in the liberation of women. Besides providing exercise and outings, it led to a change in fashion. Women had to get rid of the girdles that interfered with deep breathing, and, for safety's sake, the long, cumbersome skirts that tended to tangle in the bicycle chain. So for sportswomen by the early 20th century — exit corsets, enter culottes.

Women's spring clothes in the 19th century were crummy off the bicycle too. Imagine trudging along muddy streets while wearing an ankle-length dress, particularly one with a train. In the 1870s, trains were used for even daytime wear. A woman writer in 1872 described the predicament:

"The woman cannot be self-respecting who can trail a long skirt across a muddy street, entailing not only the ruin of the dress, but the certain bedaubing of stockings and underclothes."

Yet another opportunity for spring cleaning.

***Discovering the joy of carpentry were Phyliss Gerdes, Sandra Smith and Nancy Oman. They were building birdhouses at Loring Park in Minneapolis in 1946.***

Minneapolis Star or Tribune photo, Hennepin History Museum

Minnesota Historical Society

*Catching with bare hands and taking a vicious swipe at the ball, members of the University of Minnesota women's softball team practiced in about 1925. The 1920s offered unprecedented opportunities to women, on several fronts. They could vote. They could dance the Charleston. They could wear their hair and skirts short. And they could appear in bloomers in public. As early as the 1880s and 1890s, women wore bloomers for gymnastics and basketball, but they didn't dare go outside in them.*

Minnesota Historical Society

*A family — probably Harry Robertson of St. Paul and some of his relatives — took a leisurely boat ride at the Dalles of St. Croix, on the Minnesota-Wisconsin border, in about 1900. By our standards, they were amazingly dressed up for a casual outing. The man was buttoned up to the neck; the women wore hats. Imagine the ironing that went into getting this group presentable for a boat ride.*

Minnesota Historical Society

Minnesota Historical Society

◀ *These cool little guys showed off their scooter, trike and aviator costume in about the 1930s. There was enough mud on their shoes and rubber boots for us to guess they had a great day. It must have been chilly enough for the aviator's mom to send him out with mittens. But what's the container he carried? Was he collecting for charity? Doubtful.*

▲ *The interior of the Fred Roach Bicycle Shop at 519 Hennepin Av., Minneapolis, looked like this in about 1904. The featured bike in the window was a Merkel. We don't think the man at the door was Mr. Roach. He looks more like a streetcar conductor. The bicycle had its greatest impact from 1870 to about the time of this photo. It provided an alternative to horse-drawn transportation before the advent of affordable automobiles. People were absolutely gaga about bikes.*

Revoir Historical Collection, Red Wing

***The Red Wing Bicycle Club pedaled its way the 20 miles to Lake City in 1891 and posed for this photo at the Lyon Hotel, Lake City. These names were provided on the back of the photo: George F. Enz, Ed Mellanger, John Kulstad, Charles Steaffens, Ed Misgen, Ed Enz, Russel A. Pratt and two unidentified cyclists from Lake City. We don't know if the identifications are left to right. Do you?***

Winona County Historical Society

▲ ***When women wore long dresses and wanted to bicycle, manufacturers responded with the V-shaped frames to make the bikes easier to mount. These bikes had netting or wire over the rear wheels, probably to keep out clothing. But wouldn't you suppose the skirts got caught in the chains? Cycling was considered a proper sport for women. As cycling clubs became popular among all classes, men and women rode together and social barriers between the sexes were eroded.***

▶ ***Imagine the excitement at St. Luke's Church Fun Fest when this dandy Schwinn was unveiled as a prize in 1956. A girls' model was given away too. The woman was Jeanne McLaughlin of 95 S. Lexington, St. Paul, chairman of the annual event. The city directory listed her husband, John T., as district director of the Internal Revenue Service. With her was their daughter, Kathy, 12, and Kevin Ryan, 1001 Ashland. The parish originally was Irish Catholic.***

St. Paul Pioneer Press photo, Minnesota Historical Society

Theodore A. Sather photo, Minnesota Historical Society

◀ *The bike was called a "high-wheel safety," a variation of something called the "Boneshaker." It looked it. The tall handlebars were unusual, but bicycle manufacturers and owners in those days (about 1885) experimented and modified greatly. The man is identified as "one of the famous Bell Brothers bicyclists." Or so said the woman who donated the photo to the historical society — a sister of the famous Bell Brothers. He does have impressive medals. For what, we don't know.*

▶ *Wasn't she doll-like? Helmets were not advocated for bicyclists then, and she wore a sweet little motoring cap. The picture was taken in a photo studio. Note the outdoorsy backdrop and strip of fake grass under the wheels.*

Winona County Historical Society

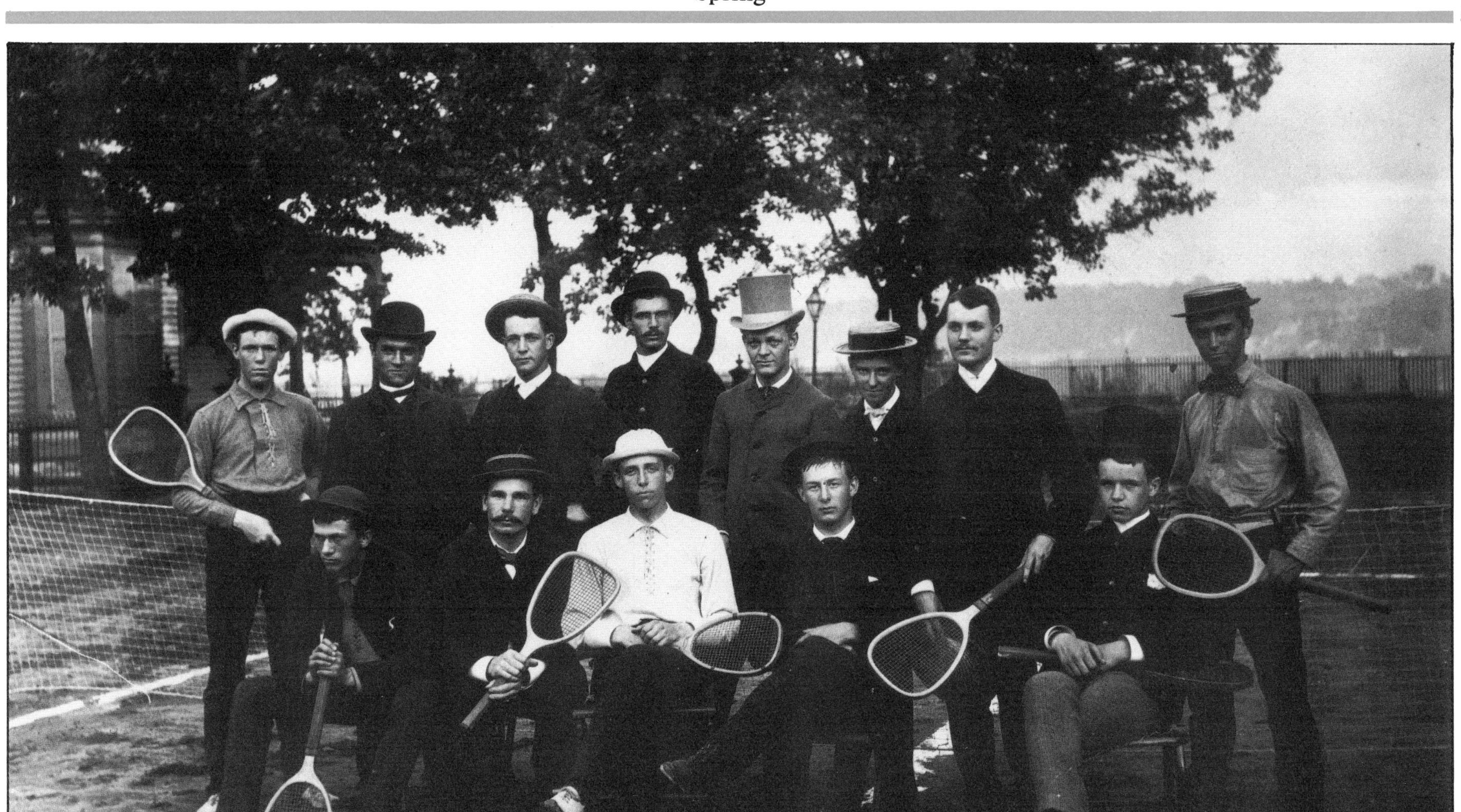

T.W. Ingersoll photo, Minnesota Historical Society

***What was claimed to be the first tennis court in St. Paul was on Walnut St. It likely was built by Henry Horn Jr., a powerful lawyer who lived in the neighborhood known as Irvine Park. His son, Harry, was to the right in this photo, taken in about 1885. These people had money, and this photographer loved to record the lives of the upper class. "Lawn tennis" got its start in 1873 in England. It was a combination of several games, including badminton, and was designed to fill a need for a rigorous outdoor sport that both women and men could play. In the early years, it was not considered necessary to have a grass surface. The only requirement was that the ground be level. Looks like they still had a bit of work to do on this St. Paul court.***

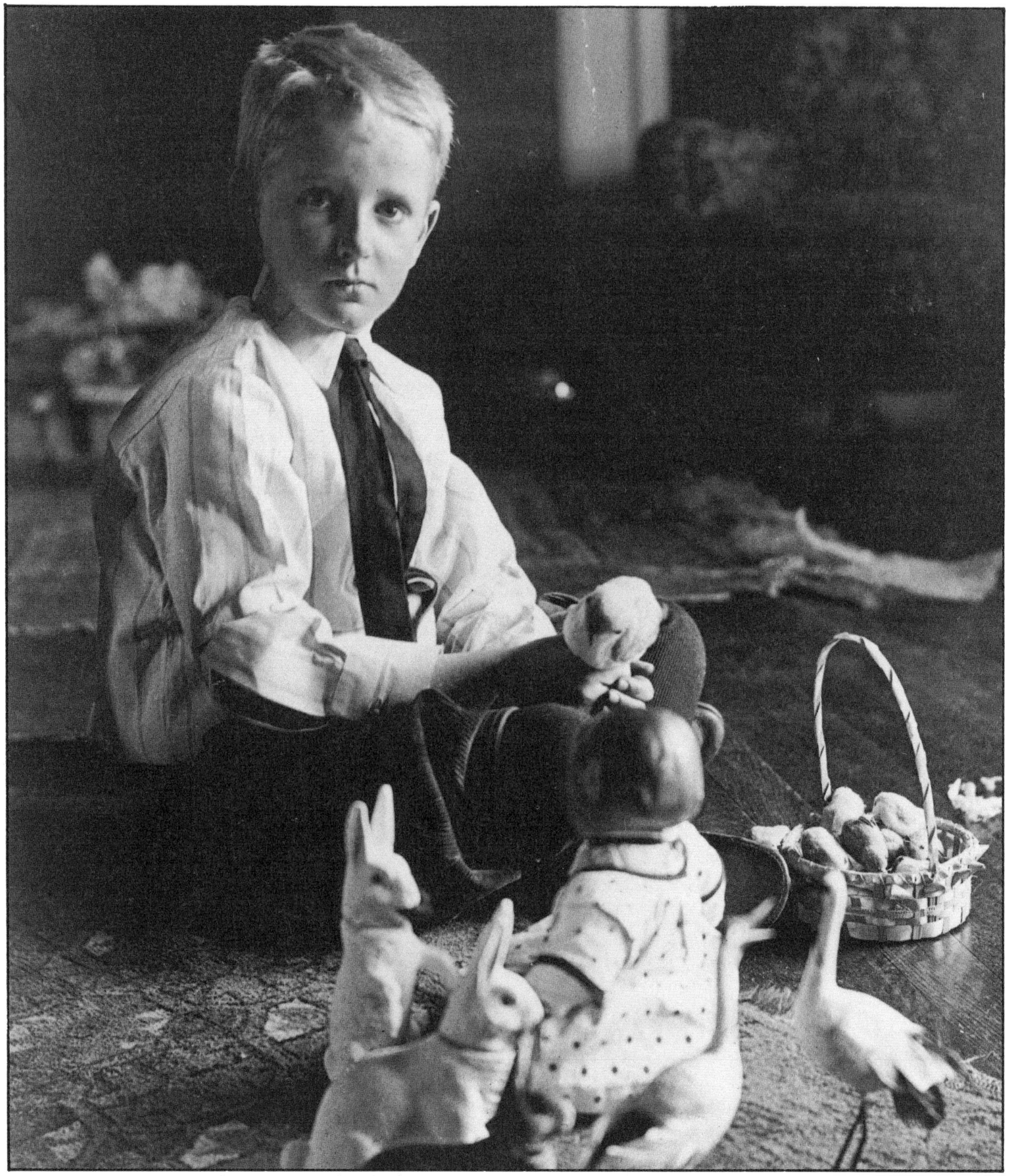

*◀ On Easter 1912, Jack Dunn examined the treasures in his Easter basket. Toy animals won out over candy, although the rabbits in the foreground were candy containers. Jack's shirt and tie look like today's, but the corduroy knickers don't. He was photographed in the living room of his family's house in St. Paul.*

*▶ Children at Tilden School, St. Paul, displayed the Easter eggs, bunny and Easter lily they were given in 1938. The school was at 1521 Albany. The kids were, left to right, David Thornes, Charlotte Miller and Caroll Lee Johnson, with the shiny patent-leather shoes. With a magnifying glass on the original photo, it's possible to see the names written on the eggs — Ralph, Doris and Gordon — proving once again that names go in and out of fashion. And further proving that these kids had other people's eggs. Why, we don't know.*

John W.G. Dunn photo, Minnesota Historical Society

Minnesota Historical Society

Brown County Historical Society

▲ ***A person can be either sad or elated that women today don't wear hats like these. The unidentified women in the oval frame celebrated spring with these elaborate creations, probably in the 1890s. Hat-making was among the few jobs open to women of the time; others were dress-making, teaching, nursing and running boarding houses. Customers could buy hats from milliners or get supplies from them to do the decorating themselves. Newspapers ran ads from milliners saying, "We sell trims."***

Minnesota Historical Society

◀ *An Ojibway woman modeled her fashionable hat at an Indian village near Grand Marais in about 1910. Notice the rose sticking out from the hat, the jewelry, the belt and the charmingly arranged handkerchief. Does anyone know the name of this striking woman?*

▶ *A milkmaid with a three-legged stool and milk pail posed in about 1900. It's an odd picture. Her fancy hat, her pressed outfit and her spanking-new milk bucket suggest this was no ordinary day in the cow barn. Perhaps, like most of us, she primped a bit in preparation for a picture. Or maybe she wanted to appear like the stereotyped view of a country woman. Or perhaps she dressed as she believed a previous generation did. Anyway, it's a hokey shot. Another mystery.*

Minnesota Historical Society

O.E. Flaten photo, Flaten/Wange Photo Collection, Clay County Historical Society

***When Minnesota's snows melt, Minnesota's floods sometimes follow, especially in rainy springs. A.W. Bowman and his unidentified cousin saw the sights in soggy Moorhead during an April 1897 flood. The land is so flat along the north-flowing Red River that flood water drains away slowly, and has since the last ice age.***

Minnesota Historical Society

***This scene was near Minneapolis' Lake Harriet, but the intersection wasn't a lake itself until a spring flood in 1905. "Weber's Lake" is what Harriet-area residents dubbed the junction of Upton Av. S. and 43rd St. You can see Henry W. Weber's grocery store in the background. The boys in the boat appeared to be having a good time, and we'd guess the kids on the curb were envious.***

H.D. Ayer photo, Minnesota Historical Society

◀ *Farmers always have had to be ingenious. This photographer worked for the University of Minnesota on the agriculture campus, so this may have been a U of M experiment. It was a transplanting machine in about 1910. The two men on the lower seat placed cabbage plants in a furrow made by the back of a shoe. A stream of water from the barrel moistened the earth. Did it work? Cabbage farmers, let us know.*

▶ *Otto Hartneck, born in New Ulm in 1863, used an ox team to plow his Brown County land, perhaps near the end of the 19th century. Farming was the region's major occupation then. It doesn't look like easy work, does it?*

Brown County Historical Society

***The photographer captured his family feeding the chickens in about 1905. That was his son, Teddy. In the middle was Marie Madison King, the photographer's second wife and Teddy's new stepmother. Teddy's mother had died. The other woman was Marie's sister-in-law, Clara Madison. The Kings, from Fulda, were visiting the Madisons in Worthington. This same little boy is shown on the next page.***

Dr. Emil King photo, Minnesota Historical Society

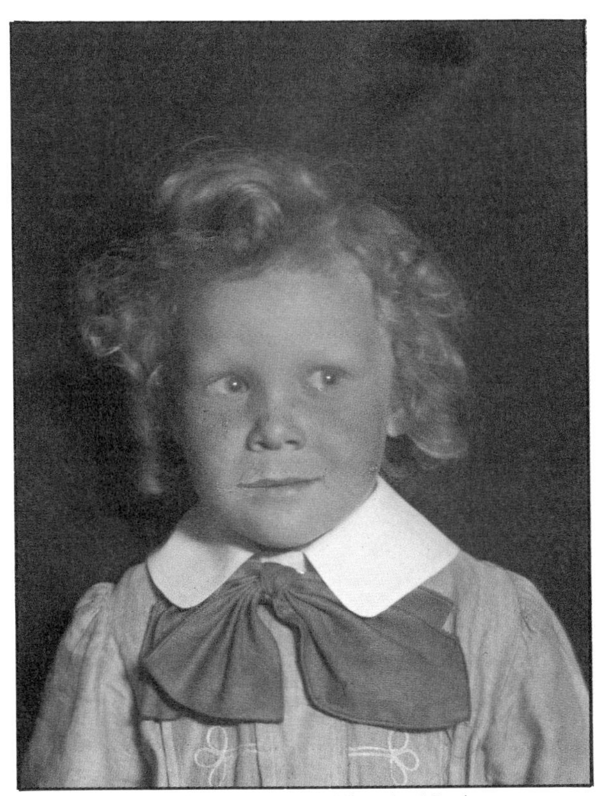

Dr. Emil King photos, Minnesota Historical Society

***Before and after his first haircut on April 14, 1906: Theodore Roosevelt (Teddy) King of Fulda, 4 years old. Eighty-six years later, he still kept a few of the blond curls snipped off that day. He remembers panicking at the barber shop. He and his father had just come from the butcher shop, and Teddy assumed the barber would use a big old meat cleaver on his little head. But the barber did a nice job, and Teddy emerged with a young man's haircut, properly parted on a side.***

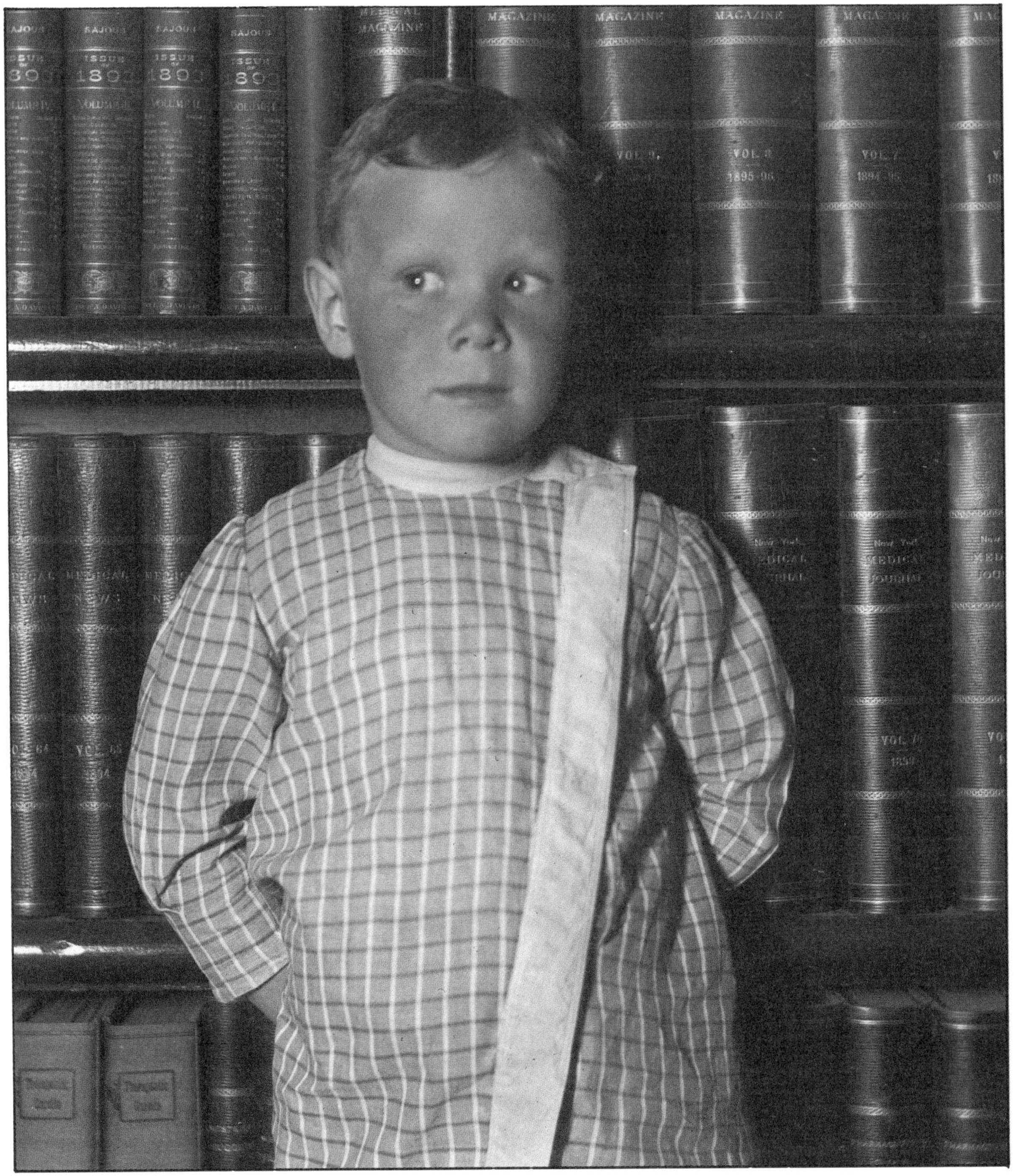

*In a Jewish neighborhood in north Minneapolis, children had their photo taken in front of a kosher grocery store in about 1908. The location was 6th Av. N. and Lyndale Av. The children may have been part of the large Jewish immigration here from Eastern Europe after the turn of the century. A popular vocation for ethnic families was running grocery stores in their neighborhoods. Little capital was needed, and if the groceries didn't sell the storekeepers could take them home for their families to eat.*

Minnesota Historical Society

St. Paul Dispatch-Pioneer Press photo, Minnesota Historical Society

***With symbols of the Jewish holiday of Passover on the table, children at Talmud Torah, a Hebrew school at 636 S. Mississippi Blvd. in St. Paul, held a seder on April 8, 1960. The 3-year-olds were Scott Zuckman of 2295 Apache, Mendota Heights; Lisa Savitt of 416 S. Fairview Av., St. Paul, and Susan Hoffman, 999 St. Paul Av. They held up matzo, the unleavened bread eaten during Passover, and on their plates were eggs and parsley.***

C.B. Johnson photo, Revoir Historical Collection, Red Wing

***Perched on top of Barn Bluff in Red Wing about 1900 were John Gross, left, and Eddie Rogers. They were all dressed up for a Sunday afternoon walk. Generations of Red Wing people have looked over the Mississippi Valley from the crest of the bluff, and high-school seniors galore have painted their graduation year up there.***

*Her plaid dress and curled hair look remarkably like those that little girls wore in the 1950s, but the high-topped shoes and the doll verify that the photo was taken about 1890. The child, apparently from a prosperous household, offered bread crumbs to a bird on the other side of the window.*

Minnesota Historical Society

*It was Arbor Day in May of 1956 when these children from St. Paul's Jefferson School planted their tree. They were Sofia Turzemanowycz, 10, who read the poem "Trees"; Brenda Jenkins, 11, who buried a bottle with the names of the 5th graders; Leroy Stockwell, 10, who held the tree, and Dale Wegleitner, 5, a kindergartner who put in the first shovelful of dirt. We hope the tree is big and thriving.*

Minnesota Historical Society

T.W. Ingersoll photo, Minnesota Historical Society

***On Memorial Day in about 1895, two children sat beside a grave decorated with flags and flowers. Was this the grave of a loved one? Hard to tell. The children didn't seem distraught or grieving. But this St. Paul photographer was well-known and expensive, and we would guess he was hired by someone with big money to shoot this picture at the gravestone of someone significant to their family.***

Henry Briol Studio of Albany photo, Minnesota Historical Society

***Albany's veterans gathered in uniform on Memorial Day 1924 to remember their fallen heroes. The name of the American Legion post was written with flowers. Services were held at the Catholic church and at the Catholic and Lutheran cemeteries. The Albany Enterprise reminded its readers, "All business places will remain closed during the forenoon exercises, and merchants as well as residents are kindly requested to decorate their homes and business houses for the parade." This photographer did a good job of recording life in small towns near St. Cloud. The grain elevator and train depot stand out as two of the most important structures in Minnesota towns, along with the churches, of course.***

*From the 1890s to about 1905, living flags were documented by many a photographer. It seemed that almost every school kid participated in the exercise to portray a huge flag. Here, each child was instructed to dress in light or dark shirts to make the stripes. Handwriting on the back of the photo says that the teacher was Miss Garva A. Millard and the date was May 30, 1900. We would bet that was Miss Millard in the white dress in the midst of the "stars."*

Charles Steaffens of Red Wing photo, Minnesota Historical Society

Guy M. Baltuff photo, Minnesota Historical Society

▲ ***This little guy, who seems to have inherited his father's personality, was named Montague. His parents' last name possibly was Baltuff, the same as the photographer's. Sorry, we know no more. The photo was shot in about 1900.***

▶ ***Looking as if they just got back from church, Carl and Alice Kisor put on their most adult faces in front of a backdrop decorated with pansies, an old-fashioned flower if ever there was one. The pose is reminiscent of wedding photos, but it was standard fare for many male-female pictures. We would guess Alice and Carl were siblings, but who knows where or when?***

Minnesota Historical Society

*Billy LaPlante, looking 2 or 3 years old, rode in a toy airplane in 1921. We don't know where he lived. His little biplane, a scooter with major modifications, seems homemade. Airplanes were a big deal by then. And six years later, Charles Lindbergh, who spent his boyhood summers in Little Falls, flew the famous solo, nonstop flight across the Atlantic in under 34 hours. Billy LaPlante would have been old enough to get a big kick out of that.*

Minnesota Historical Society

*Teatime, child version. These wee ones in their fancy clothes may have taken their china tea set to the studio for a portrait in about 1900. Perhaps their folks provided even the exquisite child-size rocking chair and a hassock for the doll. The boy is in a Little Lord Fauntleroy outfit, and he doesn't seem to mind a bit.*

Minnesota Historical Society

*Teatime, adult version. The Junior League in 1928 had the finest in china, silver and cookies for its party. Check out the strands of beads and cloche hats; they're the close-fitting, bell-shaped hats so popular at the time.*

Norton and Peel photo, Minnesota Historical Society

Minnesota Historical Society

▲ *A May Day party, complete with a Maypole, drew scads of girls to the Minneapolis home of Frederick and Dorothy Atkinson in 1921. The Atkinson house was at 104 Groveland Av. Frederick was the owner of the Atkinson Milling Co., and Dorothy was a devoted mother who delighted in her three children. The girls in this picture were probably friends of the Atkinsons' eldest child, Mary, who was about 9.*

▶ *A girl was given a spiral permanent wave, probably in the 1920s, when the procedure was tricky, stinky and sometimes downright dangerous. Many a head was scorched by the combination of heat and chemicals. This particular contraption looks more like a milking machine than a beauty maker, but hey, maybe it made great waves.*

Minnesota Historical Society

*A young man in about 1875 tried to look sophisticated with a bottle, cigarette and straw hat. This was a typical pose for a youngster wanting to be wild and crazy. The boy, about 12 years old, was Joseph Henry Sherburne, the son of Moses Sherburne, the U.S. District Judge for whom Sherburne County was named. The elder Sherburne had died in 1868, before his son became so bold.*

Minnesota Historical Society

Minnesota Historical Society

Minnesota Historical Society

▲ *"Woman's club, and pitcher of fruit juice," the caption read, probably written to make clear that alcoholic beverages were not involved. This was shot in Winona about 1900. The women look less than joyous, but smiling was considered inappropriate for most photographs of formal occasions before about 1910.*

◀ *Members of an unidentified ethnic group gathered for dinner in about 1900. The men on the left share a resemblance, and so do those on the right, but not across the table. Maybe the hostess's family was on one side, and the host's on the other. Was that homemade beer on the table? What were they eating? Were they perhaps Eastern European or Middle Eastern? The negative was damaged. This may be a good place for a reminder to store your photos and negatives on the first floor of your house. Changes in heat and humidity in the basement and attic speed deterioration.*

▶ *The Anton Johnson family had only raw potatoes to eat when relief workers and a newspaper photographer appeared at their door in March 1929. The family lived on a farm near Hollandale. Mrs. Johnson said they had had beef soup earlier in the day but had only potatoes left. The farm crisis began years before the stock-market crash in October 1929. To make things worse, there had been a crop failure in the Hollandale area in the autumn of 1928.*

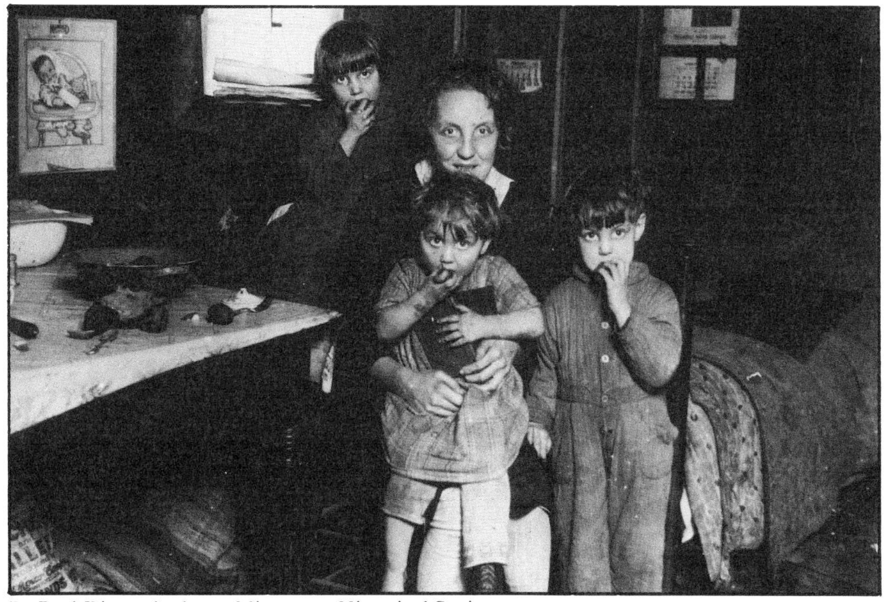

St. Paul Dispatch photo, Minnesota Historical Society

◀ *Professor Myron Reynolds took this photo of his children, Gardner and Janet, welcoming him home in about 1900. He taught veterinary medicine for the University of Minnesota's college of agriculture. The family lived in the St. Anthony Park neighborhood of St. Paul.*

▶ *This happy-go-lucky child was photographed in 1931. We don't know his name but we do know the identity of the person who made the appointment at the Minneapolis photo studio. She was Ethel Nelson. Does that ring a bell for anyone?*

M.H. Reynolds photo, Minnesota Historical Society

Norton and Peel photo, Minnesota Historical Society

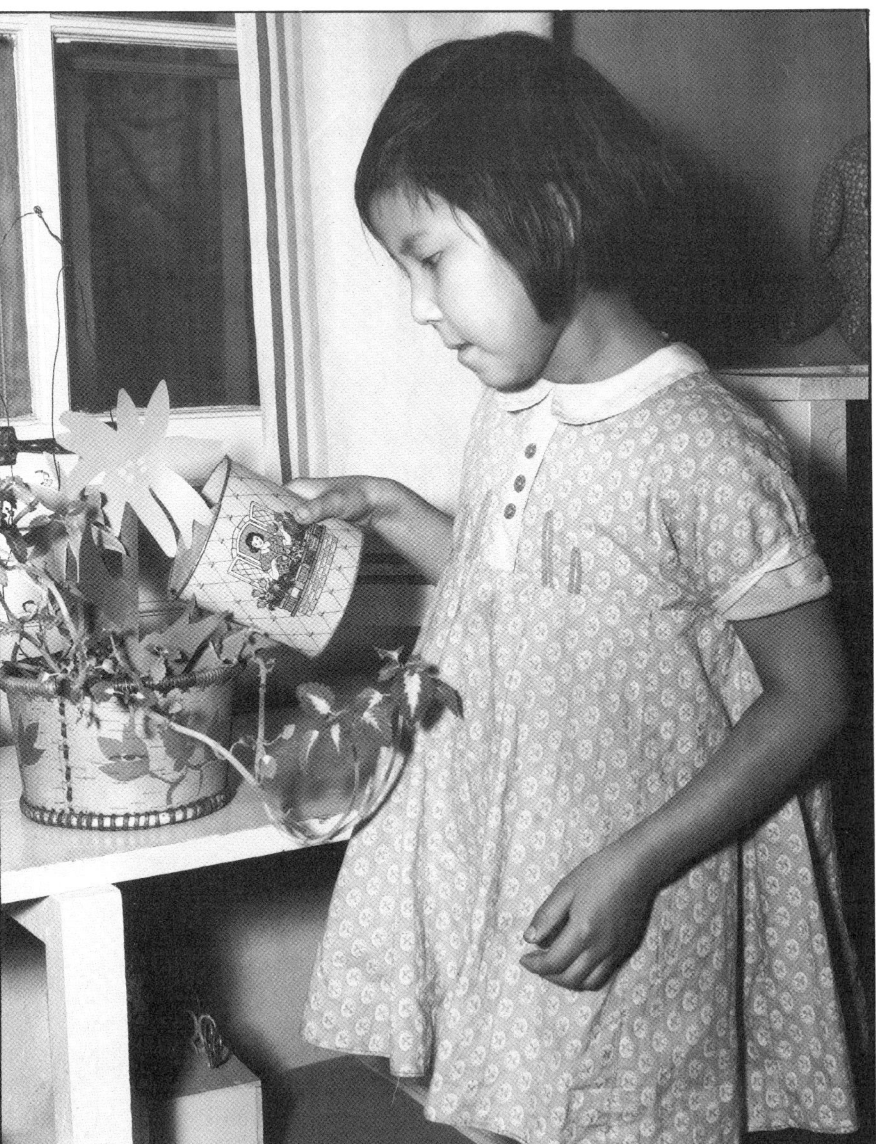

Minnesota Historical Society

***In 1938 a girl watered plants at a nursery school for Indian children at Nett Lake. The school was run during Depression times by the federal government's Works Progress Administration. The child seemed healthy and sturdy, but the coleus looked so frail and leggy that someone added construction-paper flowers.***

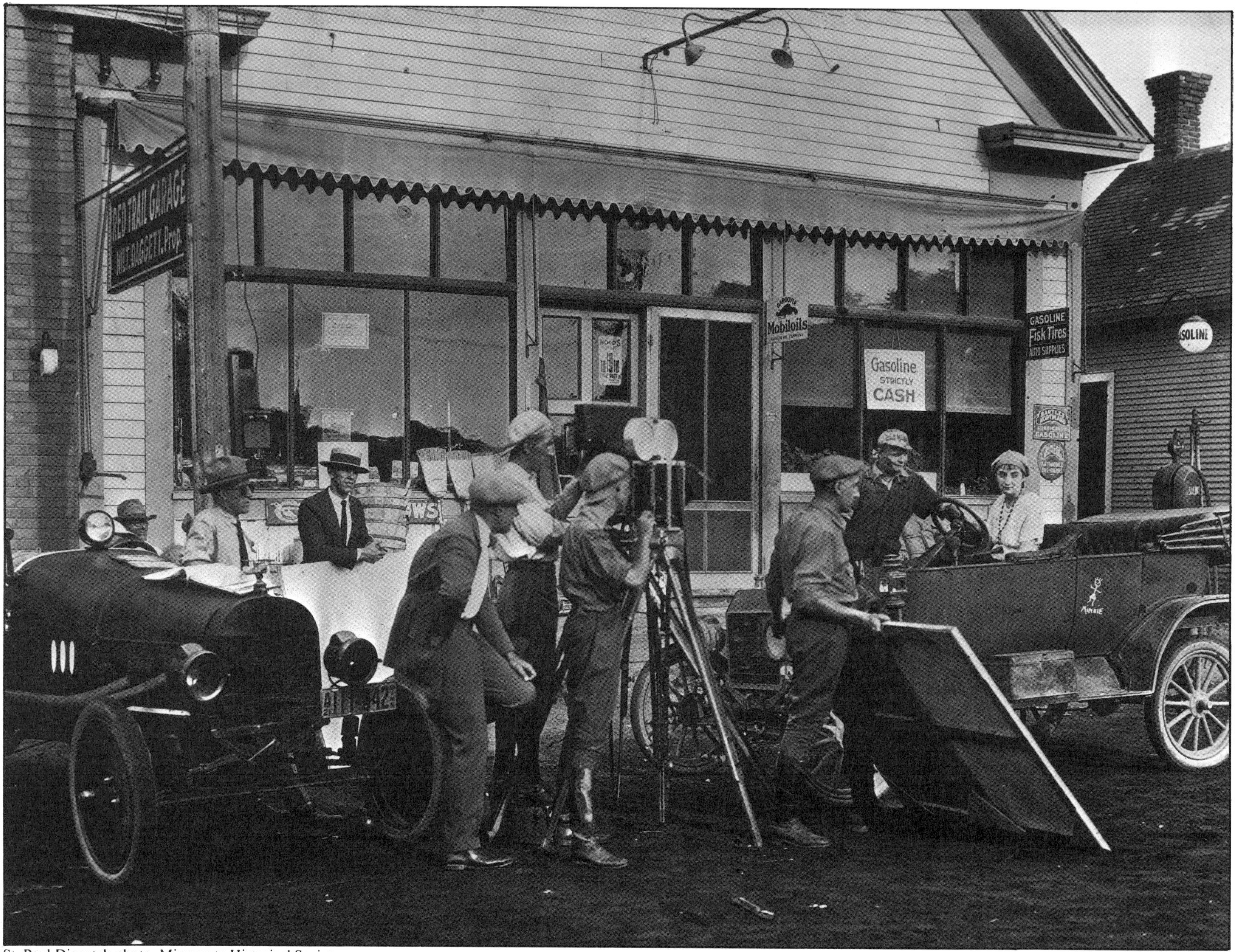

St. Paul Dispatch photo, Minnesota Historical Society

◀ *"Free Air," the first movie based on a book by Sinclair Lewis, was filmed in Rosemount in 1921. Billed as a comedy/drama, it was the story of a New York banker whose flapper daughter fell in love with a small-town Minnesota garage owner. The jodhpur-clad crew also shot scenes on the St. Paul high bridge, in Taylors Falls, Red Wing and Glacier National Park. Don't expect to find the film at your video store.*

Minnesota Historical Society

*The town band in White Earth, on the White Earth Indian Reservation, gathered for a photo in about 1908. Reclining in front was Robert G. Beaulieu, who took many photos of the White Earth Reservation in the early 1900s.*

Stearns County Historical Society

Chester S. Wilson photo, Minnesota Historical Society

*Who says you can't stop time? Philip Wilson stood on the dining-room table to interfere with the pendulum of a shelf clock in about 1900. Looking on was Martha Gast, the "hired girl." The wallpaper was a good example of the florals from the turn of the century. Philip and Martha also posed for a portrait in the photo at right.*

◀ *Spring means cleaning, and to women of German heritage, it means a thorough cleaning. The women of St. Martin Catholic Church in St. Martin gathered with pails, brooms and cleaning rags in about 1900. They wore cotton dresses ("wash dresses") and aprons.*

Chester S. Wilson photo, Minnesota Historical Society

Blue Earth County Historical Society

***All we know about this photo is that it was labeled "dancing school" and it was in the files of the historical society in Mankato. The children's clothing looks 1895-vintage.***

Minneapolis Public Library

***Dorothy Davis taught dance to a group of young girls in 1929 at Logan Park Community Center in Minneapolis.***

Hibbard photo, Minnesota Historical Society

◀ *Winged little girls, pretending to be fairies or butterflies or something, prepared to take flight in a spring pageant in Minneapolis's Lyndale Park in 1920.*

▶ *Fidelis Lauer, a St. Paul teenager, was imitating the style of dancer Isadora Duncan. The picture was shot about 1920 outside Turner Hall at Summit Av. and Wabasha St. Miss Lauer's shape and stance were less than classic ballerina, but in the 1920s everyone pirouetted and wanted to look like Duncan, the innovator of modern dance. Lauer's hair band and arm position were Duncan-like, but she blew it with the shoes: Duncan's dancers were barefooted.*

Minnesota Historical Society

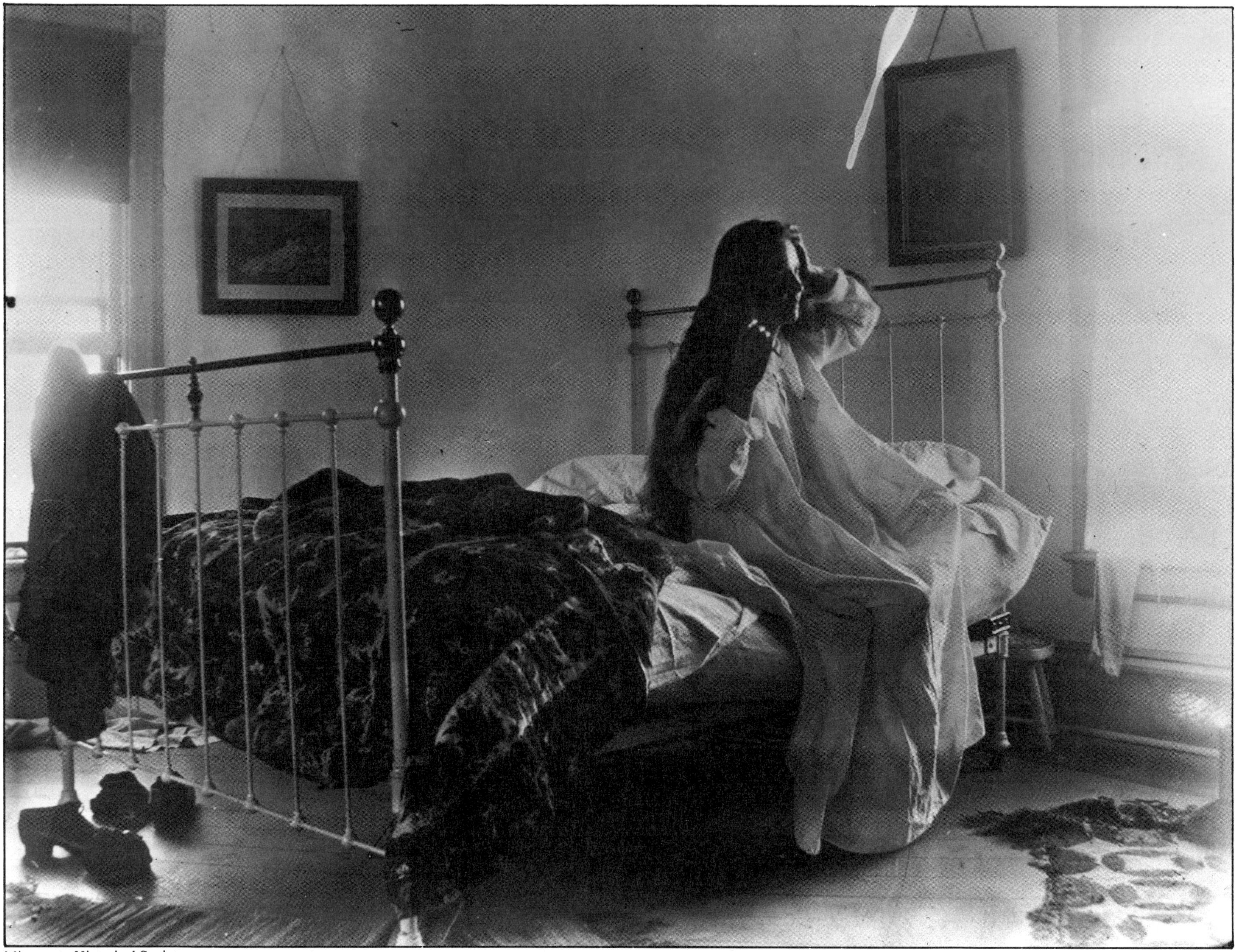

Minnesota Historical Society

◀ *As sunlight streamed into her bedroom, a woman stretched on a morning in about 1900. Private moments such as this rarely were photographed back then. Whoever took the picture apparently knew the woman well. Community standards have changed over the decades as to what are acceptable photo subjects. A more contemporary example is a baby's birth. Once absolutely taboo for photographers, now it is an almost obligatory photo opportunity.*

▶ *Agnes K. Pritchett was photographed while expecting Edward Jr. The picture was taken at 712 E. 14th St., Minneapolis, in March 1897. Flora L.S. Aldrich, a Minneapolis physician, wrote a book in 1901 called "The Boudoir Companion" that stated, "Every pregnant woman should be considered a laboratory in which she prepares a new being, to which the slightest physical or moral emotion is injurious. Childbearing is ordinarily beneficial rather than deleterious." Sounds good now, but the doctor also warned pregnant women against running a sewing machine or eating bananas. She advised against reading or sewing for a month after delivery, for fear of eye strain.*

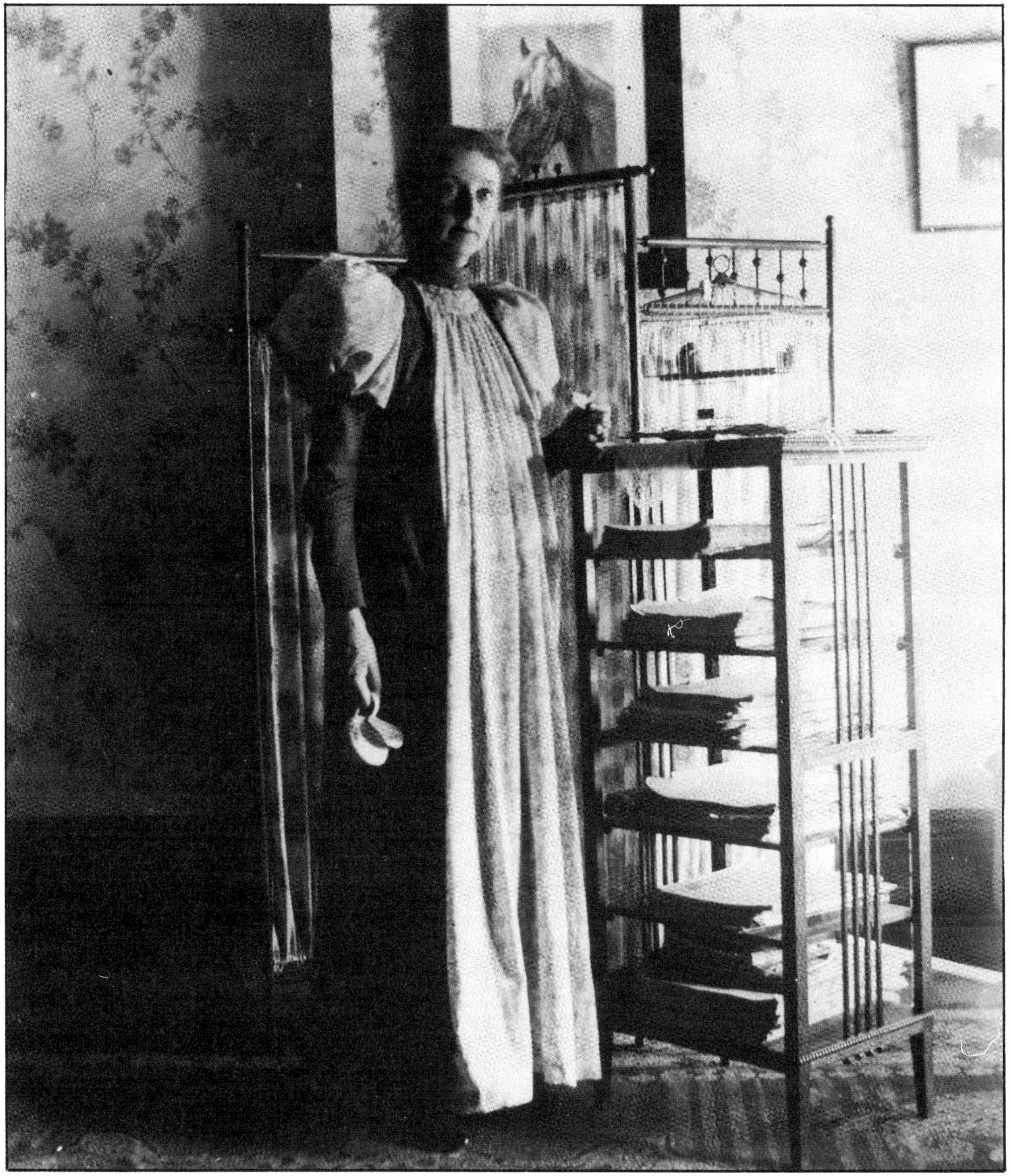

Edward Prichett photo, Minnesota Historical Society

Minnesota Historical Society

***Barn raisings were routine occurrences at the turn of the century, and many photographs were taken to prove this kind of community cooperation. This barn-raising picture, however, was unusually nicely composed. Lots of neighbors turned out to help. The print that made its way to the historical society says it was shot "down by Rainy River." Generally the women provided big pot-luck meals, and sometimes the barn raising culminated in music and dance.***

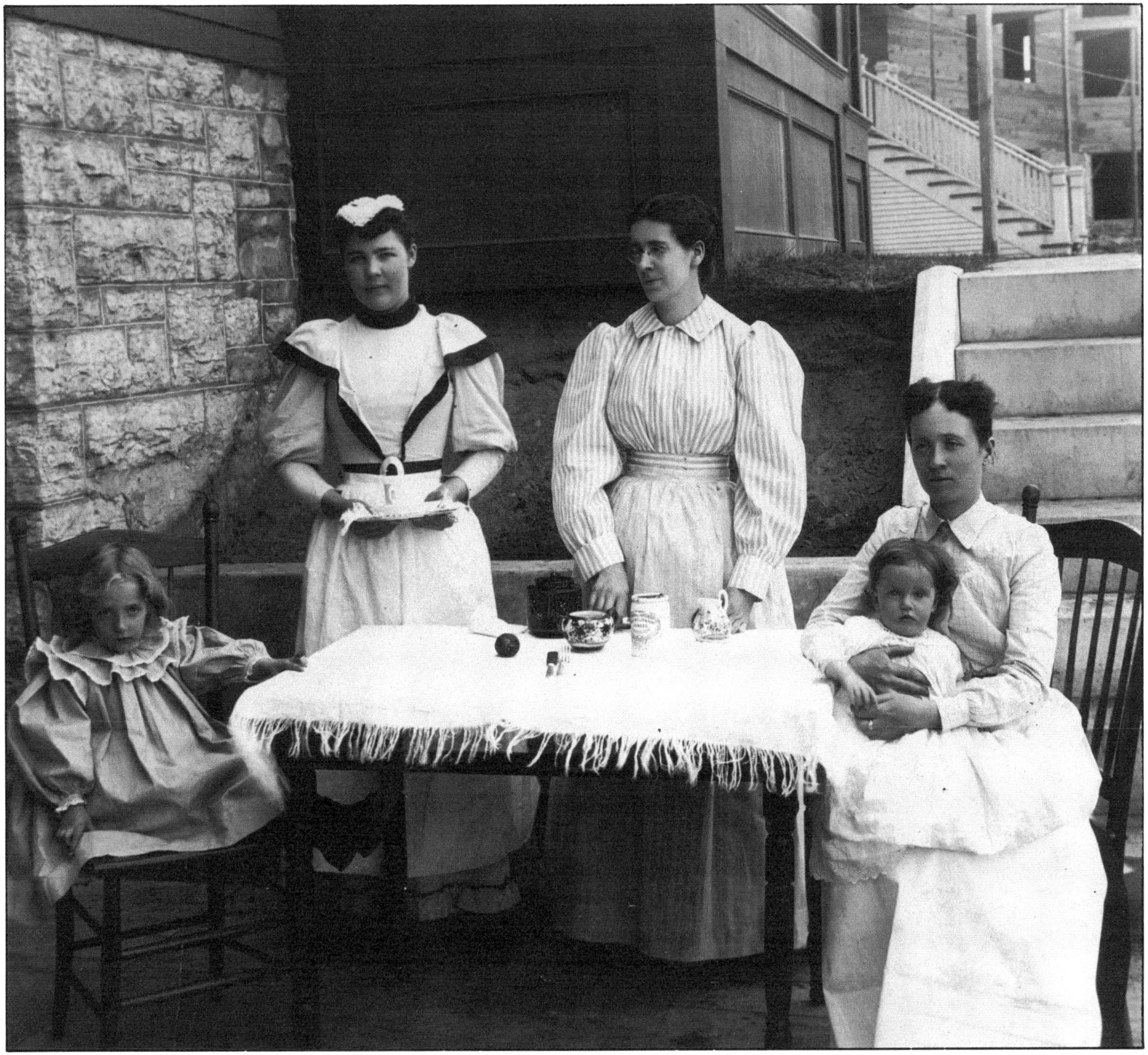

*The children's names have survived, but not the maids'. The girls are Audrey and Dorothy Walton, children of Mr. and Mrs. Edmund G. Walton. The father was a real estate developer. In 1895, the time of this photo, the family lived at 802 Mt. Curve Av. in Minneapolis. Perhaps descendants of the servants can help identify them. Their uniforms show that even work clothing reflects the fashion of the day. The maids' big sleeves and close-fitting bodices were stylish. The woman on the left was dressed to go out or to receive distinguished guests for her employers.*

Minnesota Historical Society

▶ *In another rite of passage, graduates of the University of Minnesota wound their way across campus to the armory. People in mortarboards and gowns appear timeless, but the car and the guests' clothing indicate the picture was taken in about 1911.*

Minnesota Historical Society

*Pastor Paul H. Ristau sat with his somber confirmation class at Immanuel German Lutheran Church in Lakefield in about 1905. Many clergy of the time taught religion classes in the native language of the community; you can bet these young people recited Scripture in German. Ristau was born in Germany and taught the language in the local public school. Proud of his facility with languages, he learned Slovak in order to preach to a congregation near Lakefield.*

Minnesota Historical Society

Minnesota Historical Society

◀ *With huge hats and walking suits, these women joined their spiffy men on the Milwaukee Road Station platform in Minneapolis in 1909. Railways ran excursions back then, and the couples may have been on their way to tourist attractions. Milliners would have been happy with this bunch. High-fashion hats like these cost as much as $100.*

◀ *Ain't love grand! These married people were smitten with each other. Donald Edward Ehmke and Lucille Elizabeth Williams Ehmke were in their home in Markville in 1935.*

Minnesota Historical Society

Minnesota Historical Society

Minnesota Historical Society

***Spring is a great time for family photos. The daguerreotype to the left, of a man and child, is from about 1850. Photography had barely gotten started in Minnesota by then, so chances are good that this picture was taken in the East and carried to Minnesota by an early settler. Often the subjects of early daguerreotypes looked disturbed or at least intense because they had to be very still for the slow camera. Children frequently were blurred because they couldn't hold still long enough. Above is a photo of Mrs. Paul H. Buetow with her grandson, Harry P. Buetow, at 526 W. Arlington, St. Paul, from about the 1910s.***

Minnesota Historical Society

***Above, Clarence Young and his daughter Evelyn of Two Harbors gazed into each other's eyes in about 1929. At right, Lillian Brown posed with her son, Lauren, in about 1910. Notice the sewing machine.***

Minnesota Historical Society

John W.G. Dunn photo, Minnesota Historical Society

*Waving their handkerchiefs to say hello, goodbye and isn't-childhood-grand, these children greeted the crew and passengers of a Northern Pacific train as it passed through Lindstrom in about 1913. The boy on the right was Jack Dunn, and next to him was his brother Monfort. The other children probably were residents of the Cape Horn Resort at Lindstrom, where the Dunns summered until they built cabins near Marine Mills, later called Marine on St. Croix.*

# *Spring letters and diaries*

## Drenching rain

***Jane M. Grout kept a diary of a journey in a covered wagon from near Fall River, Wis., to Luverne, Minn., in 1873. Rich prairie land in southern and southeastern Minnesota was available under the Homestead Act of 1862. She traveled with her husband, their three children and two other families. The trip took 34 days; at best, they made 20 or 25 miles a day.***

**Wednesday, May 28th, 1873.** Did not get a very early start this morning, were up late last night cooking meat & sauce. Reached Rochester between nine & ten o'clock & mailed some letters bought bread &c. G.H. Henton here left us, joined his family & went to visit his brother who lives out ten miles from Rochester. We met his brother after we left him. We find the roads very bad. Camped about half past eleven under a pretty line of willows. . . . Very good buildings around here surrounded by the white willow in almost every case. This is all the timber you will see in going from Rochester to Mantorville, a distance of seventeen miles, except when within three miles of Mantorville we came to a beautiful piece of oak timber in which we camped for the night. Traveled about twenty miles.

**Thursday, May 29.** Last night it rained terribly, but we all slept in our wagons & did not get wet. We did not get a very early start in the morning as it was very wet & some rainy. We reached Mantorville middle of forenoon while it was raining. Stopped & got some bread & enquired the way to Andrew Curtis' whose residence we reached about eleven o'clock, where we were all taken in & hospitably entertained. The weather was cold & we felt thankful to get in by the fire. Cousin Esther in tears told us of her recent affliction in the loss of her darling little baby nine & a half months old. At times she receives it as from her Father's hand for her good, then again she murmurs & thinks it so hard. Soon comes in Ella Snyder with her two little ones who I have not seen since she was five years old. I did not know that she lives so near to Esther. Esther got us a good nice dinner. It seemed a luxury to have our dinner in the house & cooked without ashes or sand in it. Libbie & I washed considerable in the afternoon. It did not rain. Esther is anxious that we all stay over until Monday hoping the mud will be dried up. The report is that the slues ahead of us are impassable. Think we shall accept their invitation to stay over sabbath.

Minnesota Historical Society, Jane M. Grout Papers

## Useful recipe

**How to make waterproof clothing:** Make the cloak, coat or trousers of linen; soak them well for a day or two in boiled oil, then hang them up in a dry place until perfectly dry, without wringing the oil out. Then paint them without turpentine or driers being in the paint, any color, put on thin & let dry.

**— Abbie T. Griffin, a Minneapolis seamstress, in about 1882**

Minnesota Historical Society, Abbie T. Griffin Diary

## Greening up

**Wednesday, April 4, 1951.** I noticed this morning a little bare spot on the lawn. Then this afternoon it had turned green. A school girl screamed when she saw it.

**— Lillian Brown, age 80, of Austin Minn.**

Minnesota Historical Society, Lillian Elizabeth Brown and Family Papers

## Frog songs

The frogs begin to sing early in April, while the nights are yet quite chilly. Along the creek, from the pond and the sloughs in the pasture, and from water-filled potholes in the fields I hear them tuning up. A few hardy ones at first, a bit rusty after the long winter layoff, then more and more joining in until the chorus is in full voice. I love to listen to them on a warm, still spring evening. The main chorus booms in from a distance, the sound rising and falling rhythmically, while nearby a few lusty soloists are holding forth on their own. There is real music and harmony in the spring frog song. I could listen to it all night and I turn away regretfully and go to bed feeling that sleep is a waste of time, that I am missing one of nature's finest concerts. It is better than Fred Waring.

**— Bennie Bengtson, a Kittson County farmer who wrote about nature in the 1940s and 1950s**

Minnesota Historical Society, Bennie Bengtson Papers

## Apples, oats and peas

***Oliver Parsons was born in Maine in 1823 and in 1849 moved to Stillwater, where he was a partner in Short, Proctor and Co., a lumber and general merchandising firm. He also operated a farm near Stillwater and kept diaries. Most farmers recorded brief, businesslike comments. Parsons was chattier. These are excerpts from his diary in the spring of 1871.***

**April 13.** Thursday, the snow is now again melted, weather today quite warm and pleasant, the boys and I have today been building fences acrost the pasture, trimming Black Raspberries. Sewed trophy Tomato seed in Boxes in the house. I have at this date 27 chickens hatched out, and eggs under 6 hens.

**April 15.** I and the boys set out seventy apple trees. Weather cool, but quite pleasant. Have finished setting out all the apple trees that we had hauled in last fall: fifty Transcendent Crab, 50 Duchess Crab and 25 Hyslop's Crab. The ground will soon be in good order. George, Mary Belle, and Mrs. P. [his wife] went to the City at 3 P.M. George had two teeth extracted, one of them had a root to it one inch long, the longest I ever saw. Mary Belle had four pieces of decayed teeth pulled out. They both had good courage and stood it well.

**April 16.** Sunday, cloudy and cool. Henry and George have gone to Sabbath School, the rest of us at home reading.

**April 17.** Monday commenced putting in my crop. Sewed 3 acres of oats.

**April 18.** George driving the horses to harrow in grain. Henry working in the Garden sewing Beet seeds.

**April 19.** Wednesday, last night we had a good deal of rain, thunder and lightning, cleared up this morning, the ground is too wet for sewing. The Boys and I set out over one hundred Black Cap Raspberries. We have commenced to cut our Early Rose Potatoes for planting. Eggs are now selling at 20 cents per doz. I have eggs under ten hens for young chickens.

**April 20.** Thursday, wet and cold, I went to town at 1:20 P.M., came home at 4:45, in a snow storm. This is rough weather for the season.

**April 22.** Saturday, tied up my Grape Vines. Sewed Early Kent and Champion of England Peas. Henry Reist has the Mumps on both sides of his face, his face is swollen and his throat is quite sore. George has the Mumps on one side of his face, his face is not as sore as Henry's.

**April 24.** Monday. Planted a few hills of Early Rose potatoes in the garden. Pleasant weather.

**April 25.** Tuesday, very warm and pleasant. Plowed the garden in the morning. Plowing ground for oats in the afternoon.

**April 26.** A very heavy rain. Corn is selling at 75 cents per Bushel, oats at 60 cents. Rose dropped her calf at 7 P.M. Doing well.

**April 27.** Cold and cloudy, very unpleasant. Willie Anderson's funeral to-day.

**April 29.** Saturday, warmer and quite pleasant, mud drying up.

**May 2.** It rained hard all night, wind N.E. It is raining now at Nine A.M. The ground is full of water, I fear this wet weather will injure the grain.

**May 3.** The weather continues cloudy, wet and cold, I think I never knew such a long spell of wet cold weather as we have had this spring.

**May 7.** Sunday, Mrs. P., Henry, Mary Bell went to church. George and I remained at home. Mr. A. Lowell and Wife called on us, it is a splendid day.

**May 11.** Thursday, finished sewing wheat. I have my crop all in except corn. I am now all out of hay. Grass is starting well. Green peas up. Onion & Beets are up and look well. Apple trees in blossom.

**May 12.** Plum trees all in blossom. Cucumbers and extra pumpkin seed planted. Mary Bell has the mumps.

**May 13.** Saturday. Plowing corn ground, weather hot. Apples, eight good sorts for Minnesota. Fameuse, very hardy, fruit good, keeps till Feb'y. Wagener! Winter apple, keeps till May. Talman's Sweet! Winter apple, keeps till May. Golden Russet, winter fruit, very hardy, early bearer. Duchesse d'Oldenbourg, late fall, keeps till March. Red Astrachan, fall, keeps till December. Sweet June, summer fruit, later bearer. Plumb Cider, late fall fruit.

**May 15.** Monday, very hot and very dry, we need some rain to wet and soften the hard ground. Sweet Corn and Cucumbers coming up, Potatoes in the garden are up.

**May 18.** Thursday, hot and dry. We need rain.

**May 19.** Friday, hot. George and Henry planting corn. 8 o'clock P.M. a small shower with the appearance of more rain, plowing ground near the house for corn, ground hard for the want of rain, hope we shall get rain to-night. Cucumbers, squash, pumpkin, sweet corn and Beans are up in the garden and look well.

**May 20.** Saturday. Last night we had a good rain, the ground is now well wet. 9 a.m. sitting out tomato plants, sit out about two hundred, they are quite small, think they will do better in the ground than in the boxes. We had another fine rain this evening.

**May 21.** Sunday, another raid on my chickens, lost six.

**May 23.** We have in 6½ acres of corn, high wind. The best time to plan corn in this latidude is when the Apple trees are in full blossom, usually about the middle of May. The Melons are up and look well, the worms and a small fly are eating my cucumbers as fast as they come up.

**May 25.** Weather very warm, corn coming up.

**May 26.** Friday hot, repairing fence, grain looks well.

**May 27.** Saturday, hot, making yard for young Turkies. The potatoe Bugs are awful, more of them than I have ever seen so early in the season. My field potatoes are just coming up and the Bugs are very thick eating them up. Rose's calf four weeks old 24th Wednesday.

Minnesota Historical Society, Oliver Parsons Diary

~

## Who says it's spring?

**March 23, 1867, St. Paul.** Had a young winter again this afternoon. "First it *snew,* and then it *blew,* and then it *friz.*"

**— Josiah Chaney, a 38-year-old St. Paul pressman**

Minnesota Historical Society, Josiah Blodgett Chaney and Family Papers

~

## Goodbye to winter

***Susan Adams and her husband, Andrew, settled in Shakopee in 1854. He was the first county surveyor of Scott County, and she was a schoolteacher. They apparently did not have children when she kept this diary in 1856. She was 29 years old.***

**March 30th.** Delightful prayer meeting. . . . Spent eve in singing and praying. Retired early. [We] talked much about religion etc. after we were in bed.

**April 1st.** Beautiful morning. . . . I went to school as usual. Wind rose and rain began to fall at noon. It looked dark and threatened a heavy storm. Still I did not dismiss school until the usual time when it began to sleet, hail & snow, in the midst of which marched home. Found a party of Swedes had taken shelter there. Very stormy night. Thought much of my husband and hoped he is in some safe comfortable place. . . . The weather more disagreeable than any I have known for months.

**April 2nd.** Clear & beautiful day. How pleasant to see the sun after such dreary days!

**April 5th.** Lovely morning. Sun soon thawed the ground. Two years to day bade adieu to Pitt. [Pittsburgh?], perhaps *forever.* How little I dreamed about any of the changes which should take place during the coming two years. How little I thought my lot would be cast in Minnesota! That I should become the wife of a *stranger* in so short a time. How different the scenes! What a contrast in my feelings!

**April 6th.** Cloudy morning but came out very bright & warm by noon. . . Had much trouble to cross the running brooks on the way. Found blades of grass long & very green. Strawberry leaves in abundance. Oh! glad sight! Herald of the happy spring time! While at church heard the music of frogs. Good bye to Winter now! Had good prayer meeting. . . . Walked home with A. Sat down by the brook and chatted together. What a pleasure thus to converse on spiritual things! May this joy be ever increasing while we live together.

***They lived together another five years. Andrew died in 1861.***

Minnesota Historical Society, Susan Maria Hazeltine Adams Diary

~

## From snow to wildflowers

***John W. Murray, a horticulturist and bee-keeper near Excelsior, witnessed spring rushing in.***

**April 25, 1866.** 60 degrees. Saw a nice bouquet of early wild flower at Mr. Sheldon's. Four days since I saw the last of the snow.

**April 26.** 68 degrees. Received my seeds from New York yesterday evening, but it is now so late in the season that I do not value them much.

**April 27.** 83 degrees. Planted my hotbed [greenhouse] this forenoon, concluding to risk it without further waiting.

Minnesota Historical Society, John W. Murray Papers

~

## Planting and patching

***Mary E. Goff grew up on Prairieview Farm in Blue Earth County. The daughter of John and Ann Goff, she was the youngest of three girls and two boys. She was 12 when she wrote this.***

**Friday, May 5, 1899.** Nice warm stir of a windy day and I took off my shoes and left them off till after dinner. Ma churned. John disced this forenoon. Pa scattered the manure around down the field. I planted some carrots, celery, parsley & okra alone and ma helped me plant some parsnip and beet. This afternoon John dragged. Pa fixed the pasture fence. Ma mended and patched. I got some of my lessons. Tonight Hattie came home from town. She rode down to the east road with Sydney Whitney and walked the rest of the way home. Jesse Kirkpatrick came home tonight on David Ham's bicycle and while Hattie and I rode on the bicycle, he and John talked.

Blue Earth County Historical Society

~

## Road trouble

**Wednesday, March 2, 1870.** Went to Brownsville with a load of wheat. Roads good to Caledonia. Then [rained] hard hard and harder then thunder mud and stones stones and mud 4 inches deep or deeper.

**— Edward Harkness, a Fillmore County farmer**

Minnesota Historical Society, Edward Harkness Diary

~

## Big suckers

**May 3d.** We have got acquainted with a bug family by name of woodticks.

**May 30th.** I can't hardly write on account of the mosquitoes. They're bigger than elephants.

**— Maude Baumann, age 15, on her family's Minnesota migration by covered wagon in 1900.**

Minnesota Historical Society, Maude Baumann Arney Journal

~

## A budding salesman

***Edward Parry was a land speculator in Mankato in the spring of 1858. Minnesota became a state that May. In letters to aunts and an uncle back home in Pennsylvania, he displayed spring fever and a salesman's drive.***

**March 20, 1858.** Thee speaks of game; the Indians in the early part of the winter brought considerable venison in the town, and it was as cheap as beef, bringing only about twelve cents a pound, it has become scarce now, and I think I haven't seen any for a couple of months. Ducks are beginning to flock on our lakes again, but until they become more abundant, I think I shall not disturb them much. Fish are also becoming abundant, and some of our young men are quite proficient in the art of catching them. Pike seem to be the most plenty at present and within the past few days I have seen some very fine ones. The fishing tackle which I brought out is all too frail, and the largest of my hooks (and I thought they would be large enough to catch most anything on) would hardly be strong enough to hold one of our common size sun fish. The cat fish beat anything that ever I have seen of the species, you could almost ride on one of their horns. Unfortunately for us, there are no trout that I know of within about a hundred miles; but it is said there are some very fine ones to the Southeast of us; as the Spring advances, they will no doubt be seen darting up and down the brooks.

You probably have noticed in the papers that the ice is rapidly thawing, and that navigation is again open in the lower Mississippi; the Minnesota is also pretty much cleared of it, and in a few days we expect to have the boats running to this point. This week quite a number of our merchants will leave for the East, to buy their Spring goods; and until about the first of May I do not expect to see much freight landing at our wharves. We are calculating largely on numerous improvements being made this Season; and in fact, there are several good sized stores and dwelling houses in the course of construction now. By this time next year I think we will number between two and three thousand inhabitants. This is a fast country, one day a woods, the next a town, and although the people direct most of their energies and talents to making money, yet they are not unmindful of pleasure, and as to extravagance I have never seen anything to beat it in proportion to the means; to illustrate it I wrote to Dick Ely a short time ago and cited the instance of a blacksmith in town who hired the use of a billiard table for three days, at the rate of two or three dollars a day. The fellow had made some two thousand dollars last year in speculating in property, and concluded he would go it whilst young. This is not an isolated case by any means. . . .

Jim Shannonhouse seems to have quite a notion of emigrating out here, and I think he couldn't do better than come, as there is a fine opening in our town for a smart Physician. He has written several letters to us on the subject, and in his last he said if we could encourage him, he would start early this Spring; and believing he would do well, I advised him accordingly. We are expecting a very large emigration, and no doubt we will not be disappointed. Already wagons are beginning to come in laden with families and household furniture.

**4th Mo. 19th 1858.** We have just passed through a most delightful winter, with just snow enough to give us an abundance of sleighing; and are entering fairly into Spring. The prairies are beginning to be carpeted with new born grass, and little flowers of various descriptions are scattered here and there, adding beauty to the scene. The little Spring birds are hopping from twig to twig, and fill the air with the music of their songs; whilst the fish chase each other beneath the limpid surface of the running brook; all hailing with delight the advent of the warmer season.

So with man; although contented whilst the keen northern blast swept around us, yet are we anxious to feel the warmer air, when we can steal away from the cares of business life for an hour, and recline on the grass beneath the outstretched arms of some shade tree. The rivers are again free from ice, and boats are running daily from this point to Saint Paul and connecting with the Mississippi line.

People are beginning to flock into the Territory from different sections of the East, and scattering over it in search of homes. In consequence of the late destructive financial hurricane [the monetary panic of 1857] that has passed through our country, and particularly the Atlantic States, thousands of emigrants will flock to the West to endeavor to build up their fortunes so recently torn down. They will not miss it much by removing out here, for if a man is prudent and attentive to any avocation which he may make choice of, he cannot well help getting along, and more than that for if he keeps his eyes open and is shrewd he must make a fortune.

Edward Parry letters, private collection of Ron Feldhaus, Edina

~

## Fit for angels

**Sunday, May 25, 1879.** Cousin Charlie's for dinner as usual. Strawberries!

**— Robert Bell, a 19-year-old University of Minnesota student**

Minnesota Historical Society, Robert M. Bell Papers

## A young man's fancy

***Michael J. Boyle was born in 1856 in Pennsylvania and moved to St. Paul as a child. In 1877 he began a 50-year career with the St. Paul dry-goods firm of Auerbach, Finch, Culbertson and Co., and its successors. Boyle advanced to manage the flannel and print departments. He fell in love in the spring of 1889. Here are glimpses of his diary that May, and later in the year, as the relationship progressed.***

**May 2.** This evening I took Leila to the People's Theater to see the company in a comedy called "The Fatal Letter." The play was good enough but it is my belief that neither of us paid any great amount of attention to it. I know that I didn't for I was completely absorbed in her, and her treatment of me in looks and manner was irresistibly winning. I honestly believe that I am beginning to feel differently toward her than I have yet felt towards Katherine or herself and it is a stronger feeling than any that has preceded it. We had a most delightful walk home.

**Aug. 15.** Leila & Bessie Taylor are visiting Mrs. Sherman of Exchange St. This morning Bessie telephoned me, inviting me to join them in a picnic at 5 o'clock. Mrs. Sherman, Leila & Jeanine McLaren rode while Bessie drove me and Baby Sherman in the phaeton [carriage]. We went down the river towards Burlington Heights that supplies a romantic spot. I never saw Leila ride before. She looks awfully swell in her riding habit and she rides most gracefully. After supper she & I took a little walk. As we were crossing a little stream, her foot slipped & I held her in my arms just for an instant. I came very near putting a momentous question to her then & there.

**Sunday Sept. 1.** Attended mass at the Cathedral at 9 o'clock after which I took breakfast in a hurry, boarded a cable car and intercepted Leila on her way to church. Leila was not in an angelic mood. Gingie was with her and the walk as far as my pleasure was concerned was a dismal failure.

**Monday Sept. 23.** A conversation by telephone.
L: Is that Mr. Boyle?
M: Yes! good morning.
L: I was very sorry I couldn't get out early yesterday but I really had to stay.
M: I was sorry too.
L: I expected to see you last night.
M: Why didn't you say so in the morning?
L: I didn't think it was necessary.
M: Oh yes it was very necessary after a late experience — but what night this week will you go to the theater?
L: Tomorrow night?
M: The play will be Othello.
L: I have seen it, but —
M: Let's go to-night to see Richard III.
L: Well! If it doesn't rain.
M: I'll come round early, we can do as we please then.
L: Alright. Goodbye!
M: Goodbye!
We went round early. It shed rain but nevertheless L. saw Keene in Richard III. He has not any definite impressions of the play but he had an evening to be remembered. L. was a little quiet but very lovely!

**Friday, Sept. 27.** While waiting on a customer about 3 o'clock I saw Leila pass in the carriage and longed to chase her up and gather her to go for a drive but circumstances of the trade forbade. A little later I was agreeably surprised to have her call me up by telephone, just for a little talk. The little talk was very nice and it whetted my desire for continuing the conversation at closer range so I quit business and went to the house at 5 o'clock. She received me in that pretty tea gown I admire so much. I persuaded her to break the "once a week" rule and she will go for a drive to-morrow afternoon. I stayed until I was sent home & very loath I was to go. At home in the evening the family played hearts for a while and then I read the new novel, "The Open Door," which Leila loaned me.

**Saturday, Oct. 12.** Went home to lunch at noon and at two o'clock I took Leila out for a drive. This was one of the momentous days of my life for I had determined to ask Leila Dean to be my wife & I carried out my resolve. We drove out Summit Ave. to the bluffs and as we sat in the October sun & gazed at the beautiful prospect up and down the river, I poured out the story of my love . . . . Her dear face become unutterably sad and all she could say was "it cannot be." What an interview that was & what a drive home! Parental opposition & religious difference were her strong objections. I asked her if there was any one else and she said, "No." Arriving at her house we had a moving parting. I clasped her in my arms, kissed her repeatedly, begged her to consider the matter and swore I would never give her up. Took the Milwaukee train at 7:30 for Chicago with Mr. & Mrs. Tom Sharp. Lay awake all night with my heart and brain on fire.

***Michael Boyle was true to his word. He never gave her up. While he had many friends and some romances, he remained a bachelor his entire life. He died in 1941, at age 84. Leila Dean did wed. In 1891, when she was 28, she married Stephen H. DeForest. They apparently had no children. She died in 1920.***

Minnesota Historical Society, Michael J. Boyle Papers

## Much enforced leisure

***Mary Whipple was an elderly widow when she wrote this letter to her sister. Her husband was George B. Whipple, an Episcopal missionary and the brother of Bishop Henry B. Whipple, known for his work with Minnesota Indians. She had been the first headmistress of St. Mary's Hall in Faribault, an Episcopal finishing school for girls.***

**Faribault, Minnesota**
**April 17, 1911**

My dear little Sister,

Your letter came, a welcome messenger Easter Even. I was so glad to hear a word from you. I have been a shut-in all winter, but have not been ill. The walks have been either snowy, wet, or icy most of the time, the icy ones being particularly dangerous for those unsteady on their feet, and snow & wet are under embargo, as far as I am concerned. Until Good Friday I had been at Church but three times since Christmas. Good Friday was a beautiful day, and I ventured out with my cane, for I have been lamer than usual since the last months. I was at one service, and yesterday I went to one. I was no worse, but I feel as though there were a snow-storm in the air. Now that I am on that prolific subject [of] myself, I may as well state that excepting rheumatism, I am very well and strong and have an excellent appetite. Early in the winter, I had a little trouble from rheumatism affecting breathing, but it did not last long. For a woman who will be 82 her next birthday, I am hale and well. I cannot, naturally, be very active, and have much enforced leisure. I potter around as much as I can and scan a great deal. As a refreshing exercise, I have taken to working Algebra — and particularly enjoy radical quantities. This year have re-read some of Dickens. We have Harper's, McClure's, Human Life, the Churchman & The Youth's Companion & Springfield Republican. Except the latter, these are all Christmas gifts. I wonder whether you are reading "The Iron Woman" in Harper's Monthly.

How nice it is that you can have the little grandchildren. People keep younger by having young people around them. If I were inclined to be serious, I should envy you your two home girls and your grandchildren. I think I do not always feel quite resigned that Eva [her daughter, adopted in Hawaii when the writer was a missionary] should have been taken [died]. I had looked forward to her being the prop and stay of my old age. But when I think about it, I say to myself, "It is well with the child."

Miss Gilmore is still with me, and we are comfortable and happy together. She needs a home, and I the family. I do not know how much longer we can go on in this way, for it is an expensive business keeping up a house. I am hardly equal in running it, I cannot do much and service is scarce and high. I hardly dare to venture on another winter here. Miriam (Miss Gilmore) thinks we must go to California in October. But at my age one has to take short views. . . .

If you can, write to me occasionally. I must close. With love to you and the girls, I am, as ever

Your affectionate
Mary J. Whipple

***Mrs. Whipple died a few months later.***

Minnesota Historical Society, William A. Wait and Family Papers

~

## Opening up the cabin

***Gracia Countryman was head librarian of the Minneapolis Public Library from 1903 to 1936. She was 66 in the spring of 1931, when she kept these journal notes about opening her cabin on the south shore of Lake Mille Lacs:***

**April 11, 1931.** Left Library at 12:40 and lunched on the way up. Roadside between Anoka and Elk River was carpeted with crocus, half a mile of them. At Princeton we went in for a cup of coffee. Just opposite the tire shop in Onamia we had a puncture. Wellington [her adopted son] changed the wheel very quickly and left it for repairs. The lake looked beautiful, Spirit Island fairy like. There was ice out on the lake, around the shore and around the island. In the centre it was grey and thin. There were two little heaps of dirty rotten snow in the woods. Spring beauties were out by the road in front of the pool, and a little clump of bloodroot. In the garden we planted gooseberries and rhubarb and dug around rasps [raspberries], transplanting some. Mr. Nelson [the caretaker] moved the iris over to a place by the pool where we covered it with leaves. He had cut off the top of the tree by the porch. The snow fence was still up. Mr. Benson came to see about the wavey floor in the kitchen. Phoebes wakened us early and robins and woodpeckers. We also heard bluebirds and song sparrows. Hoot owls screeched. Gulls sailed along on cakes of ice. Wellington said he heard wolves in the night.

***The next year she wrote:***

**May 15, 1932.** Came up late for the first time. We went to New Orleans in April. . . . Spring very late, leaves just bursting. Bloodroot, Dutchman's Breeches, dog tooth violets and trillium all out at same time. . . . Cottage was in good shape except dusty. The water tank has split, will have to have a new one. Mr. Benson has not yet connected the water pipes, nor put in the docks, but Mr. Nelson has the garden in fine shape. Yesterday the day was very hot. 88 degrees on the porch. We cleaned the upstairs but could not work in the garden. Asparagus bed bearing heavily. Ate a big mess and carried a lot home. Today it is cooler — cold in fact. About 5 o'clock a big thunder storm came up. Sharp lightning and much rain. We went up in the evening to Mr. Boxell's for milk from our own Jersey cows. Too dark to see cows. Got stuck badly in his driveway. Rained a lot in the night. Blew a gale for awhile. But lake calmed down later in the morning and many fishermen were out. Good reports of fishing. Cleaned downstairs today. House looks fine for family to come up next week.

Minnesota Historical Society, Gracia Alta Countryman Papers

~

# And now about your photos. . .

If you enjoy these old black-and-white photographs, I have a few suggestions for you about the photos you take and the way you store them.

Most people assume that their color snapshots and portraits will survive in family albums, shoeboxes and picture frames just as well as the old black-and-white photos did. Wrong! If you live another 30 or 40 years, you're likely to outlive your color photos.

So it would be smart for you to shoot some black-and-white film. If processed correctly, it lasts 200 or 300 years. Heat, light and humidity — the chief enemies of photos — harm black-and-white negatives and pictures far less than they do color. All color film and prints fade. Color prints, slides, Polaroids and videos all slowly disappear to nothingness. Some color images show marked deterioration in only 10 years. Most color photos last fewer than 50 years.

Take a look at your color prints and slides from the 1950s. Have they turned blue or yellow? Then you'll probably get my point. Unless you take precautions to preserve your color photos — precautions that few of us amateurs bother with — the images are likely to be gone in a few generations.

You may be thinking, "That's silly! Nobody will want to see my snapshots in 50 years." (I can read minds.) My rebuttal: Look around your house. Aren't some of your favorite possessions the old family photos? Probably some of the black-and-whites are from long-gone generations. Just as you love to see those faces, study their features and guess how they lived, your descendants might someday like to have photos of you.

It's important to take at least a few black-and-white photos on special occasions, such as births, religious celebrations, weddings, birthdays, anniversaries and family reunions.

But as the everyday photos in this book show, black-and-white photography can be wonderful to document the "ordinary" times that sometimes are sublime. I'd suggest you load your camera with a roll of black-and-white to photograph the baby in her bathtub, the Little Leaguer at bat, your new car, colleagues at work, pets and other "everyday" photo opportunities.

Some professional photographers will shoot black-and-white portraits and wedding photos, even though demand, unfortunately, has declined dramatically. I know several couples who recently had both black-and-white and color pictures taken and, much to their surprise, prefer the black-and-white. They're glad they sought out photographers who were familiar with black-and-white work.

Heat and humidity rapidly age photos. The worst place to store old photographs is in the basement (too damp) or attic (too hot). Fireplace mantels and walls with heat sources nearby also are poor choices. What's optimal is a cool, dry, dark place. A closet shelf in an air-conditioned, first-floor room may be best. Keep the negatives there too. Black-and-white negatives last even better than prints, so put them in a safe place too.

Because people tend to display their best photos, we actually single out our favorites for destruction: Sunlight and fluorescent light fade photos noticeably in only 10 to 15 years. Display color pictures only if they are expendable or if you have a copy in dark storage. Have duplicates made of special slides and use the duplicates for projecting; the light wears them out.

Do yourself and your family another favor — label your photos. Even a few notes with names, dates, locations and occasions are appreciated when memories fade. Write on back of the photos — never the front — with a soft pencil. Ball-point pens leave indentations; felt-tip pens smear. Special pencils for writing on photos are available in photo shops for a small price.

Don't take apart photo albums, not even strangers' albums that were bought for a song at estate sales. Albums reveal a great deal more about the person or family than individual photos do.

Don't try to repair a damaged photo yourself. Soaking curled pictures or taping ripped ones promises disaster. Paper clips rust and ruin photos. Tape grows yellow and crispy, staining the photos. If you absolutely insist on taping photos, at least work from the back.

Select a photo album that will protect your photos, not ruin them as many albums do. Most inexpensive albums wreck pictures. Beware of "magnetic" photo albums, the kind that work by gripping photos on sticky cardboard with plastic overlays. This kind of album causes rapid fading and discoloration. Look for albums that have plastic enclosures of archival quality; the packaging will say that. But the best method is probably the one our grandmothers used: Corner mounts in a scrapbook. The glue touches only the page, not the print.

All the evidence isn't in yet for videotape, but its useful life may be as short as 15 years or as long as 50. It is known that videos start to deteriorate after 50 playings. Don't count on them as momentos for future generations. Make a back-up copy of a special tape, file the original and show the copy. Then if it breaks or deteriorates, you can make another copy.

If you want to shoot color pictures, use the most stable materials to begin with. These would be Kodachrome slides and Cibachrome prints (which can be made only from slides). Put the negatives for color snapshots in a sleeve so they won't get scratched. A new print can be made from the negative after the old print starts to fade.

If you have wonderful old photos, I hope you'll consider giving them or copies of them to an historical society. Your county society might be interested in local scenes and people; the state society might want your most fascinating photos.

I'm sorry to be so preachy about preserving your photos. But it is a tragedy that the billions of color photos taken every year will be goners. Soon there will be a big gap in photo collections, beginning in the 1950s and 1960s when black-and-white photography went out of favor. There will be a lost era in photography — in our photo albums, historical societies, museums and in our culture.

You can take steps to be sure your family photos survive.

# Thanks

This project depended on the good will of many historians and other fine people. The "we" in this book refers to the dozens who shared their knowledge with me. I didn't keep good enough notes to name them all, but I want to acknowledge those to whom I am especially indebted.

I did much of my research at the Minnesota Historical Society in St. Paul. These staff members were particularly helpful: Toni Anderson, Nina Archabal, Tino Avaloz, Tracey Baker, Ruth Ellen Bauer, Denise Carlson, Nancy Erickson, Lila Goff, Mark Haidet, Patricia Harpole, Nordis Heyerdahl-Fowler, Phil Hutchins, Bill Johnson, Sarah Jordan, Mary Klauda, Dallas Lindgren, Kathy Marquis, Linda McShannock, Debbie Miller, Steve Nielsen, Al Ominsky, Bonnie Palmquist, Alissa Rosenberg, Brigid Shields, Dona Sieden, F. Hampton Smith, Cheryl Thies, Bonnie Wilson and Alan Woolworth.

The people at many other historical societies, plus libraries and universities, opened their photo archives and provided information about the pictures. My thanks to these persons and institutions:

Blue Earth County Historical Society, Linda Henry, Jeff Kroke and Susan Schoettler; Brown County Historical Society, Darla Gebhard; Clay County Historical Society, Mark Peihl and Pam Burkhardt; Cokato Historical Society and Museum, Irene Bender; Dakota County Historical Society, Gary Phelps; Fillmore County Historical Society, Jerry Henke and Alma Syvertson; Goodhue County Historical Society, Jean Chesley, Orville Olson and Shirley Brunner; Hamline University, Thelma Boeder and Barbara Laskin; Hennepin History Museum, Dorothea Guiney, Dorothy Burke and Nicole Pettit; Hinckley Fire Museum, Jeanne Coffey; Iron Range Research Center in Chisholm, Bud Gazelka, Don Hildreth and Ed Nelson; Jewish Historical Society of the Upper Midwest, Linda Schloff; Lake County Historical Society, Marj Carol and Jeff McMorrow; the Library of Congress; Minneapolis Public Library, Bev Anderson, Erin Foley, Edward Kukla and Judy Mosiniak; Minnesota Landscape Arboretum, Richard T. Isaacson; Minnesota State Fair, Sue Ritt; Morrison County Historical Society, Jan Warner; Nicollet County Historical Society; Northeast Minnesota Historical Center in Duluth, Patricia Maus; Otter Tail County Historical Society, Chris Schuelke; Ramsey County Historical Society; Redwood County Historical Society, Bernice Tyson; St. John's Abbey, Father Vincent Tegeder; St. John's University, Annette Atkins; Star Tribune library, Bob Jansen, Sylvia Frisch and Roberta Hovde; Stearns County Historical Society, Kevin Britz, John Decker and Bob Lommel; University of Minnesota Archives, Penelope Krosch and Carol O'Brien, and Winona County Historical Society, Ginger Keith.

Other historians who helped included James Taylor Dunn, Marine on St. Croix; Ron Feldhaus, Edina; Steve Keillor, Askov; Phil Revoir, Red Wing, and John Wickre, St. Paul and Connecticut. People who provided permission to publish photos and identifications include Harriet Huneke, Burton Huneke, Don Prinz and Audrey Brunner.

My supervisors at the Star Tribune who granted me a sabbatical to work on this book were Tim McGuire and Linda Picone.

Special thanks to Jarrett Smith, the designer of this book, who was part of the project from the beginning. Carol Evans-Smith assisted with production. Phil Ford helped us with photo selection and keylining. Ingrid Sundstrom, Bob Lundegaard, Liz McConnell, Al Sicherman and Sue Peterson provided proofreading assistance. Linda James prepared the index. Megan O'Hara and R.T. Rybak contributed marketing ideas.

And a heartfelt thanks to good friends who urged me on: Jane Curry, Kris Jensen and Rebecca Lindholm.

Al Sicherman, Bruce Adomeit, Brian Cravens and Bob Quick got me out of computer messes. Yes, computers help, even when dealing with historic photos.

Any errors are mine. Set me straight. Write to me. The address is on the back cover. Also, please send information you have about the photos. I'll forward it to the appropriate historical societies. Hey, thanks.

# Index

## G



## H



## I



## J



## K

## Index compiled by Linda James

## Photo credits

Blue Earth County Historical Society, 24, 276
Brown County Historical Society, 48, 55, 127, 161, 186, 246, 251
Clay County Historical Society, 27, 53, 67, 70, 72, 164, 165, 188, 248
Cokato Historical Society, 187
Feldhaus, Ron, photo collection, 199, 201
Fillmore County Historical Society, 35, 54, 58, 97
Goodhue County Historical Society, 123, 196
Hennepin History Museum, 4, 53, 62, 112, 116, 124, 212, 213, 214, 217, 235
Hinckley Fire Museum, 135
Iron Range Research Center, 59
Library of Congress, 69, 74, 108, 117, 133, 137, 141
Minneapolis Journal, 23, 37, 121, 132, 170, 208
Minneapolis Public Library, 14, 25, 75, 163, 167, 168, 174, 210, 277
Minneapolis Star, 41, 200
Minneapolis Star-Journal, 106, 107, 113, 159, 160, 207
Minneapolis Star or Tribune, 235
Minneapolis Times-Tribune, 163
Minneapolis Tribune, 75, 140, 210
Minnesota Historical Society, 1, 7, 8, 10, 11, 12, 17, 18, 19, 20, 21, 23, 26, 28, 29, 30, 31, 32, 33, 34, 36, 37, 38, 39, 40, 41, 42, 43, 44, 46, 47, 49, 50, 52, 56, 57, 60, 61, 63, 64, 65, 66, 67, 71, 72, 73, 74, 76, 77, 85, 88, 89, 90, 91, 92, 93, 94, 95, 98, 99, 100, 101, 102, 103, 104, 105, 106, 107, 108, 109, 110, 111, 113, 114, 118, 119, 120, 121, 122, 123, 125, 127, 128, 129, 131, 132, 133, 134, 137, 138, 139, 140, 142, 143, 149, 152, 153, 155, 157, 158, 159, 160, 161, 162, 163, 164, 166, 169, 170, 171, 172, 173, 175, 176, 177, 180, 181, 182, 183, 184, 189, 190, 192, 193, 194, 195, 197, 198, 199, 200, 202, 203, 204, 205, 206, 207, 208, 209, 211, 215, 216, 218, 219, 229, 233, 236, 237, 238, 239, 241, 242, 243, 244, 245, 246, 247, 249, 250, 252, 253, 254, 255, 257, 258, 259, 260, 261, 262, 263, 264, 265, 266, 267, 268, 269, 270, 271, 272, 273, 275, 278, 279, 280, 281, 282, 283, 284, 285, 286, 287, 288, 289, 290
National Archives, 45
Northeast Minnesota Historical Center, 11, 16, 28, 51, 68, 156, 179, 191
Otter Tail County Historical Society, 9, 31, 36, 49, 105, 130, 157, 183
Revoir Historical Collection, Red Wing, front cover, 13, 15, 45, 126, 136, 240, 256
St. John's University Archives, 115
St. Paul Daily News, 42, 134, 164, 175
St. Paul Dispatch, 20, 269, 272
St. Paul Dispatch-Pioneer Press, 255
St. Paul Pioneer Press, 121, 200, 241
St. Paul Press, 67
Stearns County Historical Society, 5, 22, 24, 96, 178, 185, 274
Winona County Historical Society, 208, 241, 242
YMCA Archives, 181

**Other books by Peg Meier**

"Bring Warm Clothes"

"The Pie Lady of Winthrop"
(written with Dave Wood)

"Coffee Made Her Insane"

"The Last of the Tearoom Ladies"